AF712207

Code Blue

Health Science Edition Four

Richard E. McDermott, Ph.D.

Traemus Books
2481 West 1425 South
Syracuse, Utah 84075
Phone (801) 525-9643
Fax (801) 773-7669
www.traemus-books.com
carol@traemus.com

 For questions or inquiries contact: Traemus Books, 2481 W 1425 South, Syracuse, UT 84075, phone (801) 525-9643, fax (801) 773-7669, email carol@traemus.com.

To order copies, see **Order Information** on last page.

Instructors: To order instructors materials including test bank, answers to student questions, and PowerPoint lecture slides, e-mail author at carol@traemus-books.com. Include name, title, institution, department, mailing address, e-mail address, phone, and the course for which materials will be used.

Table of Contents

Major Characters

All characters are fictional

Dr. Paige Adams—Professor of Human Resource Management, Weber State University

Dr. Ashton Amos—President of the Medical Staff, Board Member, Cardiac Surgeon

Birdie Bankhead—Secretary to the Administrator

David Brannan—Chairperson of the Board of Brannan Community Hospital, Son of James and Rachel Brannan, brother of Matthew Brannan

James Brannan—Wealthy hospital benefactor, son of Peter Brannan

Matt Brannan—Physician, Son of James and Rachel Brannan, friend of Amy Castleton

Mike Brannan—First member of the Brannan Clan to settle Park City, Silver Baron

Peter Brannan—Son of Mike Brannan, husband of Sara, hospital founder and benefactor

Rachel Brannan—Wife of James Brannan, mother of Matt and David Brannan

Sara Brannan—Wife of Peter Brannan, hospital founder

Amy Castleton—Daughter of Hap Castleton

Hap Castleton—Former Administrator of Brannan Community Hospital

Helen Castleton—Wife of Hap Castleton

Emma Chandler—Acting Controller, Brannan Community Hospital

Del Cluff—Budget Director

Tony Devecchi—Real Estate Developer and Entrepreneur

Wes Douglas—Interim Administrator, Brannan Community Hospital

Kayla Elmore—Health Occupations Students of America Volunteer

Elizabeth Flannigan—Director of Nurses

Dr. Emil Flagg—Physician and Board Member

Thayne Ford—Newspaper Editor

June Hammer—Chief Dietitian

Karisa Holyoak—Managing Partner, Hospital CPA Firm

David Hull—Administrator, Snowline Regional Medical Center

Helen Ingersol—Board Member

Dr. Herb Krimmel—Health Economist, University Hospital

Al Kuxhausen—FBI Agent

Dr. Allison Lindberg—Medical Director, University Hospital

Pete Lister—Director of Marketing, St. Matthew's Hospital

Peter O'Malley—Sergeant, Park City Police Department

Madeline McMillan—Utah Healthcare Association Director

Martha Nelson—Paradigm Medical Systems Accountant

Larry Ortega—Director of Reimbursement, University Hospital

Ryan Ramer—Chief Pharmacist

Dr. Lindsey Reese—Nursing Professor

Parker Richards—New Assistant Administrator, Brannan Community Hospital

Liam Russell—President, Park City State Bank

Roger Selman—Hap Castleton's Controller

Jerry Smith—FAA Investigator

Charles Stoker—HMO Director, University Hospital

Hank Ulman—Self Appointed Union Steward

Jaxon White—Architect

Arnold Wilson—Vice President, Park City State Bank

Edward S. Wycoff—Chairperson of the Finance Committee of Brannan Community Hospital

Don Yanamura—Human Resources Director, Brannan Community Hospital

Barry Zaugg—Underworld figure

Acknowledgments

Appreciation to the following who reviewed the book and provided helpful insights:

Denise Abbott, R.N., Instructor in medical anatomy and physiology, Timpview High School, Orem, Utah

Steven Bateman, M.H.A. Administrator, St. Mark's Hospital, Sandy, Utah

Kristen Davidson, R.N., Instructor in medical anatomy and physiology, Northridge High School, Layton, Utah: National President, HOSA 2008

Spencer Elmore, **D.D.S.,** Colorado Springs, Colorado

Mark J. Howard, Administrator, Mountainview Hospital, Las Vegas, Nevada

Joseph McDermott, M.D., Pathologist, San Antonio, Texas

Richard McDermott Jr., D.D.S., Orthodontist, St. Louis, Missouri

Robert Parker, M.H.A., President, Emergency Physicians Inc.

Christine Pounds, R.N., Syracuse, Utah

Lindsey Reese, R.N., Research and Editorial Consultant, Clearfield, Utah

Candadai Seshachari, Ph.D., Emeritus Professor of English, Weber State University, Ogden, Utah

Kevin Stocks, Ph.D., CPA, Professor of Accountancy, Brigham Young University, Provo, Utah

Debie Todd, Kaysville, Utah

Melissa White, R.N., Lakenheath, England

Preface

What you are about to read represents a new way of teaching technical material. As the approach is unorthodox, an explanation is warranted. The format is that of a textbook/novel. It tells the story of an accountant asked to become the interim administrator of a failing rural hospital after the death of the hospital administrator. Before he can save the hospital, he must understand how the healthcare industry differs from other industries where he has worked.

Why a textbook/novel? I believe fiction is an effective tool for teaching technical material. For thousands of years, civilizations passed knowledge to succeeding generations through stories—folk tales, poems, myths, and epics that taught values to succeeding generations of their societies. Even the Bible—a reference for many cultures—is not a list of rules. It is a series of stories explaining what happens when people follow (or fail to follow) the concepts taught in the text.

A well-written textbook/novel can provide the following:

- **A smoother transition from school to the world of work.** The author—a former hospital administrator—observed the cultural shock that occurs when students graduate from school and enter the hospital. Traditional textbooks have difficulty portraying some of the more difficult issues employees face involving ethics, power, and politics. *Code Blue* is designed to soften the adjustment by giving students a simulated work experience in the healthcare environment.
- **Learning in context**. Students learn better when they can see how ideas taught apply to real-world settings. Instructors report that difficult ideas are more easily understood when an author immediately illustrates theory with examples.
- **Richer classroom discussions**. Fiction allows the instructor to interact with students in meaningful classroom discussions. Discussions are more interesting than lectures, as they involve students in learning. Classroom discussions teach assertiveness, communication, and critical thinking.
- **Better integration of topics**. Fiction gives instructors the opportunity to explain how issues like cost, quality, and medical ethics relate to each other. In a textbook/novel, students can see how professionals balance competing interests.
- **Exploration of ideas from different viewpoints.** In the world of work, well-meaning people can look at the same data and come to

different conclusions. Fiction allows students to explore diverse viewpoints through the eyes of those with different values, agendas, and backgrounds.

- **Conflict Resolution.** A well-written textbook/novel shows conflict resolution in high-stress environments.

- **Instruction in critical thinking.** Most textbooks are good at teaching students to find *correct answers*. They give the question, and supply all the data needed for the *solution*. Many fail, however, to teach students how to *ask the right question*. If you ask the wrong question, you are likely to get the wrong answer.

  Fiction can teach students to distinguish between problems, and symptoms. A well-written textbook/novel teaches, that in the real world, there is often not one right answer.

- **Experience in resolving ethical issues.** In work, issues are not always black and white.

  As health costs consume an ever-increasing share of the gross national product, our nation may soon face rationing of healthcare products and services.

  Is it better to spend scarce resources on prevention, or should it be spent on catastrophic care?

  Is it better to save money, or to save lives?

  These are issues the next generation will be forced to address. *Code Blue* explains problems healthcare professionals face when reconciling cost, quality, and accessibility.

- **Increased communication skill.** *Code Blue* gives students the opportunity to develop written communication skills by preparing memos on issues and events portrayed in the story. It adds life to what otherwise might be viewed as "dry writing assignments."

  Code Blue also improves communication skills through presentations and role-playing exercises.

- **Increased Learning.** Finally, education is more effective when it is fun. A murder mystery is more interesting than a traditional textbook.

TOPICS COVERED

Topics covered include:

- The history of the American healthcare delivery system
- The history and theory of managed care
- The Affordable Care Act of 2010 (the Patient Protection and Affordable Care Act)
- Pay for performance
- An exploration of the question: *"Why are costs so high?"*
- An introduction to legal and ethical issues
- Total quality management
- The effect of technology on cost and quality
- Legislation and regulation
- Critical thinking and problem solving
- The role of the professional
- Hospital organization
- Power and politics in healthcare organizations
- Teamwork
- Systems
- Cultural diversity
- Discrimination
- Quality, safety, and risk management
- Medical and administrative terminology

Supplementary Teaching Materials

Supplementary questions at the end of chapters give the instructor an opportunity to test students' knowledge. Test banks and PowerPoint slides cut preparation time.

There is a PowerPoint lecture for every chapter with technical material. Teachers can reproduce copies of the PowerPoint handouts and give them to students as teaching aids.

Teaching Suggestions

Code Blue was designed as a supplement. Educators have used it in a variety of courses to introduce students to current issues in healthcare. We recommend teachers cover the book in a three-to-six week period, preferably at the start of a course. They can then use the topics taught as a framework to build on when teaching from the primary textbook of the course.

We strongly encourage instructors to allow students to read the entire novel, excluding discussion questions, before covering the chapters in class, as students become impatient to find out how the story ends.

There are multiple ways to add structure to the course. One is to use the first 20 minutes of the class reviewing the chapter terms and theory using the PowerPoint slides. The instructor can then use the rest of the class period to discuss the questions at the end of the chapter. A second approach is to use the lesson plans on the CD.

Code Blue is pre-professional reading. It includes some non-clinical material such as power and politics, ethics, managed care, and prospective reimbursement, all of which influence the way healthcare is practiced at all levels in the 21st century. The author has tried to present the material in an interesting format. As with any topic, however, mastery of the material requires genuine study.

My goal in writing *Code Blue* was to increase learning by presenting technical material in a fun and entertaining manner. I encourage educators and students to e-mail me with questions or suggestions on how I can improve the textbook/novel and its supplements. I will be responsive to your suggestions.

Richard E. McDermott, Ph.D.
Professor of Healthcare Administration and Accountancy
Weber State University
remcdermott@weber.edu
June 2013

1

Trip to McCall

September 4, 1999—Salt Lake City International Airport

Administrator. The manager of the hospital.

Finance department. The department responsible for accounting and finance within a hospital.

It was 7:30 a.m. and the shadows of the Wasatch Mountains blanketed runway three-four-left as a blue and white Cessna 340 pulled out of the hangar, rolled onto the taxiway, and stopped. The roar of the twin 335 horsepower engines severed the crisp morning air, resonating angrily off the metal buildings to the west. Inside the private aircraft, the pilot, Hap Castleton, pulled his flight plan from a dog-eared navigation book and studied it for the route that would take him to Twin Falls, Boise, and finally, McCall, Idaho.

Hap had a broad, generous face, graying brown hair, and a large frame. Deep creases mapped a face that weathered the storms of 30 years as **administrator** of a small hospital in Park City, Utah. Satisfied with the flight plan, he gently nudged his traveling companion, Del Cluff, and traced the route on the map with his index finger.

Cluff, a thin man with receding brown hair, looked up from an accounting journal. His rooster like eyes pecked at the map momentarily. Nodding at Hap, he returned to his journal.

Hap had invited Cluff to discuss changes in the **finance department**. The board was pushing for a major change in the way the hospital was being run, and finance was a good place to start. Hap folded the aviation map and placed it next to his seat. Picking up the mike, he contacted ground control.

"Salt Lake ground—Cessna two-six Charlie requests taxi to runway three-four-left."

"Cessna two-six Charlie—cleared to taxi."

Hap increased his throttle, turning the plane onto the taxiway that would lead him to the assigned runway. The morning air was cool and the takeoff would be smooth. He tuned the radio to 118.3—the Salt Lake tower.

"Cessna two-six-Charlie requests clearance for takeoff."

"Cessna two-six-Charlie cleared for takeoff. Fly heading 320, climb to one-three thousand feet, contact departure on 124.3," was the tower's reply.

Hap felt the freedom surge deep within him as he released the brakes, pushed forward on the throttle, and started his takeoff roll. Flying and fishing were his favorite hobbies, but heavy responsibilities at Brannan Community Hospital made it difficult to find time for either. Today would be different.

The plane accelerated. At 100 knots, Hap gently pulled back on the control **yoke**. With a soft thump, the wheels left the runway and the plane lunged skyward. The plane climbed to 13,000 feet and turned onto its assigned heading of 320 degrees. Hap studied the **altimeter** and compass, checked his airspeed, and adjusted the trim. Satisfied the plane was on course, he turned his attention to Cluff.

Del Cluff had been with the hospital for nine months. A meticulous accountant, he was a major source of irritation to Hap. It wasn't just that Cluff was a bean counter, although that didn't help. Why anyone would want to spend his day with his nose buried in accounting records puzzled Hap. It wasn't even the preference shown to Cluff by Edward Wycoff, **chairperson of the finance committee**, although anyone who could get along with Wycoff was suspect in Hap's eyes. No—there was something more to it, something he couldn't quite put his finger on.

Grabbing a sack from under his seat, Hap nudged Cluff on the leg. "Something to eat?"

Cluff managed a nauseous smile. Pointing to his stomach, he shook his head—negative. Hap snatched a sandwich and took a generous bite, wiping his fingers on his flight suit. *Nervous stomach? Cluff takes life too seriously,* Hap thought. The smell of eggs and mayonnaise filled the cockpit. Chewing ferociously, Hap tuned his navigation radio to the next **VOR** as the plane crossed the first **radio beacon**.

From the right seat, Del Cluff watched the pilot adjust the radio and wondered why he accepted the invitation to fly with Hap Castleton. *Hope this yo-yo knows more about flying than he does about hospital administration,* he thought. Palms sweating, he tightened his seat belt.

Hap's management style was an increasing source of frustration to Del Cluff. He created more problems in a day than Cluff and a small flock of hospital accountants could fix in a month. Although his larger than life personality made him a hero to most of his employees, he was no hero to Cluff.

The situation at the hospital was desperate. There were rumors the **Board of Trustees** was planning a major change prompted by Edward Wycoff chair of the finance committee. For the past couple months Wycoff had been snooping around the department, reviewing records and quietly interviewing members of the staff.

Altimeter. An instrument in the cockpit of an aircraft that reports the aircraft's altitude.

Board of Trustees. A group of individuals who oversee the operation of the hospital. The board of trustees has the authority to hire and fire the hospital administrator, approve the strategic plan and budget, and approve applications of doctors for membership on the medical staff.

Chairperson of the finance committee. A member of a hospital board who has responsibility for monitoring the financial health of the hospital. In Code Blue, Edward Wycoff has this responsibility.

Finance committee. A committee of the Board of Trustees responsible for supervising the financial operation of the hospital.

Radio beam. In the context of aviation, a beam emitted for navigation purposes.

VOR. Acronym for very high frequency omni directional range. An aviation radio navigation system.

Yoke. The "steering wheel" of an airplane.

Auditor. A person who reviews records to verify that transactions have been accurately reported.

Budget director. The person responsible for preparing and monitoring the hospital's budget.

Cardiac arrest. A condition where the heart has stopped beating.

Code blue. A distress call broadcast over the hospital intercom announcing to doctors that there is a cardiac arrest and that aid is needed.

Consultant. An expert who has knowledge that an organization lacks. Consultants are hired to provide this knowledge for a fee. Hospitals use many consultants as the medical field is complex and most hospitals cannot afford to employ full-time employees in every area in which expertise is needed.

Controller. The individual responsible for managing the financial activities of a hospital. Responsibilities include accounting, working with banks to borrow money, and supervising the collection of accounts receivables (amounts owed by patients who have received care but not yet paid the bill).

CPA. Abbreviation for certified public accountant. A certified public accountant has passed an exam that shows a minimum level of knowledge in accounting and tax.

The operation needed a good review, but Wycoff scared the wits out of most of the employees. His efforts only made things worse. The hospital was in dire straits. If it were a patient, it would be in cardiac arrest, in nursing terms—a code blue. Cluff folded his journal, slid it under his seat, and retrieved Hap's navigation map. He studied it, and then squinted nervously at the hostile terrain below. To the north lay Mount Ben Lomond, capped with snow from a storm that moved through the Rocky Mountains two days earlier.

To the east, the cliffs of the rugged Wasatch Range reached skyward, thrust high by catastrophic earthquakes thousands of years ago. To the west, the frigid waters of the Great Salt Lake reflected the purple mountains of Antelope Island. Cluff shivered involuntarily. Folding the map, he returned it to the pocket by Hap's seat.

"Heard the rumors about Selman?" Hap asked, the irritation in his voice sawing the cold morning air. "Board's pushing for a change—Wycoff plans on firing him Monday." Hap worked his jaw—his habit when irritated. "As soon as Selman's gone, Wycoff wants to install you as **controller."**

Cluff's eyes, a good indicator of his emotions, jumped in surprise. Cluff would welcome a change—he and Selman often disagreed. He would even welcome the chance to run the department his way, but he wasn't sure the promotion would be up—*it might be out.* Cluff said nothing while Hap struggled to control his anger.

"Accept the job and you'll get two new responsibilities." Hap's words were short and clipped. "The first is **budget director**—Wycoff wants three million dollars cut from the budget—I want you to oppose him!"

Fat chance! Cluff thought. *Half of our suppliers have us on a cash only basis; we aren't even sure we can meet payroll.* This wasn't the first time Hap locked horns with Wycoff. He had no ally in Del Cluff.

"The second . . .?" Cluff asked.

"Project coordinator for a new accounting system." The yoke of the small aircraft started to pull. Hap adjusted the trim.

"Six months ago I asked a **consultant** to look at the operation, see if he could propose something to cut losses. Insurance companies are killing us. The board isn't going to allow me to take another contract until we have a better handle on our **costs**."

Cluff smiled and nodded, his eyes narrowing with approval. "Our **auditors** have been after Selman for a year to get a system up and running," Cluff said. "They think this should be our number-one priority."

Hap nodded decisively. "It's now *your* number-one priority. Wycoff's hired a **CPA**, a fellow named Wes Douglas, to serve as a consultant on the project. Wycoff wrote him a memo—read it."

Cluff smirked sarcastically. He'd seen the memo. Wes was an Eastern accountant and knew nothing about rural hospitals. He'd be more trouble than he was worth.

Earlier that morning, Hap received a briefing at the weather desk. An unstable air mass with high moisture content from Canada had moved into

Cowling. The shield or covering of an aircraft engine.

Horizontal stabilizer. The short horizontal wing on the tail of an aircraft.

Localizer. A transmitter used in an instrument landing system that provides the pilot with information regarding his alignment with the runway centerline during a landing approach.

Vector. A magnetic direction used in aviation.

the region, lifted high by the steep terrain of the Rocky Mountains. Severe thunderstorms were probable.

Hap studied a dark bank of cumulus clouds at twelve o'clock. On his present heading he'd hit the storm head on. He fished in his shirt pocket for a note card, and then pointed to a scuffed manual on the floor.

"I need a radio frequency—Twin Falls **localizer**. Think the frequency is 122.4 but I'm not . . ."

Hap aborted the sentence. Mouth wide open, he studied his instrument panel, then gaped out the window as his expression changed from disbelief to terror. Simultaneously, a cold wave of anxiety engulfed Cluff. "What's wrong?' he asked.

"The right engine—" Hap choked, the color draining from his face.

A thin ribbon of blue smoke was trailing from the **cowling**. Hap reached for the throttle, but before he could cut power, an explosion rocked the plane, whipping Cluff's head so violently he could taste the pain.

Hap grabbed the yoke in an attempt to regain control of the aircraft.

"Fire!" Cluff screamed.

The plane banked dangerously while Hap reached for the radio.

"Mayday, Mayday, Mayday," he shouted into the mike. "Cessna two-six Charlie, lost an engine . . . on board fire." He glanced at the altimeter "Descending out of one-two-niner. Request immediate **vector**—emergency landing!"

One engine dead, the Cessna pulled right, the centrifugal force created by the right engine threatening to pull the plane into a flat spin. A spin would give the aircraft the flight characteristics of a pitching anvil—no lift; just spin, speed, and mass. "Can't hold it!" Hap shouted, jamming his foot down on the left rudder.

"Throttle back . . . cut the left engine!" Hap whispered to himself. He lunged for the throttles, accidentally cutting power to both engines. The plane shuddered—then dropped like a roller coaster. Unable to pull it out, Hap wrapped both arms around the control yoke. The veins in his neck protruded like steel cables as he pulled with all the strength of his 250-pound frame.

At 280 knots, the burning engine separated, its broken cowling ripping the **horizontal stabilizer** from the tail as it cleared the aircraft. A side window blew out.

Cluff grabbed for something to hold on to—the ride down got rougher still.

Still struggling with the yoke, Hap turned the plane north towards Highway 82. It was clear from the glide slope they wouldn't reach it. An alarm sounded—red and amber lights exploded on the instrument panel.

Heart pounding like a sledgehammer, Cluff gaped at the rapidly approaching terrain below. To the west, he saw homes and apartment buildings. To the east, nothing but the foothills of the jagged Wasatch Mountains. Direct in front lay a freshly harvested hay field.

A farmer watching the plummeting aircraft jumped from his tractor and ran for cover. Cluff's eyes desperately drank every detail of the approaching terrain as he searched for a way out.

The field was flat—but too short for a landing. At the far end was an elementary school. Children were already playing in the yard, waiting for the morning bell to ring. Cluff pointed. "Try for the field!"

"We'll hit the kids."

"They'll scatter."

"Can't chance it . . ."

This idiot's gonna kill us!

Hap banked the plane east toward the foothills. Completing the turn, he dropped his flaps. An alarm sounded—the landing gear wasn't down.

Rough terrain—bring her in on her belly. To minimize the chance of a fire on impact, Hap turned off the electrical system. The blue and white Cessna, both engines silent, skimmed a row of cottonwood trees, the yoke heavy and unresponsive. As Cluff screamed in terror, Hap Castleton tightened his harness and braced himself for the crash.

Discussion One–Communication

"It takes two." For communication to take place one person must create a message and another person must receive, interpret, and evaluate it. The person sending the message is the sender. The person receiving it is the receiver.

A sender can use words (spoken or written), pictures, or nonverbal cues such as facial expression, actions, and body movement to suggest meaning. The receiver responds to a message based on his or her perception of what the sender has said.

Discussion Questions

1. *From what you have read in chapter one, complete the following personality profile for Hap Castleton and Del Cluff.*

Attribute	*Hap Castleton*	*Del Cluff*
Focuses on details		
Focuses on the big picture		
Motivated by facts		
Motivated by feelings		
Focuses on the possible		
Motivated by dreams		
Analytic		
Sympathetic		
Interested in things		
Interested in people		
Inclined to gather a lot of information before making a decision.		
Inclined to decide quickly based on emotion rather than facts.		

2. *Why is it important to understand the values, personalities, and decision making model of a person you wish to communicate with?*
3. *It is obvious Del Cluff has not established a good rapport with his boss Hap Castleton. To what do you attribute this problem?*
4. *What are the differences in the ways Del Cluff and Hap Castleton process information, and therefore make decisions?*
5. *Given the differences in personality, values, and decision-making style, how could Del Cluff be more effective in communicating his concern about the hospital's financial condition to his boss Hap Castleton?*

Writing Exercise

6. *Assume you are Del Cluff. From what you know about Hap Castleton, prepare a written memo explaining your concerns about the hospital's losses. Explain why you will not oppose Edward Wycoff's efforts to cut the hospital budget.*

2

The Board

Chief dietician. A dietician is an individual who has been trained to use nutrition to treat illness. Dieticians work in the dietary department where food is prepared for hospital patients. The chief dietician is the supervisor of the dietary department.

Dietary department. The department responsible for preparing patient meals.

President of medical staff. An elected officer of the medical staff who represents the medical staff to the board and administration.

Transportation aide. A person responsible for transporting food, supplies, or patients throughout the hospital.

Edward Wycoff arrived at the hospital at 6:30 on Monday morning—a half-hour before an emergency meeting of the Board of Trustees. Exploding down the hall, he ignored the greetings of the housekeepers. Without breaking stride, he threw open the large walnut doors of the boardroom and switched on the lights.

Throwing his briefcase on a small telephone desk, he inspected the room. A retired officer in the Army Reserves, he knew how to conduct an inspection. Pity the employee who failed to meet his expectations!

Consistent with his instructions, the housekeepers had vacuumed the carpets and polished the conference room table until it shone like the brass on a general's uniform. He picked up the phone and punched in the extension of the **dietary department**. The **chief dietician** answered.

"Wycoff here!" His commanding tone never failed to catch an employee's attention. "I ordered breakfast for the board!"

Telephone in one hand, the chief dietitian motioned frantically at a **transportation aide** with the other. The aide clumsily shoved the heavy cart toward a service elevator. "Cart's on the way, Mr. Wycoff. Would've been there earlier but—"

Wycoff hung up, unwilling to satisfy her with an explanation. For a moment, the room was silent as he admired his reflection on the marble surface of the boardroom table. His most distinguishing features were his eyes—small and deliberate, the color of chipped ice. As always, he was unstirred by currents of self-doubt. *Hesitate—even for a moment—and you'll lose,* he thought. *Compassion now would only dull the victory . . .*

Dr. Ashton Amos stuck his head through the door. At six-foot-one, he looked more like a basketball player than the newly elected **president of the medical staff**. His boyish mannerisms—coordinated awkwardness and large grin—made him popular with employees and doctors alike—a characteristic Wycoff would capitalize on.

Attending physician. The doctor who admits and supervises the care of a specific hospital patient.

Coronary care unit (CCU). The medical unit where patients with coronary (heart) diseases are treated and housed.

Critical condition. The most serious classification of patient illness.

Double bypass. An operation where two arteries are grafted to divert blood beyond an obstruction.

Emergency call. Physicians at some hospitals are required to provide coverage of the emergency room. This is referred to as emergency call.

FAA. Acronym for Federal Aviation Administration.

Life flight. A group that transports critically ill patients by aircraft to the hospital.

Rounds. In this situation, the morning visit by a doctor to his or her patients in the hospital. The term originated at Johns Hopkins Hospital in the late nineteenth century, where patient wings radiated off a central circular hall causing doctors completing their daily visits to do "rounds."

Weariness from a 28-hour shift in the **coronary care unit** lined Dr. Amos' voice. "Got your message," he said. "Just finished **rounds** . . . can talk now if you'd like."

Wycoff nodded. "Come in," he said evenly.

Dr. Amos crossed the room, seating himself in a large leather chair across from Wycoff. Pulling a clean handkerchief from his pocket, he wiped his face and then blew his nose.

"Spent the night at the hospital?" Wycoff asked.

The doctor's mouth drew into a grim line. He nodded. "Fifty-one-year-old patient." Removing his glasses, he slowly massaged his eyes. **"Double bypass**—complications."

Wycoff was unmoved.

"Any word on Hap's accident?" Amos asked, moving on to a new subject.

Wycoff shook his head. "The plane hit 50 feet below the summit. Sheriff thinks they were trying to reach Mountain Road. An **FAA** team arrived Saturday—I don't think they know anything yet. Have you heard anything about Hap's funeral?"

"It's scheduled for Monday—noon. I've canceled surgery."

Wycoff nodded. "What's the report on Cluff?" Dr. Amos had **emergency call** the night they brought in Cluff.

"**Life flighted** to University Hospital. Called his **attending physician** this morning. Listed in **critical condition** but they think he'll make it."

The room was silent as Wycoff digested the information. The young doctor knew Wycoff hadn't called him in to report on Del Cluff. Unless Wycoff needed Cluff's services again—an unlikely probability considering the severity of his injuries—Wycoff would give no further thought to Cluff's welfare.

"What's the board going to do about a new administrator?" Amos asked.

Wycoff pursed his lips as though it was the first time he'd considered the question. "It's been a difficult weekend for me," he began, mouthing the words he so carefully rehearsed early that morning. "Hap and I disagreed—disagreed often," he said, nodding in agreement with himself. "Still, I had a great deal of respect for the man."

Wycoff was lying. He had nothing but contempt for the former administrator. He didn't think Amos would know the difference. He was wrong.

Wycoff steepled his fingers, a gesture of authority he'd used with good effect on Wall Street. "I've spent the past two days agonizing over the best course of action for the hospital." He hesitated. "I have a proposal, but I'm not sure if the board will buy it."

An ingratiating smile played on Wycoff's lips as he leaned forward. He pointed a crooked arthritic finger at Amos. "I need someone with your prestige to explain it to them," Wycoff continued. "Someone they respect, someone they'll listen to!"

Department head. Hospitals are complex organizations. To make them easier to manage, administrators organize them into departments, usually by function. There are clinical departments such as nursing and laboratory that provide medical services; and support departments such as medical records, administration, accounting and housekeeping that provide support services. The supervisor of a hospital department is usually referred to as a department head or sometimes department supervisor. Department heads usually report directly to the hospital administrator, or in larger hospitals, to an assistant administrator.

Interim administrator. A temporary hospital administrator who serves at the discretion of the board until a permanent replacement is found.

Managed care. An approach to cost control that includes preauthorization for expensive procedures, incentive reimbursement, retrospective (after-the-fact) quality audits, and second opinions.

Rigor mortis. The stiffening of the body that occurs after death.

Everyone knew how patronizing Wycoff could be when he wanted something. The thin layer of goodwill, however, failed to veil the cold **rigor mortis** of his eyes—the reflection of a thousand enemies ruthlessly eliminated.

"It's been my experience the board rarely turns down one of your recommendations," Amos replied, his face masked and expressionless.

"It's essential the board pick the right man to replace Hap," Wycoff continued. "It won't happen overnight. While we're interviewing candidates, we need an **interim administrator**. Someone strong enough," Wycoff continued, "to fully implement **managed care** at Brannan Community Hospital."

Amos nodded, his face softening with relief. There were rumors Wycoff planned to bring one of his hired guns in from New York to run the hospital. An interim administrator would be okay. It would give the hospital an opportunity to recover from the death of Hap while providing the time to organize the medical staff, if Wycoff still planned a takeover.

"Candidates?"

"None of our **department heads** qualify," Wycoff replied. We need a *financial man*," Wycoff said with emphasis. Someone who can lead us through the current budget crisis."

"Who do you suggest?" Amos asked.

"There's a new CPA in the community—a fellow named Wes Douglas. The hospital hired him a few weeks ago for a consulting project. He has no preconceived notions and isn't involved in hospital politics."

"Does he have the time?" Dr. Amos asked.

Wycoff nodded. "I phoned him last night. He's still building his practice. He's not only got the time; he needs the money."

Amos smiled. Wycoff could always identify a person's vulnerabilities—he obviously found Wes's. Dr. Amos rose thoughtfully and walked to the French doors overlooking the west patio. It was 7:00 a.m. and the morning shift was arriving. Mary Hammond, a widow with six children was parking her car. Hammond worked as a clerk in the operating room. She pulled a lunch bag from the front seat of her battered Honda as she hurried off to her workstation. As Dr. Amos watched, he reflected on the effect closure would have on its employees. He turned to Wycoff. "I don't have a better idea," he said with a shrug. "I'll support the recommendation. Of course, I can't speak for the other members of the board."

Discussion One—Power and Politics

In this chapter, we learn the reaction of the board to the death of the hospital administrator. We also are introduced to power and politics in the hospital. Financial problems facing the board are also briefly discussed. Selecting a new administrator will be a difficult task. The board has several options:

- *Select an administrator who has been formally trained by an accredited program in healthcare administration and has experience in hospital management. If the Board of Trustees chooses this alternative, they probably will not be able to fill the job immediately. Any person they hire will have to give their present employer several weeks' notice.*
- *Select someone who has business experience, but no hospital experience, perhaps a local businessperson. The problem with this alternative is the issues involved in running a hospital are different from those involved in running a retail, manufacturing, or construction firm. By the time the new administrator knows the rules, the game may be over.*
- *Choose someone from the hospital to succeed the old administrator. This person would have the advantage of understanding the hospital's problems. Department heads don't always make the best hospital administrators, however. Many come from technical backgrounds and have little or no formal training in management.*
- *Recruit a local doctor to fill the job. A high salary and a lack of business training are the major disadvantages of this alternative.*
- *Select an outside interim administrator who can guide the hospital through the current crisis and provide the Board of Trustees time to find a permanent replacement. The advantage of this alternative is the hospital will have someone immediately to address the financial problems the hospital is having. The disadvantage is that it is difficult to find a temporary administrator with previous experience. The hospital staff will also have to adjust to two administrators (the interim administrator and his or her replacement).*

Discussion Question

1. *What are the advantages and disadvantages of selecting an interim administrator?*

3

A Change of Seasons

Joint Commission on Accreditation of Healthcare Organizations (JCAHO). An organization that accredits hospitals and other healthcare organizations. Accreditation provides legitimacy in the eyes of the consumer, who is often unable to judge the quality of healthcare services.

Thirty-one year old Wes Douglas stepped from his car to the sidewalk. He stretched the knots out of his back as he surveyed the wooded grounds of Brannan Community Hospital. The change of seasons had come suddenly this year. Colorful leaves blanketed the lawn like the patchwork quilts sold in the gift shop. Wes enjoyed all the seasons, but Fall—the season of change—was his favorite. As he watched a gust of wind stir the colored leaves, he pondered the changes awaiting him.

Wes stood with Hap Castleton on this very spot in mid-September. Hap explained the crisis that motivated him to hire Wes as a consultant. The Board of Trustees was concerned the hospital was losing money. They blamed it on managed care, a program designed by insurance companies to control cost. Hap asked Wes to design a new information system that would allow the hospital to track their cost. For the consulting engagement, the board agreed to pay Wes $50,000.

Although Wes spent less than a week working with Hap, the administrator impressed him with his energy and enthusiasm. Hap was an extrovert. His expressive style won the admiration of employees and medical staff. Hap understood people and was a master at hospital politics. He was weak, however, in operations, an area where Wes excelled. At Lytle, Morehouse, and Butler, his former CPA firm, Wes consulted with a host of manufacturing firms and helped design over a dozen accounting systems to control costs. Wes had a mind for detail. He was also a workaholic. Long after the staff went home, Wes pored over production reports and product flow diagrams, identifying inefficiencies that slowed production and raised cost.

Wes reflected on the difference between himself and Hap Castleton during his first interview with Edward Wycoff, and Dr. Lindsey Reese, a former nursing professor who now worked for the **Joint Commission on Accreditation of Health Organizations**. Since Dr. Reese traveled extensively, she could choose where she wanted to live and had settled in Park City. The three had finished dinner and retired to a richly paneled lounge on the second floor of the Yarrow Inn.

Bankruptcy. A situation where a person or organization is unable to pay its bills. Often in bankruptcy, the court seizes the bankrupt person's or organization's assets and sells them to pay creditors (the people to whom debts are owed).

"I want to tell you a story," Wycoff said, lighting a cigar as he settled into a large wing back chair. "One of my neighbors in New York, a fellow named Eric Rose, was vice president of General Electric. When he retired, he had 30 years with the company. Four of the company's officers retired at the same time—three vice presidents and a director. Thanks to General Electric's generous retirement plan, they retired wealthy men, certain of their business ability."

Wycoff removed his glasses, placing them on a table by his chair. "Wes, sixty-five is too young to do nothing," he said. "After long vacations, Eric and the three other officers started businesses of their own. They were filled with confidence."

Wycoff paused for emphasis. "In three years, each lost his investment! One of them even took out **bankruptcy**. For a long time, I wondered why people who ran a billion dollar corporation couldn't succeed with their own company." His eyebrows rose inquiringly and he pointed his cigar at Wes. "Want to guess why they failed?"

Wes shrugged. "Inexperience in a new industry?"

"That contributed, but I think the main reason was they no longer had the support and discipline of a *team*. At General Electric, the vice president of research had the vice president of marketing to remind him he had to develop a product that would sell. The vice president of marketing had the discipline of the vice president of engineering to assure he wouldn't sell a product they couldn't build.

"The manufacturing vice president had the vice president of finance looking over his shoulders, urging him to cut cost so he could price the product at a level the customer could afford. The vice president of finance had the other three vice presidents to remind him without marketing, engineering, and research, none of them would have a job!"

Wycoff smiled reproachfully. "My friends failed because they chose partners that were just like them—not only in experience, but in aptitude."

"They failed to select people who could compensate for their blind spots," Wes affirmed.

"That's why I'm interested in your experience." Wycoff pressed his lips into a fine line as he studied the young consultant. Wycoff leaned forward as though he was going to share a secret. "I'll admit Castleton is great with people," he whispered, "but he's poor with details." He shook his head. "Spend a little time with him, for example, and you'll learn he knows nothing about finance. He couldn't balance his own checkbook if his life depended on it."

Wycoff continued: "Hap understands hospital politics, but you understand management and cost control. *Alone*, neither of you could run a business as complex as Brannan Community Hospital. As a *team*, however, I think you'd be unbeatable!"

Dr. Reese didn't care for Wycoff much—*he puts too much emphasis on money* she thought. She had accepted the dinner invitation to interview Wes only out of her interest to the community in which she lived. While she wasn't on the board, she followed its activities closely through articles in the newspaper. "I agree with Wycoff's concern about the financial condition of the hospital," Reese said. "But we have other problems as well, problems I think you could help us with.

"I haven't talked with Wycoff about it, but I think he ought to hire you as a permanent consultant to the board. I see your experience helping the clinical staff in a whole host of areas." She pulled a list from her pocket.

"The first is **quality assurance,"** she said. "**Continuous quality improvement** is a big issue in manufacturing where the Japanese are cutting the American's grass. Just look at the beating Ford and General Motors are taking from Honda and Toyota.

"Administration and the board know almost nothing about the subject," Reese continued, "and the hospital employees know even less." She cocked one eyebrow. "Any idea of how you compare on issues of **morbidity** and **mortality** when compared to hospitals in Salt Lake City?" she asked Wycoff.

Wycoff shook his head to the negative.

"Neither does anyone else," she replied. "Patients need more information on quality and cost, and we give them neither."

Dr. Reese turned to the second item on her list. "There are legal issues relating to the delivery of care that I think you could help us with," she continued. "Ever heard of **HIPAA** or **EMTALA**?" she asked.

The question drew a blank stare from both Edward Wycoff and Wes Douglas.

"Administration is doing nothing to educate nurses, respiratory therapists and the like on issues that could cost you hundreds of thousands of dollars in lawsuits. I know you're not a lawyer, Wes, but CPAs are accustomed to working with regulations, and where you don't know the answers you can get them.

"Diversity is another issue you've ignored," she said, directing her comments to Wycoff. "To a financer, diversity means carrying more than one credit card," she said sarcastically. The jab was not lost on Wycoff who shot an abrasive scowl.

"Park City is somewhat of an isolated place," she continued. "People here know nothing about the cultures of people who are moving here from all parts of the globe. You need to be more sensitive to patient's cultures when providing care.

"**Risk management**," Dr. Reese said pointing to the next item on her list. "You know what that is?"

Wes nodded. "I installed a new program in a plant in Hartford, Connecticut."

Continuous quality improvement (CQI). An approach to providing products that stresses that the organization should never be satisfied with its product—that ways should be found to constantly improve quality.

EMTALA. Acronym for Emergency Medical Treatment and Active Labor Act, also known the Patient Anti-Dumping Law. This law is designed to keep hospitals from transferring patients who cannot pay for their care to other hospitals. Heavy fines are involved for those who do.

HIPAA. Acronym for the Health Insurance Portability and Accountability Act. HIPAA was enacted by the U.S. Congress in 1996. One objective is to protect confidentiality of health information.

Morbidity. The number of cases of a specific disease in relation to the general population.

Mortality. The hospital's death rate. The number of hospital deaths divided by the number of people in a specific population.

Quality assurance. Procedures taken to assure a high degree of excellence.

Risk Management. A department or specialty that anticipates and tries to prevent risks to employees, patients and visitors. Slipping on an icy sidewalk would be a risk this program might address.

Administration. The department responsible for the management of the hospital. The hospital administrator heads this department.

Cresyl violet. A dye used in staining slide specimens to be examined under a microscope.

Ethyl alcohol. Synonymous with rubbing alcohol. It is often used as a disinfectant.

"Big issue in healthcare," Reese said. "Except for here. I'm not sure that anyone at Brannan knows what it means."

Wycoff nodded. That was one issue he agreed with. A poor risk management program could cost the hospital millions of dollars."

"You see," Lindsey Reese continued, "we have students coming out of professional programs that think that all they have to know is the clinical side of medicine. While our clinicians are busy providing patient care, they have let the administrators, lawyers and accountants assume the role of running the system. Unless clinicians re-involve themselves in the management of hospitals, we are going to lose the entire health care system. It will be one huge corporate or governmental bureaucracy."

"And they can't do that unless clinicians know more about the issues you are discussing," Wes affirmed.

"Right—but presently they lack the knowledge and training."

The room was quiet while Wes absorbed Reese's message.

After an appropriate pause, Wycoff insisted on the last word.

"The final item we need your help on is finance and accounting," Wycoff said. We are four weeks or less from not meeting payroll—no payroll, no hospital."

Standing now on the front lawn of Brannan Community Hospital, two weeks after the first conversation, Wes realized the proposals were no longer relevant. Hap was gone, and without him, there was no team, and without a team, there was no contract.

Forcing a smile, he picked up his briefcase and crossed the lawn, entering the hospital through the large brass doors of the visitors' lobby.

A row of wooden chairs with straight, upright backs stood sentry at the entrance to the lobby, and the scent of **ethyl alcohol** and **cresyl violet** seeped into the hall from the small laboratory on the first floor. Wes's leather-soled shoes squeaked on the highly waxed linoleum floor as he crossed the lobby to the information desk. He spoke briefly with the receptionist, and then went directly to **administration** where Birdie Bankhead, secretary to the administrator, greeted him.

Birdie, a 56 year-old divorcee, had worked at the hospital as long as Hap. She looked up from the newspaper. Hap Castleton's picture was on the front page. Wes noticed her red eyes and splotched cheeks.

"I'm Mr. Douglas," he said softly, "I'm here to meet with the board."

Birdie nodded in recognition. "They're running a few minutes late. Would you care for some coffee while you wait?"

"No, I'm fine."

Birdie wiped the corners of her eyes with a handkerchief. She opened her purse and retrieved a small makeup compact. "Sorry," she said as she

Chairperson of the board. The person appointed to lead the board. The chairperson usually sets the board agenda, appoints committees, and represents the board to the administrator and medical staff.

Formaldehyde. A pungent gas used as an antiseptic and disinfectant.

Pathologist. A medical specialty focusing on the diagnosis of disease through changes in tissues.

excused herself. "It's been a difficult morning. I'll be gone for a few minutes. If you need anything, Mary Anne in the next office can help."

Wes nodded as Birdie left. Hands in his pockets, he scanned the room. The office was 20 feet square and served as the reception area for the administrator's office and the boardroom. The door to the boardroom was slightly ajar, and from the conversation drifting through the door, he could tell the meeting was winding down. A woman was speaking.

"I'm not sure there's anything we can do but what you suggest," she said. "While I don't like it, you've convinced me it's our best alternative."

"All in favor?" a male voice said. There was a volley of "Ayes."

"Those opposed?" There was one vigorous voice of dissent.

The door to the boardroom opened wide, and Dr. Ashton Amos emerged, extending his hand in a generous greeting. Wes shook it as the doctor apologized for the delay. "Hope you haven't been here long," Amos said. Wes shook his head no and Amos gestured for him to enter the boardroom.

Inside, four members huddled in quiet conversation around a large conference table. Octagon in shape, it was cut from a one-inch slab of white Tennessee marble. It rested solidly on a square platform of polished walnut. In the center stood an architect's model of the new hospital Hap Castleton hoped to build—a project canceled just three days before his death.

"I don't think you've met the entire board," Amos said as his eyes swept the room. This is David Brannan, **chairperson of the board**." Dr. Amos pointed to a well-dressed man in his early thirties. Amos ginned. "From his last name, you can tell his family has played an important role in the history of the hospital." Wes smiled in acknowledgment, while Brannan stood and shook his hand.

"Next to David is Dr. Emil Flagg, the medical staff's representative on the board." Dr. Flagg, a **pathologist** in his early sixties, had a dyspeptic smile and smelled vaguely of **formaldehyde**. Stretch wrinkles radiated from the single button of an enormous white lab coat that struggled to corral his rotund torso. Flagg glowered as he scanned Wes from head to toe, and gave a brief nod.

"Helen Ingersol, president of Ingersol Construction is next. This is Helen's first meeting with the committee." Helen Ingersol, a strong administrative type with short brown hair and piercing blue eyes, smiled acknowledgment.

"And last, but not least, is Ed Wycoff. You already know Mr. Wycoff." Wycoff motioned for Wes to take the chair next to him.

"The tragic events of the weekend have forced us to come to some difficult decisions," Wycoff said, his lips compressing into a cold, thin line.

Credit limit. The maximum amount, as determined by the bank, an individual or firm can borrow.

Financial analyst. A person who earns his or her living by studying the financial statements of companies and making recommendations, often about investments.

Financial reports. Reports that show the financial condition of a firm. The three most common financial reports are the income statement, the balance sheet, and the statement of cash flows. The income statement shows revenues minus expenses. The balance sheet lists assets (items that have economic value), liabilities (debts), and owner equity (the value of the owner's investment in the firm). The statement of cash flows shows cash that has been received and disbursed by the firm during the accounting period.

"As these involve your consulting contract, we felt we should involve you in the discussion."

Wycoff paused. "Before addressing the issue, however, we have one other item of business. Dr. Amos, would you invite Roger Selman in?" As Amos left the room, Wycoff turned to Wes. "Roger is the controller," he whispered.

In the summer before college, Wes worked for his grandfather, herding sheep to the mountain pastures. Sometimes dark thunderheads appeared on the horizon, churning their way toward the summer pasture. Even though the air was deathly still, an unfathomable uneasiness preceded the pyrotechnics soon to come. That same atmosphere filled the room as Amos returned with Selman. Each took their seats—Amos next to Wycoff, and Selman next to Wes Douglas.

Except for the drumming of Wycoff's fingers on the cold marble table, the room was silent. Wycoff studied the concerned face of each board member. Satisfied he had their attention; he removed the hospital's **financial report** from a manila folder and carefully placed it on the table. He gazed at it for a moment, quickly withdrawing his hands for dramatic effect.

"Lady and gentlemen," he said with a theatrical flair, "Mr. Selman has provided us with an unusual document! In my 20 years as a **financial analyst**, I have never seen anything like it." He paused for emphasis. "You are to be congratulated, Mr. Selman!"

Wycoff's sarcasm was not lost on Selman who squirmed uncomfortably in his chair.

"Mr. Selman, when you joined the hospital five years ago, we had a successful business. No debts—one million dollars in the bank." Wycoff took a drink of ice water, and then wiped his mouth with a handkerchief.

Beads of perspiration formed on Selman's forehead. With a beefy forefinger, he tugged on his collar, loosening the knot of his necktie, which seemed to tighten even as Wycoff spoke.

Wycoff's eyes narrowed. "The report given this morning shows a substantial reversal," he said glacially. Still staring at Selman, he methodically flipped—one by one—through the pages of the report.

"During the previous twelve months," he continued, "we produced a loss of three million dollars. Monday morning, our borrowing reached *two million dollars,* taking us within $150,000 of our **credit limit**. With less than $150,000 of cash in the bank, we are dangerously close to not being able to meet payroll. Why, Mr. Selman," he said with obvious sarcasm, "you and your associates have taken us to the edge of bankruptcy!" The room seemed to hold its breath as no one spoke.

After a long pause, Helen Ingersol, president of Ingersol Construction spoke. "I'm not an accountant," she began, addressing David Brannan, "but this is the first time I've seen the hospital's financial report, and there are a couple of questions I need answered before I decide if I'm going to remain on the board."

"Shoot," Brannan said.

"Mr. Selman, your reports show the hospital's volume is up, but so are its losses. Your costs haven't risen dramatically—in my business, this would signal a pricing problem. How do your prices compare to those of your competitors?"

"We aren't sure," Selman replied. "Our competitors don't publish their prices. Even if they did, it wouldn't matter. We work with over twenty insurance companies. Everyone pays a different price."

Ignersol gave a tenuous frown, unable to comprehend twenty different billing systems. "But what about your costs?" she asked. Are they competitive?

"Don't know." Selman replied. "Our competitors don't publish their costs."

Wycoff interrupted. "That's understandable, we don't' publish ours either" he said. "What isn't understandable is we don't even know what they are."

This was a different business than anything Ingersol had ever encountered. "How is that possible?" she asked.

"Our accounting system tracks costs by department, but not by product," he said.

Wycoff cut him off. "The problem isn't accounting!" he shouted. "The problem is management! You don't plan. You spend your time putting out fires."

"Actually Mr. Wycoff," Selman said, breaking in.

"Don't interrupt me!" Wycoff snapped. "The reputation of the hospital is plummeting. Employee morale is low, productivity is lower, and service is rotten. I can't attend Rotary without someone jumping me about some problem they had with the hospital. I'm fed up with it!" he shouted angrily.

"Eighteen months ago," Wycoff continued, "I opposed bidding on the Mountainlands insurance contract without cost data," Wycoff continued. Hap Castleton moved ahead anyway—on your recommendation!"

"If we hadn't bid the contract, we would have lost the business to competitors." Selman replied. "I don't know if we could have survived the drop in volume."

"There's much you don't know!" Wycoff replied sarcastically.

From the expression on their faces, it was obvious the board was not comfortable with the caustic approach Wycoff was taking. Still, no one spoke.

Roger Selman took a deep breath and released it slowly. "It's been a difficult year," he admitted, "but the worst is behind us. Yes, we've lost money, but we can fix the problem. That's why Wes Douglas is here, isn't it?"

Breaking the lock of Wycoff's gaze, Selman shot a plea for help to David Brannan. David had always been more sympathetic than the rest.

"Give me three or four months," said Selman, "and you'll see a dramatic change in our position."

Wycoff slammed the table. "We can't survive that long! For the past three years, the hospital's financial strength has plummeted. Although we can't hold you solely responsible, your inability to provide cost information has crippled our ability to run the hospital."

Wycoff's voice lowered as he sighted in on Roger Selman for the final kill. "Mr. Selman," he said, "with the death of Hap Castleton, we have decided to reorganize your department," he said. "As a part of the reorganization, we are asking for your resignation." Wycoff forced his lips into a glacial smile as his voice dropped "If you don't resign," he said barely above a whisper, "I will personally fire you."

Selman gasped as though he had been hit in the abdomen. He scanned the faces of the board, searching for any sign of support—none was offered. Denied a reprieve, he settled back in the large leather chair. In a minute or so, the tight lines around his mouth relaxed as fatigue replaced shock.

Roger Selman was 62-years-old—and he was tired. He was tired of fighting administration and the board. He was tired of running a department with few resources. Most of all he was tired of the long hours it took to fix the problems created by well-meaning but inefficient Hap Castleton.

His emotions surprised him. He was no longer angry; he was relieved. *Without Wycoff, I might live another ten years,* he thought. *The money isn't important. I can find another job; maybe I'll even start enjoying life again.*

Selman turned to Wycoff, who watched the transformation with quiet curiosity. Selman decided to give a speech he had rehearsed often but never found courage to deliver.

"The world has changed, but the board is still living in the 1960s," he started. "Healthcare is no longer a charitable enterprise—it's a business. For five years I've told you we need a new accounting system—something that will allow us to bid intelligently on insurance contracts while giving our supervisors the information they need to control their costs."

Now Roger Selman addressed his comments primarily to Edward Wycoff. "It's the board's responsibility to provide direction and control. You provided neither. You failed to respond to a changing environment, and the hospital's reaped the consequences.

"The doctors complain about inefficiencies," Selman continued, turning to Flagg. "But most doctors haven't got a clue about what it takes to run a hospital profitably. You talk about teamwork and unity, but the medical staff can't agree on even the most mundane issues.

"The hospital *is* in trouble," Selman continued. "But firing me isn't going to fix that. The hospital needs change, but it is doubtful this will happen as long as you dinosaurs are in control." Wycoff stiffened, obviously insulted.

Roger Selman straightened himself with dignity. He folded his papers and stuffed them into the large envelope he had carried into the meeting.

Interim Administrator. A temporary hospital administrator that serves at the discretion of the board until a permanent replacement can be found.

Line of credit. Many organizations need to borrow money to meet short-term obligations. Supplies must be purchased, and employees must be paid before payment for the services provided is received from the patient or insurance company. A line of credit from the bank is designed to temporarily provide these funds.

Medicaid. A governmental program funded with state and federal funds to provide healthcare to the poor.

Standing, he shook his head in quiet disgust at Wycoff, and then crossed the room. "Welcome to the 21st century," he said as he shut the massive walnut door behind him.

The room was silent as board members studied one another, uncertain how they felt about Wycoff's action—or Selman's response. Before anyone could respond, Wycoff spoke.

"Mr. Douglas," he said, "the board has empowered me to offer you a contract to serve as **interim administrator** of Brannan Community Hospital—only until we find a permanent replacement. We know you're not a hospital administrator, but you have had some experience with the hospital, and right now we don't have many other candidates.

Wes looked up in surprise. *Interim administrator?* Unwilling to speak until he thought the offer through, Wes studied the board members. In the two weeks Wes worked with the hospital on the projects Wycoff outlined, he had lost much of his enthusiasm for Edward Wycoff. Wycoff would be a difficult person to work with.

On the other hand, Wes had consulted with other small firms in trouble and enjoyed the challenge. His practice was small, and he did have the time. If he was successful, it might lead to future consulting jobs in the community. Accepting the assignment would be a good way to increase his visibility in Park City.

"I think we can work something out," Wes said.

"I'm prepared to offer you $5,000 a month for six months," Wycoff said.

Wes did the calculation in his head. "That's about $30 an hour. My consulting rate is four times that."

Wycoff shook his head with firm determination. "The hospital's in trouble, Wes. We can't afford that. Five thousand a month is our best offer, guaranteed for six months if you perform to our expectations—longer if it takes more time to get a permanent replacement."

Wes thought about his new accounting practice. He only billed 28 out of a possible of 160 hours last month. In a week or so, he could complete his current jobs and sublease his office. He turned the offer over in his mind. His eyes softened and he settled on a decision. "I accept," he said.

Wycoff smiled smugly as he sank back into the large wingback chair. Expressions of the other board members ranged from happiness, to relief, to despair.

David Brannan broke the silence. "I don't mean to change the subject, Ed, but I have a meeting downtown in 20 minutes. Do we have enough cash to meet the payroll Friday?"

"I spoke with the Business Office last night." replied Wycoff. "They're expecting a $400,000 payment from **Medicaid** . . . should arrive by Wednesday. With that, and our remaining **line of credit**, we should be able to squeak by."

"Any chance it won't be here in time?" Brannan queried.

"If it's not here by Wednesday, I'll drive to Salt Lake City and walk the check through their accounting department myself," Wycoff said. He had done that before.

"If payroll is covered, then I suggest we adjourn," said Brannan, smiling with relief. "Do I have a motion we adjourn?"

"I so move!" said Dr. Ashton Amos.

It was evening when Wes entered the administrator's office for the first time since assuming the job. No one had touched it since Hap died. He gazed at Hap's personal items—family photos, a dusty rainbow trout, and a pair of running shoes—and remembered his last visit. Hap's beaming personality permeated the room like the rays of sun that poured in through the French doors behind his desk.

It was different today. The forest green drapes were drawn, and except for the light from a small corner lamp, the office was dark and tomblike. Wes turned on the lights, opened the curtains, and settled into the large green armchair facing the desk.

The administrative wing was empty and he was grateful for the silence. Had Wycoff asked him, Wes would have opposed firing Roger Selman. Even if the controller was incompetent, he took with him knowledge and experience that would have been helpful to a new administrator. Besides, firing hospital personnel was the job of the administrator, not the board. Wycoff had overreached his authority.

Wycoff justified himself by telling others the action was inevitable. "I was just wiping the slate clean," he bragged, "taking care of a dirty job so Wes wouldn't have to handle it." Although Wycoff's intent may have been good, it clearly backfired. The employees liked Selman. His dismissal, so soon after Hap's death, shocked some and offended most. This hostility was evident at a meeting held later that morning when Wycoff introduced Wes as the new boss.

As Wycoff told of the dismissal of Selman, two women employees on the front row cried, and a supervisor stormed from the meeting. It was true that three department managers introduced themselves after the meeting in an attempt to be friendly, but it was also obvious that most blamed Wes for the firing of Selman. *If Wycoff planned to set me up to fail, he couldn't have a done a better job*, Wes thought. Wycoff was not well tuned to the sensitivities of other people. The word on the street was he was bright, but ruthless.

Wes' thoughts were interrupted as Birdie Bankhead, secretary to the administrator, entered the room. She carried a large yellow envelope which she handed to the new administrator.

Wes looked up in surprise. "I thought you left for the day," he said.

Accreditation. An evaluation by an official organization to assure that another organization meets minimum standards of quality. In healthcare, accreditation is an activity conducted by a group named the Joint Commission on Accreditation of Healthcare Organizations. Since patients are usually unable to judge the quality provided by a hospital, accreditation is designed to guarantee that the hospital provides a high level of care.

"I did," she replied. Birdie's lips were drawn tight, a signal to Wes that she was struggling with pretty strong emotions. "This is the first year we are applying for **accreditation**, however, and the application needs a signature."

As he opened the envelope she continued. "The application has to be in Chicago by Friday."

"Sign here," she said pointing to the bottom line, "and I'll drop them by the post office tonight." He signed them and handed them back. She snatched them with hostility, not apparent before Roger Selman's dismissal. Her eyes glistened as they caught the picture of Hap's family on the desk. "You'll want Hap's belongings out of your office," she said stiffly. "I'll remove them tomorrow."

"There's no hurry," Wes said waving the comment off. "Let his family do it—at their convenience."

Birdie studied Wes through the cobwebs of reddened eyes. She hadn't slept for two nights, *or maybe she was asleep still.* This week was a living nightmare. From deep inside, a mournful sob shook her frame.

Wes stood up and took her hand. "Listen Birdie," he said. "I don't agree with everything that's gone on. Let's not rush the family. I can work around this stuff for a few days."

Observing Wes's sensitivity, the lines around Birdie's eyes softened. *I wonder if he knows what he's got himself into,* she thought. At first Birdie hadn't understood why the board hired someone with no experience to take the reins from Hap. She was starting to suspect it was to take a fall—deflect the blame from Wycoff and the board if the hospital folded. Her sympathy rose as she contemplated the consequences of failure for this naïve new administrator.

She took a deep breath and released it slowly. "I'm sorry about the reception you got at the meeting," she said, starting anew. "The employees are good people. They're still in shock over Hap's death, and now with the firing of Roger Selman—."

Wes nodded. "I understand," he said. "I'm not happy about the way things were handled today." He smiled weakly. She smiled sadly in return.

"Is there anything I can do before leaving this evening?" she asked, nodding at a pile of mail on his desk.

"I'm flying to Seattle to complete a consulting assignment," he replied. "Watch over the department while I'm gone."

"When will you be back?"

"I told the board I could start a week from Monday."

Birdie raised her eyebrows in contradiction. "There's a phone call from Wycoff that might change your plans," She crossed to his desk where she tore a phone message from a notepad. "Mr. Wycoff called an hour ago. The bank is calling the hospital's line of credit. Without it the hospital can't meet payroll."

Wes looked up with a start, and then shook his head in disbelief.

Job description. A document detailing a position's: (1) job title, (2) salary range, (3) reporting line, and (4) duties.

She continued. "And did you see tonight's paper?" she continued, handing him the evening edition of the *Park City Sentinel.* The headline read:

Hospital Employees Threaten Walkout

Vote "no confidence" on appointment of new administrator

Wes blinked with bafflement as he read the lead article. Removing his glasses, he rubbed his eyes, and then stared out the French doors. Dark storm clouds were rolling in from the West.

Deep in thought, Wes reviewed his options. Finally he spoke, each word heavy with the responsibility he had unwittingly assumed.

"Cancel my flight," he replied.

Discussion One–Employability Skills

Wes Douglas interviewed for a new job. The Board of Trustees interviews potential candidates and selects the winner.

What do employers look for in hiring a new employee? Surveys reveal the following characteristics:

- *Ability to do the job*
- *Ability to get along with people*
- *Willingness and ability to fit the corporate culture*
- *Integrity and loyalty*
- *Adaptability to change*

Ability to do the Job

High in priority for any employer is the ability of the employee to perform the tasks needed by the job. Before interviewing applicants, employers often prepare a ***job description****, giving the title of the job, the place of employment, who the employee reports to, and a list of tasks the employee must complete to perform the job successfully.*

Aptitude. Natural ability.

Certification. Recognition by a nongovernmental regulatory body that a person meets minimum standards to provide healthcare services.

Licensure. Official recognition by a governmental body that a person meets minimal educational requirements, and has the knowledge and skill to practice a specific profession.

Aptitude

Aptitude *is defined as "natural talent, an ability to learn easily and quickly, a set of factors that employers can assess that show what occupation a person is best suited for."*[1]

Different people have different aptitudes. People with strengths in one area often have weaknesses in another. A good mathematician may be a poor writer. An able mechanic may have poor people skills.

Before selecting a career, one should research the aptitudes needed for the specific job. A dentist, for example, needs manual dexterity and good people skills.

Some people spend years qualifying for an occupation, only to find after graduation that they don't enjoy the work or its environment. How does one avoid making a mistake when selecting an academic course of study?

- *Talk with people who work in the industry. Ask them what they do during a typical day. Ask about their work environment, the type of people they associate with, the aspects of the job they find enjoyable, and the aspects they find boring or distasteful.*
- *Work in the industry before seeking a degree in a specific field. Many medical schools, for example, encourage students to work as Certified Nurse Assistants (CNAs), before applying to medical school.*
- *Take a vocational aptitude test.*

Education and Training

Many professional jobs need **licensure** *or* **certification**. *Professional associations like the American Medical Association, the American Nursing Association, and the American Hospital Association can help identify requirements for a specific profession.*

In addition, most healthcare jobs require some college or technical school education. Realize, however, knowledge is expanding at an ever-increasing rate. Much of what you learn in school will be obsolete within 15 years of the time you get your degree. Continuing education is a requirement for most professions.

[1] *The New Lexicon Webster's Dictionary of the English Language*, Lexicon Publications, Inc. Danbury, Ct.

Internship. A training program, usually one or two years in length, immediately following graduation from medical school, designed to give the medical school graduate real world experience in applying the theoretical concepts learned in class.

Experience

Some employers want real-world work experience before they hire an applicant. One way to satisfy this requirement is through an ***internship****. Check with a local college to see if they offer internships.*

Ability to Get Along with People

Another important characteristic employers look for is an ability to work with people. The most common reason people are fired is not technical incompetence, but an inability to get along with people.

Most work in the healthcare industry is done in teams. The ability to work in a team takes skills sometimes not taught in high schools and colleges. These include:

- *An ability to identify the goals of the team, and to put these ahead of personal agendas.*
- *The ability to take responsibility for a specific task and complete it without supervision or prodding.*
- *The ability to communicate; to understand other people's points of view; and to compromise.*
- *The ability to coordinate time schedules.*
- *The ability to coordinate tasks with other people.*
- *A willingness to share credit for a job well done.*

Ability to Fit the Corporate Culture

Corporate culture is defined as "what behavior is acceptable at our place of work." A corporate culture defines the dress code, codes of conduct, and so on. The corporate culture varies from company to company. At one time the corporate culture at IBM mandated a white shirt, blue or gray suit, and a conservative tie. At Microsoft the corporate culture permitted t-shirts and sandals.

How do you know when an organization is "a good fit?" One way is to visit the firm before applying for the job. Another is to talk to employees about the culture, expectations, environment, and so on.

Integrity and Loyalty

Studies have shown that many firms favor loyalty above honesty. Both are important.

Adaptability to Change

The only constant in the modern world of work is change. New technology, global competition, and emerging world economies are changing the way employees work. Employees must commit to lifetime learning and continuous adaptation to changing environments.

Discussion Two--Terminology

During his first week on the job, Wes Douglas encountered many technical terms. He remarked that it was almost as if each department had a separate language. He recognized that effective communication would require him to learn new terminology.

One way to do this is to memorize certain Greek and Latin roots that serve as the basis for many medical terms. The list is provided on the next page for memorization.

a- *not, without, less*
acantho- *thorn*
adeno- *gland*
adip- *fat*
albo- *white*
algesi- *pain*
ambly- *dull*
angi- *vessel*
anti- *opposing*
aque- *water*
arteri- *artery*
audio- *hearing*
aut- *self*
bi- *twice, double*
bacterio- *bacteria*
brachi- *arm*
carcin- *cancer*
cardi- *heart*
carpo- *wrist*
cephal- *the head*
chemo- *chemistry*
crani- *cranium*
cry- *cold*
crypto- *hidden*
cyan- *blue*
cyst- *bladder, cyst*
cyte- *cell*
dactul- *finger, toe*
deca- *ten*
dent- *tooth*
derm- *skin*
duo- *two*
dys- *bad, difficult*
ect- *outer, outside*
encephalo- *brain*
epi- *upon or following*
ergo- *work*
erythro- *red*
esthesio- *sensation*
gastr- *stomach*
galact- *milk*
gingiv- *gums*
gloss- *tongue*
glycol- *sugar*
gyn- *woman*
hem- *blood*
hepat- *liver*
hist- *tissue*
homeo- *same*
hydro- *water*
hyper- *excessive*
hypo- *beneath*
infra- *below*
intro- *within*
-ism *disease*
-itis *inflammation*

kerat- *cornea*
laryng- *larynx*
-lepsy *seizure*
lipo- *fat*
lith- *stone*
-logy *study of*
macr- *large*
melan- *black*
morph- *shape*
naso- *nose*
necro- *death*
nephr- *kidney*
neur- *nerve*
odont- *tooth*
oma- *tumor*
opthalmo- *eye*
ortho- *straight*
ossi- *bone*
para- *abnormal*
patho- *disease*
ped- *child, foot*
peri- *around*
pharmaco- *drugs*
-philia *attraction*
phleb- *vein*
phobia- *fear*
phon- *sound, speech*
photo- *light*
-phylaxis *protection*
plasma- *plasma*
pleur- *rib, side*
pnea- *breath*
pod- *foot*
poly- *many*
pre- *before*
pseud- *false*
psych- *mind*
ren- *kidney*
rhin- *nose*
-rrhagia *discharge*
schizo- *split*
scope- *look*
sin- *sinus*
somat- *body*
spasmo- *spasm*
spiro- *breathing*
spleen- *spleen*
stom- *mouth*
super- *in excess*
sub- *beneath*
supra- *above*
syn- *together*
tachy- *rapid*
tel- *distant*
thorac- *chest*
therm- *heat*
thromb- *clot*
thyro- *thyroid*
tomy- *cut*
toxi- *toxin*
trache- *trachea*
ultra- *beyond*
uni- *one*
uro- *urine*
vas- *vessel*
xanth- *yellow*
zo- *life*

Discussion Questions

1. *Edward Wycoff felt Hap Castleton and Wes Douglas would make a good team, as each would complement the strengths and weaknesses of the other. What are the strengths and weaknesses of Hap and Wes?*
2. *Edward Wycoff related the story of several vice presidents of a large Fortune 500 company who were successful while holding important jobs within the company, but lost their fortunes when they tried to go into business for themselves. Why did this happen? What can a supervisor learn from this experience?*
3. *Why did Wes accept the offer to serve as interim administrator of Brannan Community Hospital? What did Wes Douglas have to win by accepting this offer, and what might he have to lose? Place yourself in the role of Wes Douglas. Would you accept the job?*
4. *It has often been said; How someone does something is as important as what he or she does. If you were chairperson of the board, would you have fired Roger Selman? Is there anything you would have done differently?*
5. *Assuming it was necessary to fire Roger Selman, what do you think of Wycoff's timing?*
6. *What was the response of hospital employees to the appointment of Wes Douglas as administrator? What might the board have done to ease his transition?*
7. *So long as the board does the right thing, does it matter what the employees or the medical staff think of their actions?*
8. *Where does authority come from: a title, or credibility?*
9. *What will Wes Douglas have to do to build his credibility with the board, the medical staff, and the employees?*
10. *If an allied health employee has good technical skills, why is it important for him or her to have political savvy and good communication skills as well?*
11. *Birdie Bankhead, Hap Castleton's secretary, believes Edward Wycoff may have hidden motives in selecting Wes Douglas as the new hospital administrator. What might these motives be? If Bankhead is correct, what can Wes Douglas do to protect himself?*
12. *Identify the root words of each of the following terms. From the roots, explain what you think the term might mean. Using a medical dictionary, write the definition:*

Cyanotic. Blue

cystitis

gingivitis

hematology

histology

hypodermic

liposuction

necrophobia

necrosis

ophthalmologist

orthodontist

pathology

tracheoscopic

13. *Assume you are a healthcare practitioner talking to someone with no medical training about a loved one who has been admitted to the hospital. Translate the following into simple English the family can understand.*
    a. *I believe your 100 year-old aunt is necrophobic.*
    b. *The child was* ***cyanotic*** *at admission.*
    c. *Your father was suffering from apnea when he called us.*
    d. *Your son has severe gingivitis.*

Writing Exercise

14. *Assume you were asked to fire Roger Selman. Prepare an outline of what you would say. Role-play the situation with another student in front of the class, showing courtesy and kindness.*

Using the tools taught in Discussion One—Employability Skills develop a plan to explore a specific healthcare career. Consider (a) personal aptitudes, (b) education and training requirements, (c) pay and job opportunities, and (d) work environment.

Role-Playing Assignment

15. *Select a team of six or more people to role-play the Board of Trustees of Brannan Community Hospital and the administrator before the class. Have the board develop a plan to save the hospital in the next 30 days. Address the following problems: (1) the hospital is not producing enough cash to pay its bills, (2) employee morale is at an all-time low, (3) the newspaper is running unfavorable editorials about the operation of the hospital, (4) the community is losing confidence in the quality of services provided by the hospital, and (5) there is talk of an initiative to close the hospital down.*

4

Resolve and Regret

Paramedic. A person trained to provide emergency care.

Through an open window in his small apartment, Wes listened to the noise from the street below. A freight truck was backing into an alley, and someone was shouting instructions to the driver in Spanish. The freight dock for the hotel next door was directly beneath his window.

Wes rolled over and checked his alarm—5:00 a.m. The weatherman had forecast stormy weather. Wes smelled the rain as it hit the dusty asphalt below. A gust of wind snatched a newspaper high in the air above the alley, and thunder rumbled in the distant mountains.

Wes stumbled to his feet to shut the window. He returned to his bed. Sinking into the pillow, he took a deep breath, held it, and slowly released it. *If I could just relax the muscles in my back.*

He eyed the medicine on the nightstand, tempted for a moment to swallow another painkiller. He reconsidered. They dulled his thinking, and he would need all of his mental resources to handle the problems of his second day.

He gently straightened. It had been six months since the automobile accident, and this morning the pain in his lower back was as severe as the night they pulled him from his mangled automobile. He vaguely remembered being lowered onto an ambulance litter before passing out. Sometime later he drifted in consciousness. A **paramedic** had started an IV and was reading Wes's vital signs over the radio to a nurse at the hospital.

"Kathryn? . . . Where is Kathryn?" he whispered.

"It's going to be all right buddy," the paramedic answered. The paramedic lied—nothing would ever be right again.

Friends told him time would soften the loss. Someday life would again have meaning. For now, the only relief was the distraction of hard work that left little time to think about anything else.

Even so, his mind burned with her memory. Rarely an hour passed he didn't think of Kathryn—her slender figure, twinkling green eyes—the impish smile that played at her mouth just before he kissed her. He closed his eyes, his mind clouding with visions of the past.

Bond. A type of borrowing instrument. Hospitals can issue bonds to borrow money to pay for buildings and equipment.

Director of Nursing. The chief nursing officer (CNO). This person has line responsibility for all nursing activities in the hospital.

Stock. A share certifying the holder owns part of a corporation.

Unable to sleep, he sat up—*carefully*. He took a deep breath, and then nodded with firm resolve. It had been six months since he realized it was time to move on; find a new job, new friends. His answer was to relocate to a new part of the country. He picked Park City from a ski magazine.

Erasing memories, however, was easier said than done. Often, in the slumber of the early morning, he would return to the evening of the accident. In the recurring nightmare he would feel the play of the steering as the tires slipped on the wet pavement, the crushing impact of the crash; the blackness that blended the smells of burning rubber and gasoline mingled with pain, and the sound of the rain as it hit the dusty asphalt below.

Wes's body was heavy with fatigue as he drove to work an hour later. To focus his thoughts, he reviewed the events of the previous day. At 1:00 PM he met with Elizabeth Flannigan, the **director of nursing**.

Flannigan was a fierce woman. She handled herself with the authority of a staff sergeant and rarely took direction from anyone. Focusing on the hospital's financial problems, Wes quizzed her about nursing costs and discussed the possibility of cutting staff.

He shouldn't have done that—not during their introductory meeting. Flannigan and her staff were already paranoid. Alarmed, she ran to Dr. Emil Flagg, who confronted Wes in his office, pouncing on him with the fury of a Rocky Mountain thunderstorm.

"Hell-bound financiers like Wycoff are destroying healthcare!" Flagg shouted, his enormous fists smashing a stack of financial reports on Wes's desk. "Wycoff, the miserable rodent, thinks he can run this place like a bank. This isn't Wall Street, and our patients aren't **stocks** and **bonds**!"

The meeting lasted for an hour. Flagg was angry at insurance companies, paperwork, hospital administrators, and the other members of the board. Wes, in his eyes, was one with Wycoff.

Wes assured him of his concern for the welfare of the employees. His voice was firm, however, when he reminded the doctor that the hospital was losing money and the board had hired him to do all in his power to save it from bankruptcy. The meeting ended in a stalemate.

As Wes's car pulled into the parking lot, it occurred to him that accepting the job might have been a mistake. He didn't' have the background to run a hospital, and botching the job now would reflect negatively on his new CPA practice. He shook the thought off. Negative thinking never solved anything. Having committed himself, he would give the job his full effort. Three hundred fifty employees depended on him. The hospital had served the residents of Park City for 65 years. It might fail—but not on his watch.

Employee council. A committee of hospital employees, often elected, whose purpose is to represent the viewpoints and concerns of the employees to management.

Maintenance department. The hospital department responsible for maintaining buildings and equipment.

On-call nurse. A nurse not assigned a specific time to work, but who agrees to be available to be called in on short notice.

"Good morning, Mr. Douglas!" A noticeably more chipper Birdie Bankhead looked up from her computer and smiled brightly. The puffiness was gone from her eyes, and her voice was as sunny as the yellow pantsuit she wore. Wes smiled, grateful for the change.

"You're here early," he said, nodding at the clock above her desk.

"Had a ton of letters to finish before the phone started ringing," she replied. She continued typing, and then looked up with a start. "That reminds me," she said. "Hank Ulman, president of the **employee council**, called me at home last night. He wants to meet with you—this morning at 10:00 a.m. at the Pipe Fitters Union Hall. I wrote the address down."

She reached for her purse. Retrieving a small notepad, she tore the message off and handed it to Wes. "920 South Brannan Avenue," she said. "Small red building—second floor—just above the bakery."

Wes's brows pulled into a scowl as he read the note. "Didn't know we had a union."

"Technically, we don't, but there's been talk of one since Wycoff vetoed the budget," she replied continuing to type. "He wanted Hap to cut salaries by 12%. Someone leaked the story to the newspaper. Caused quite a stir among the employees. That's when the union talk began. Guess the issue is surfacing again," she sniffed, returning to her typing.

"Hank Ulman," Wes said, turning the note over in his hand. "One of our employees?"

Birdie nodded. "Works in the **maintenance department**. Moonlights part-time as a mechanic for a flight service in Salt Lake City. He has a reputation as a troublemaker. Ran once for city council—American Socialist Party ticket. Got seven votes.

"Historically most of our employees ignored him. Four months ago, however, when Wycoff started getting involved in running the hospital, the employees elected him president of the employee council."

Wes frowned. "What do you mean by 'Wycoff started getting involved in running the hospital?'?"

"He manipulated the board into appointing him budget director," Birdie replied. "Once he got control of the budget, he had control of the hospital."

"The Golden Rule," Wes replied. "He who controls the gold makes the rules."

"Right," Birdie replied. "Hap planned to take the responsibility back. He got Wycoff to agree to transfer the title to Del Cluff." She sighed, "Of course, that was before the accident."

A dozen thoughts flashed across Wes's face as he considered the issue. "Call Ulman," he said finally "and tell him there'll be no meeting, not with him, and not at the Union Hall. Then arrange a meeting with our employees for 10:30. Ask scheduling to pull in all **on-call nurses** for staffing coverage—I want as many of our full-time staff there as possible."

"Do you want supervisors at the meeting?" Birdie asked.

"No, I'll meet with them tomorrow."

Carotid artery. The artery that supplies the brain with blood.

Deposition. Written testimony under oath.

Malpractice. An act of professional negligence that injures a patient.

Medical executive committee (MEC). The primary governing committee of the medical staff. The goal of the MEC is to conduct business in the hospital for and in behalf of the medical staff.

Birdie scratched a note in her planner.

Energized by completing his first official act, Wes was hungry. "Think I'll catch breakfast," he said brightly. "When I get back, let's meet to plan the rest of the day."

This was Wes's first visit to the cafeteria. An arrow pointed to the basement. Taking the exit, he plowed down the stairs, shaking hands with two doctors on the landing. They asked for a meeting at his earliest convenience. "Schedule it with Birdie," he replied cordially as he continued down the stairs.

During Wes's first interview, he found the lobby cold and uninviting. It reminded him of the lobby of a bus depot. He was pleasantly surprised, therefore, to find the cafeteria warm and cheerful. Nothing fancy—if anything, a little homespun—checkered red and white tablecloth and yellow walls.

Canyon Elementary School had decorated the south wall with crayon drawings depicting brightly colored surgeons helped by chalk-white nurses. The aroma of eggs, bacon, and coffee drifted from a spotless kitchen. A radio was playing country music, and the room hummed with the pleasant chatter of 50 or so employees and visitors.

Wes selected a tray and headed for the cafeteria line, confident few employees would recognize him as the new administrator. *A good chance for a little reconnaissance.* He grabbed a packet of silverware.

An attorney friend once told him about a hospital **malpractice** case he handled. It involved a doctor who severed a **carotid artery** during surgery. For two days the attorney interviewed the surgeon and operating room personnel. Frustrated at his inability to crack the case, he sent two clerks to the hospital. Posing as visitors, they spent three days in the cafeteria, drinking coffee and eavesdropping on the conversations of hospital employees. "Get a group of nurses on break and they'll gossip," he said. "Over coffee and rolls they gossiped about the case, the incompetence of the surgeon, and the **medical executive committee's** long-standing inability to control or discipline the doctor being sued."

Having discovered more from cafeteria gossip than they would have learned in ten months of **depositions**, the attorneys approached hospital administration with their newfound evidence. They settled out of court for two million dollars.

Wes paid for breakfast and took a table near the center of the cafeteria, not far from a group of housekeepers seated at a large round table. "Did ya hear they fired poor old Mister Selman?" a heavy woman in a blue housekeeping uniform said to her companions as she buttered a thick pancake. From a picture in the hospital newsletter, Wes recognized her as Betsy Flint, a long-term employee.

CEO. An acronym for chief executive officer. In a hospital, the CEO is the hospital administrator.

Operations. Relating to the functioning or management of an organization.

"It was Wycoff that got him," replied a coworker, a frail woman with a thin rooster nose. "Now Mr. Castleton's dead, Wycoff's going to have his evil way with the hospital," she blathered, pointing with her fork to a picture of the hospital on the wall. Her dark eyes turned bitter. "Doc Flagg said he's been pushing staffing cuts for three months. He'll have us all on unemployment if he gets his way." The employees at her table nodded ominously.

"He don't believe in unemployment insurance," another housekeeper hooted. "He'll have us on the street!"

"Hap would never have stood for that," Betsy said, her eyes widening with resentment. She took a hearty bite of her cheese omelet and leaned forward conspiratorially. "Say, what's this new administrator like?"

"He's a real dandy," her companion replied, mirroring Betsy's facial expression. "Flagg says he's Wycoff's man—a guy from back East, a fancy finance fella. Doc says he doesn't know nothin' 'bout hospitals."

A flash of alarm exploded across Betsy's stout face. "Good Jehosophat!" she said, rocking back in her cafeteria chair. Wes held his breath as the vintage chair—a survivor from the original hospital—groaned under her weight. It held, and a worker's compensation injury was avoided.

Wes's eavesdropping was interrupted by the cafeteria intercom. "Mr. Douglas, line four," the operator announced. Several employees scanned the cafeteria for a look at their new boss. When the interest died down, he quietly made his way to the hall where he took the call.

"Wes speaking," he said.

Birdie was on the other end. Her voice registered concern. "I have Mr. Wycoff on the line. Told him you were unavailable. He insisted I track you down," she said.

"Put him on," Wes said softly.

The phone clicked and Wycoff spoke. "Read the article in last night's paper," he began, his words coming in short staccato-like bursts. "I'll be down shortly. Want to meet with the employee council. I've dealt with threats like this before," his voice dripping with contempt. "Don't know who they think they are, but I'll nip this in the bud."

"Understand your concern, Mr. Wycoff," Wes said politely, "but I'll handle it."

"You can't meet with them alone,—" Wycoff said. Wes sensed the surprise in Wycoff's voice.

"That's my intent," Wes said calmly. *It was important to establish policy early.* "The board establishes policy and evaluates the administrator. The administrator runs the hospital. This is an operational issue—my turf."

"Don't be a fool," Wycoff said dropping the polite facade. "A good **CEO** uses the talents of his board."

"Not in **operations** he doesn't."

Operational issues. Issues relating to the management or operation of a hospital.

Union steward. An in-house union representative.

Wycoff gasped at Wes's boldness. "As chairperson of the finance committee, I'm going to meet with our supervisors on the financial crisis," he announced with all the authority he could command.

Wes held his ground. "As chairperson of the finance committee, you will meet *only* with the board. The board will set policy. I will relay that policy to employees," he said.

Wycoff sputtered. "I have several issues to discuss with the employees. The budget, our new organizational structure. . ."

"Those are **operational issues**," Wes repeated firmly.

Wycoff simmered silently.

"I appreciate your concern," Wes continued. "If I need your help, I'll call."

Wes waved cheerfully at Dr. Flagg who stormed by without speaking.

"Good-bye, Wes," Wycoff said.

Was that a farewell . . . or a threat? Wes wondered as the phone clicked dead.

It took a heroic effort by Housekeeping to prepare the cafeteria for a meeting on such short notice. The dietary department shut the breakfast line down promptly at 10:00 a.m.—30 minutes early as a team of housekeepers quickly descended on the department, removing tables, sweeping floors, and setting up chairs. Wes had one goal for the meeting— *prevent a walkout.*

The room filled quickly. Wes entered from the rear, and walked briskly to a portable podium at the front. He stood there as the room quieted.

"I'm Wes Douglas, your new administrator," he began. "I know my appointment as interim administrator surprised many of you—none of you more than I." *A feeble attempt at humor—no one smiled.*

Wes noticed the audience was divided into three groups. A small cluster standing in the back exchanged guffaws with their ringleader—a stocky maintenance man with a barrel chest and large animated arms that swung out from his body like hams as he mimicked Wes. From an earlier description, Wes assumed the comedian was Hank Ulman—the self-appointed **union steward**.

A second group, scattered throughout the audience, watched dispassionately, arms folded, faces skeptical. *Convince us the board didn't make a mistake*, their expressions seemed to say.

The third group—10 or 12 people on the front row—were receptive. But being few in number, they seemed intimidated by others in the audience.

"I'd like to begin by explaining my management philosophy," Wes continued. For the next ten minutes he discussed the goals he had set for the hospital, the most important of which was to keep the hospital from closing.

"I've had my say," he concluded. "Now, tell me your concerns."

Reagent. A substance used in the laboratory to detect or measure another substance.

The room was silent. Finally, an employee from the business office raised her hand. "I have a complaint," she said. "The board never consults us; we don't know what's going on. There isn't a single employee who has ever heard of you. Suddenly you're the new boss." The room hummed with agreement.

"The newspaper editor knows more about what's happening here than we do," she continued. "Hap never told us about a financial crisis." Her face twisted with skepticism. "How do we know it's real?"

"It's real," Wes replied.

"Can you guarantee there'll be no layoffs?" a nurse demanded.

"No, but I'll consult with your supervisors before cutting staff. There'll be no secrets."

A lab technician raised his hand. "There's a rumor you're an accountant. I've got a complaint about the accounting department. The employees get blamed for the hospital's losses, but it's not our fault—accounting's pricing policies are the problem. We're doing some of our lab tests for less than the cost of **reagents**."

"Waste is another problem," a nurse added. "Last week we threw away several hundred dollars of sterile products because they were outdated. This is a problem on all units."

Wes took notes. "Helpful input," he said. Complaints continued for another 20 minutes.

Finally, Wes summarized. "There was a time in my career when I blamed employees for poor quality. Experience has changed my mind. I realized the problem is poor management. Give me a few days to find out what is going on," he said, "and we'll hit the issues straight on."

His approach was working. Many employees smiled—a few applauded. It was time to discuss the threatened walkout. As the morale of the meeting improved, Hank Ulman's hostility rose. Suddenly he left the room, taking with him two coworkers.

Good riddance, Wes thought.

Wes was in striking distance of his goal—or so he thought. He cleared his throat. "There's one more issue I want to discuss," he said as the employees quieted. "An article in the paper reported a threatened employee walkout. The hospital has problems, a walk out won't solve them—"

A muffled explosion interrupted his words. A loud hissing noise followed as a stream of boiling water, red with rust, gushed through the opening under the boiler room door and swirled over the feet of the employees. A laundry worker in low cut shoes screamed in pain as she grabbed her ankles. A coworker grabbed her arm, but slipped on the wet floor and fell in the scalding water. Two men pulled them to their feet.

Hank Ulman appeared in the doorway. Interestingly enough he was wearing hip boots. "A pipe to the boiler's broken!" he shouted. "Everyone out!"

Stakeholder. A person who has an interest in an organization, project or concept.

The room exploded in commotion as the crowd convulsed to the front of the room, knocking over chairs in their efforts to escape the scalding flow. An employee hit the crash bar to the emergency exit, setting off the alarm as workers pushed one another through the door and up the stairwell. Ulman had successfully ended the meeting.

Thirty minutes later, Wes met Hank Ulman in the hall.

"Like I tol' Hap, the boiler's old—needs replacin'." Ulman smiled, exposing a broken, chestnut colored tooth. "Gonna kill somebody someday. The steam pipe came right off the wall. It's good I was there. If I wasn't, things might have turned out differently."

"I'm sure that's true," Wes replied flatly.

Discussion One–Assuming the Reins

In this chapter, Wes Douglas assumes the reins of Brannan Community Hospital. Many people will offer advice and help. Some will try to get the new administrator to take sides on issues they support or oppose.

Here is some good counsel for anyone moving into a position of authority in a new organization:

1. *Don't commit yourself to a course of action on major issues until you understand what is going on. There will be people who will try to get you to take a stand on an issue favoring their interests before you have all the facts.*
2. *Until you understand all the issues, listen more and talk less. Remember the famous quotation by Mark Twain: "It's better to remain silent and be thought a fool, than to open one's mouth and dispel all doubt." Some people try to impress others with their knowledge by talking too much—that doesn't work. One advantage of quality listening is that you may actually learn something. When you finally do speak, you will do so with knowledge and authority.*
3. *Build rapport with your employees before taking major action. Some novice managers mistakenly believe the shortest distance between two points is a straight line. Often the quickest course of action, especially when you are dealing with people, is not the best approach. Before you start giving orders, strive to understand each* ***stakeholder's*** *point of view and to build consensus.*

Interdisciplinary team. A group of people with different educational backgrounds who come together for a specific project.

4. *Remember how you do something is often as important as what you do. It is not enough to be sincere, you must be right. However, it is still not enough to be right, you must be effective. Many supervisors fail by doing the right thing, but in the wrong way. We no longer live in an economy where a title alone carries authority. A supervisor must gain the employees' respect before he or she can lead.*

5. *Don't criticize your predecessor, even if he or she was incompetent. Your successor will have friends among your employees, whom you will alienate if you bad-mouth their former boss.*

Discussion Two—Teamwork

Wes Douglas is seeking the help of his employees as he tries to save Brannan Community Hospital. He recognizes he can only solve the hospital's problems with a team effort. Most work in the healthcare industry is done in teams.

What is a team? It is a group working for a common goal. Hospitals use ***interdisciplinary teams****—teams composed of people with different educational backgrounds—to work together in the care and treatment of hospital patients. Team members include the doctor who diagnoses the patient and develops a plan for care, registered nurses who supervise and direct hospital care, and non-licensed staff who perform duties assigned.*

Good team leaders delegate the right task, in the right circumstance, to the right person, who has the proper license and training. Effective team leaders direct, communicate, supervise, and give feedback on employee performance.

Many schools do a poor job of teaching teamwork. Most students compete for grades with assignments individually completed. Usually there are penalties for working together on an assignment. This is unfortunate, as the ability to work with others is one of the most important characteristics employers look for in new employees.

What characterizes a successful team? Researchers have identified seven elements:

- *Leadership*
- *Common goals*
- *An understanding of the role of each team member*
- *Attention to activities that build team spirit*
- *An ability to meet the needs of each person on the team*
- *Trust*

Human resources. The personnel department.

- *Good communication*
- *Respect for facts*

Leadership

Although there are many effective management styles, successful leaders share several characteristics. Successful leaders:

- *Understand the goal to be reached*
- *Accept responsibility*
- *Seek input from all team members*
- *Break complex goals into tasks that they can delegate*
- *Possess the ability to inspire and manage people*
- *Understand the importance of* **human resources**
- *Have good listening skills*
- *Understand and respect diversity*
- *Supervise and give feedback*

Good team leaders are service oriented. The greatest leader is one who serves.

Common Goals

Successful teams have mutual goals or objectives and share a sense of urgency in completing those goals. A nursing team's goal is to treat patients.

An Understanding of the Role of Each Team Member

Members of successful teams understand the responsibilities of each player. They know what they can expect from each member and realize that everyone contributes to the team effort.

Attention to Activities that Build Team Spirit

Successful teams recognize how important team spirit is and devote time and resources to building that spirit. Team building activities include:

- *Periodic meetings to set goals and measure progress*
- *Newsletters*

- *Certificates of appreciation*
- *Thank you cards*
- *On the spot rewards (for example, movie tickets for nurses asked to work a double shift)*
- *Parties and other fun activities to celebrate accomplishments*

Successful teams celebrate cooperative effort—they will not intentionally allow one member to benefit at the expense of another.

Ability to Meet the Needs of Team Players

Successful teams meet the needs of each team member. Team members need:

- *A sense of accomplishment*
- *Control over their environment*
- *Freedom of thought, action, and growth*
- *Recognition and prestige*
- *A sense of belonging*
- *Security*

Trust

Without trust, team members are unwilling to rely on the experience, judgment, or personal commitment of others. Trust involves:

- *Respect for the talents and roles of each team member*
- *Acceptance of different backgrounds, opinions, and contributions*
- *Willingness to take the risk of interdependence*
- *Problem solving, rather than bargaining*
- *Willingness to allow others to make mistakes*
    - *Mistakes are often stepping-stones to success. There is no such thing as innovation without error. When employees make mistakes, the emphasis should be on learning, not punishment.*
    - *This is not to say teams should allow mistakes to occur through carelessness or a lack of planning.*

Good Communication

In healthcare, a failure to communicate can lead to the injury or death of a patient. Communication is an important part of teamwork. Communication can be verbal or nonverbal. Nonverbal communication improves and supports verbal communication, and includes body language, facial expressions, and gestures.

Good communication has four ingredients:

- *The sender*
- *The message*
- *The receiver*
- *Feedback*

When communicating with patients:

- *Consider the listener's education and understanding.*
- *Keep it simple. Avoid using technical language the listener will not understand.*
- *If a patient speaks another language, get an interpreter.*
- *If the patient is hearing impaired, speak loudly and clearly, but never shout.*
- *Reinforce your message with nonverbal communication.*
- *If the patient is confused, simplify your message. Use short, clear sentences*
- *Face the patient andd use proper eye contact.*
- *Seek feedback to assure the listener understands what has been said*
    - *Ask the patient if he or she understands the message.*
    - *More important, have the patient repeat what has been said.*
- *Always show courtesy and respect.*

Respect for Facts

Successful teams have an ability to collect and analyze data. They rely on facts, not opinion.

Discussion Questions

1. *The first meeting of Wes Douglas with Elizabeth Flannigan, director of nursing, didn't go well. If you were the new administrator, explain how you might have established rapport with your new nursing director before exploring a controversial topic such as cost reduction.*
2. *How can planning for an important meeting with a supervisor, coworker, or subordinate raise your chance of success? What issues might you want to include in such a planning session?*
3. *Emil Flagg, the representative of the medical staff on the board of Trustees, is an important stakeholder in the operation of the hospital. What would have been your approach in defusing Dr. Flagg's anger during his first meeting with the new hospital administrator?*
4. *From the conversations of hospital employees Wes Douglas monitored in the hospital cafeteria, it is obvious the employees have a negative impression of their new administrator. List possible reasons for this. If you were interim administrator, how would you address this problem?*
5. *Sometimes, people jump before they think. Wes Douglas, for example, is having second thoughts about accepting the job of administration. Given that he has accepted the job, what do you think is his best course of action? Should he bail out, walking away from the commitments he has made to the board, or hang in there and try to salvage the situation?*
6. *Hank Ulman, president of the employee council, thinks he sees a vacuum in leadership—one he is eager to fill. What are his motives? Does he have the best interests of the hospital at heart? List several alternative courses of action Wes Douglas might take in neutralizing Ulman's efforts. List the advantages and disadvantages of each course of action, telling what you would do if you were the interim administrator.*
7. *According to Wes Douglas, what is the role of the board, and what is the role of the hospital administrator?*
8. *Wes Douglas canceled the meeting with Hank Ulman at the Union Hall. Why did he take this course of action? How would you handle the situation?*
9. *During a telephone conversation between Wes and Edward Wycoff, Wycoff expressed his wish to involve himself in solving the hospital's operating problems. What are the advantages and disadvantages of having a board member involved in daily operations?*
10. *Why are elevators and hospital cafeterias a good place for reconnaissance by attorneys who have malpractice suits against the hospital? What ramifications does this have for patient privacy? Is there a lesson for hospital employees?*

11. *What do employees think of Edward Wycoff, chairperson of the finance committee? Why do they think Wes Douglas is in Wycoff's camp? Should Wes Douglas distance himself from Wycoff?*
12. *If an employee believes she has two bosses, is there a possibility she will play the one against the other?*
13. *By telling Wycoff to stay out of operations, Wes offended one of his few allies on the board. Was this the right action to take?*
14. *What do you believe Wes Douglas's purpose was in meeting with the employees this early in his administration? What message would you have sent to your employees in your first meeting?*
15. *List five characteristics of successful teams.*
16. *List four ingredients of good communication.*

5

Amy

Credentials committee. The medical staff committee that reviews the application of physicians to perform specific procedures in the hospital and recommends to the hospital Board of Trustees that the physician be given or denied these privileges.

The following morning was filled with meetings with community leaders concerned about the future of the hospital and the impact a closure might have on the local economy. It was noon when Wes returned to the hospital. Birdie Bankhead was leaving for lunch when he met her in the employee parking lot. "There are several messages on your desk," she said, fishing in her purse for her keys. Her eyes widened. "That reminds me," she said. "Hap's daughter Amy came by this morning to clean out his office. She's still there. You'll enjoy meeting her."

Wes nodded and headed for the employee entrance. By now, everyone recognized him as the new administrator. Just navigating from the parking lot to administration was a difficult chore, as doctors, supervisors, and employees collared him to voice complaints and give advice. It took 20 minutes from the time he entered the building to the time he arrived at administration.

By the time he reached his office, his arms were full of three-ring binders with past minutes of the **credentials committee** the secretary of the medical staff asked him to review and sign. Nudging the door closed, he leaned against it and caught his breath. He dropped the binders on Birdie's desk.

With the interruptions, he had forgotten about Amy Castleton. He was surprised when, through the door of Hap's old office, he saw her reading from a stack of papers on the massive walnut desk. Her head was turned gently to one side, exposing a slender white neck. She had long, amber hair that glowed softly in the sunlight that poured through the French doors leading to the patio. Mute, he stared at her as she read from a letter she picked up from Hap's desk. She looked up, startled.

"Hi," he said, "I'm Wes Douglas."

Pursing her lips, she studied him for a moment—then her eyes lit with recognition. "Wes Douglas—of course . . . Father's new financial consultant," she hesitated, "and now his replacement." She smiled sadly and held out her hand. Wes gently shook it as he sat in the chair next to hers.

“Dad was pleased with your decision to consult with the hospital,” she said. “I’m sorry you didn’t have more time to work together.”

“I’m sorry too,” he said gently.

A shadow crossed Amy’s face and her brown eyes filled with tears. Looking down at the letter she was holding, she bit softly on her lower lip. It was the first time he’d felt clumsy around a girl since he fell in love with Carol Reimschussel in the sixth grade. As he stared into her eyes, an unfamiliar intensity overcame him.

It took a moment for him to realize he was still holding—squeezing actually—her hand. She looked at their hands and then into his face. A questioning look stole across her eyes. Blushing, he released her hand. Anxious to start anew, he pointed to a painting on the wall above the credenza. “Interesting picture,” he said. “I noticed it when I first met your father—is it yours?”

Color touched her cheeks. She smiled and nodded. “I painted it when I was five-years-old,” she stated. “Dad framed it and hung it in his office—I was so proud.”

Her eyes, soft and sentimental, slowly surveyed the room. “Some of my happiest hours were spent here on Saturday mornings,” she said. “Mom was taking a class at the university, and Dad would bring me with him while he opened the mail and caught up on correspondence. I’d read, or draw, or paint.”

The picture, painted with acrylics, was six by eight inches and framed in walnut to match the paneling of the office. A drawing of a large man holding three balloons dominated the picture. At his side was a small girl holding a flower. A huge tree, the sun, flowers, chipmunks, and stop signs, in all their profusion of color, filled the remaining white space.

“Those were all the things I knew how to draw at that age,” she explained, an impish smile playing at the corners of her mouth.

“Dad wasn’t given much to worrying,” she continued, “but during the last few weeks of his life things changed.” Her eyes narrowed as she searched for the right words. “He acted as though something was wrong, but he wouldn’t talk about it. Six weeks before the accident, he took out a life insurance policy.

“People sometimes have premonitions,” Wes said.

“We hoped the fishing trip would restore his enthusiasm,” Amy said sadly. “He seemed so tired—” Neither spoke as she examined the belongings she had removed from his desk.

“I was finishing when you came in,” she continued. “In a few more minutes I’ll have all of Dad’s belongings, but I can finish later if you need the office.”

“Take your time,” he said. “I’ve other errands to run.”

Radiology. A branch of science that uses radiant source energy (especially x-rays) in the diagnosis and treatment of disease.

Sociologist. One who specializes in the history and function of human society.

Amy's eyes softened as she shook her head and smiled. "I hope you will visit us," she said. "I know Mother would enjoy meeting you."

He nodded and turned to leave. As he did, her hand gently brushed his. As he walked to the parking lot, he wondered if there was something else she wanted to tell him.

Wes Douglas had settled into a routine. Often, in the evenings he would visit the nursing stations. It was a good chance to meet employees and talk to patients. Both were a good source of suggestions.

One patient asked for a clock in the room so she would know when to take her medications. Wes got her one. If he ever built a hospital, there would be a clock in every room.

The food carts were noisy early in the morning when most patients were trying to sleep. He talked to the dietary director about training the transportation aides to be quieter.

"Could you invent a modest hospital gown?" a young executive asked. It was a good idea. From his own experience as a patient, Wes remembered having to hold his gown together to keep from exposing his backside when he walked.

"I was cold when they wheeled me to **radiology** for tests," a patient reported. From then on, patients were gowned, and covered with cotton blankets when transported through the halls.

"Ever take a ride through the hospital on a gurney?" a patient asked. "You'll see things people don't see standing up." It triggered Wes's curiosity. He tried it. The next morning he directed Housekeeping to wash the ceilings and remove the cobwebs.

A **sociologist** from the University of Wyoming was admitted after a hiking accident. "Your hospital has a way of dehumanizing people," the professor said, "of stripping them of their personal identity. You replace their clothes with a generic gown. Anything that differentiates them from others, including jewelry, is impounded.

"It's insulting not to be called by your name. I'm not *the gallbladder in room 247*, I'm Robert Hansen!"

Wes took notes. If he survived the financial crisis, he would find ways to humanize the hospital experience.

One evening Wes was visiting patients on the second and third floors. As he exited the elevator, he bumped into a ten-year old boy in a wheelchair. The kid wasn't seriously injured, but obviously had done something bizarre. Both legs were in casts, his hands were bandaged, his hair was singed, and his eyelashes were missing.

Wes smiled. He remembered how easy it was to get in trouble at age ten. One of these days, he'd have to apologize for the anxiety he and his younger brother put their parents through.

Circle electric bed. A bed for patients who cannot or should not move. A circle electric bed looks like a Ferris wheel. The patient is strapped in the position of one of the spokes, enabling him or her to be rotated from time to time to remove pressure from parts of the body that may develop sores called decubitus ulcers. Decubitus ulcers are painful and difficult to cure.

Ependymoma. Cancer of the spinal cord.

Hepatitis. Inflammation of the liver, often caused by infection.

"What did you *do*?" he asked curiously.

"Climbed a power pole to catch a bird," the boy replied. His face sobered. "When I touched the wire," he said slowly, "I stayed in the air . . . but my body dropped. I watched it fall . . ." His singed eyebrows rose in astonishment. "When it hit the fence," he said, "I went back into it."

The boy looked as though he expected Wes to answer a question he himself wasn't old enough to put into words. Wes was silent as he studied the boy quietly, not exactly sure how to respond. Finally, he nodded. "Well," he said, his voice soft but upbeat, "We're glad you're back!"

Down the hall, in room 352, was a 16 year-old boy with spiked green hair, a tattoo, and three body piercings. Since his admission, the patient oscillated between ominous silence and violent rage. A drug user, he was admitted the previous evening with his second case of **hepatitis**—*a dirty syringe.*

"Keep this up," his doctor said, "and your next visit will be to the morgue."

The boy cursed loudly, his face twisted with rage. His doctor ordered a psychiatric consult. Wes visited only once. The young man blew him into the hallway with a volley of profanity. Wes continued down the hall, hopeful someone would help him before it was too late.

In the next room, in a **circle electric bed**, was a young police officer from Heber, Utah. His name was Don Hemphill. Initially, there was a problem with his insurance. The hospital was at fault. Wes resolved it and apologized. Since then, Wes visited whenever he was on the floor, and they had become friends.

Hemphill was 32 years of age and had a wife and two little girls, one four and one six. They visited each evening. Tonight they were there in bright red dresses that matched the valentines they were giving their father—never mind that it was October.

"God has been good to me," Don told Wes earlier that evening. "I'm going to beat this you know." Wes admired his optimism, but Don was wrong. A few minutes later the doctor told Connie Hemphill that Don had an **ependymoma**—a cancer of the spinal cord. He would be dead by December. Connie returned home and retrieved the love notes his daughters had made but were saving for Valentine's Day—hence, the valentines in October.

Wes paused outside the doorway, not wanting to interrupt. His expression was still and serious. *I don't understand. Down the hall, we have a teenager who has given himself hepatitis—twice. He's throwing his life away, says he doesn't care if he lives—but he will. And here, we have a young father who wants so desperately to live—but won't.*

Wes continued down the hall. As a hospital administrator, he was often confronted with issues for which his business degree provided little, if any preparation.

Administrative council. Department heads that meet regularly to coordinate activities of the hospital.

Medical record. A record created on admission that records the treatment provided during the patient's hospital stay.

Discussion One–Patients' Bill of Rights

Wes Douglas is concerned with the way patients are treated by doctors, nurses, and allied healthcare workers. In this chapter, he visits with a sociologist who accuses the hospital of dehumanizing patients. In their desire to apply the best scientific techniques possible in treating disease, healthcare workers sometimes ignore the rights and feelings of patients.

In response to this criticism, Wes directs the ***Administrative Council*** *to develop a patient bill of rights for Brannan Community Hospital. Wes Douglas appoints Elizabeth Flannigan as chairwoman of the committee and she submits the following draft.*

Brannan Community Hospital—Patients' Bill of Rights

Brannan Community Hospital shall have a hospital ethics committee, the purpose of which shall be education, policy review and development, and case review.

The staff of Brannan Community Hospital recognizes patients have the following rights:

1. *To know the name and professional status of all people providing healthcare.*
2. *To know the name of their attending doctor.*
3. *To receive complete information on their diagnosis and treatment.*
4. *To be given the prognosis for their illness.*
5. *To review all of the information in their* ***medical record****.*
6. *To have every procedure, treatment, or drug therapy explained to them in language they can understand.*
7. *To know the possible risks, benefits, and costs of every procedure, treatment, or drug therapy.*
8. *To accept or refuse treatment.*
9. *To prepare, in advance, treatment directives and to expect these will be honored.*

Ethics. The study of the principles of right and wrong.

Law. A minimal rule of conduct enforceable by a controlling authority, usually a governmental entity.

Morals. Personal standards of right and wrong.

Standard. A performance goal.

10. *To appoint a person to make decisions about their care, if they become mentally disabled.*
11. *To have personal privacy.*
12. *To receive compassionate care and proper management of pain.*
13. *To seek a second opinion.*
14. *To ask that the Hospital Ethics Committee review their case.*

Discussion Two—Healthcare Ethics

Definitions

- ***Ethics*** *is the study of the principles of right and wrong.*
- ***Morals*** *are personal* ***standards*** *of right and wrong.*
- ***Laws*** *are rules that enforce behavior.*

Just because something is legal, or cannot be proven illegal, does not always mean it is moral. Ethical conduct is dependent on personal morality.

Importance of Healthcare Ethics

The field of ethics concerns itself with the way that individuals behave, the manner in which they exercise their power, and the impact it has on their fellow human beings. A subcategory is biomedical ethics, which has received increasing attention in recent years. The reasons for this include:

- *New technologies that have prolonged life and changed the definition of death.*
- *A society that increasingly looks to lawsuits as a way of resolving unsatisfactory medical outcomes.*
- *An increased sensitivity to individual rights.*
- *A willingness of society to examine controversial issues, such as abortion and euthanasia.*

A Framework for Ethical Thought

How should one approach ethical issues? There are two common schools of thought.

- *Deontological School*: *The Greek Word "deon" means "duty." This school studies moral obligations. Followers believe in the existence of good and evil and that individuals have an obligation to do good for other people.*

- <u>Teleological School</u>: *The Greek Word telos means "end." This school believes the end is all that matters. The teleological school focuses on that which provides the most positive result for the greatest number of people. The Teleological school believes: "The end justifies the means."*

Rules for the Healthcare Ethicist

Since an examination of the strengths and weaknesses of deontological and teleological arguments is beyond the scope of this book, we will use another model, one that focuses on seven principles accepted by most ethicists as being useful in resolving biomedical ethical issues. These principles are:

- *Free agency*
- *Equality*
- *Kindness*
- *The obligation to do good*
- *The obligation to do no harm*
- *Honesty*
- *Legality*

<u>Free Agency</u>: *A patient has a right to make decisions about his or her own body without outside control.*

Difficult Questions Raised:

1. *In making decisions about one's own body, does one have the duty to consider the impact those decisions might have on others (i.e. children, members of society who sometimes must pick up the bill, and so on)? For example, does a parent who plans to commit suicide have a moral duty to his or her loved ones?*

2. *If society is responsible for treating individuals with preventable illnesses, what (if any) responsibility does a person have to avoid unhealthy habits and practices?*

Equality: *The healthcare system has a duty to treat all patients fairly.*

Difficult Questions Raised:

1. *Is equality possible? Resources are scarce. How do you treat 100 patients needing a heart transplant equitably, when there are only 50 hearts available?*

2. *Should patients who cause their illness through poor lifestyles have the same access to transplants and other expensive procedures as those who have tried to take care of their health?*

Kindness: A patient has a right to expect that a healthcare worker will be merciful, kind, and charitable.

Difficult Questions Raised:

1. *What is kindness? Is there a universal definition? If not, whose definition do we use?*
2. *Is it kind to inflict pain to raise the likelihood a disease will be cured?*
3. *Is it kind to increase the length of life when the quality of that life is low?*
4. *Is euthanasia against one's will ever kind?*

Obligation to do Good for Others: Health-care workers are obligated to take the action that will result in the best outcome for the patient.

Difficult Questions Raised:

1. *Is there a universal definition of "the best outcome?" If not, whose definition should be used?*
2. *If death is viewed by one as a supreme evil, then is saving life at any cost (including suffering and pain) an ultimate good?*
3. *What if the patient does not want to live? How does the duty of the health professional to "do good" relate with the patient's right to free agency?*

Obligation to do no harm: The first obligation of a healthcare practitioner is to avoid injury to his or her patient.

Difficult Questions Raised:

1. *What about experimental procedures that may not help, and may harm the patient? Is it okay to risk a patient's life to develop a surgical technique that may save patients in the future?*

Honesty: A healthcare worker should be honest.

Difficult Questions Raised:

1. *Is it always good to tell the truth? What if telling the truth in the opinion of the family will reduce the quality of life of the remaining days of the patient?*
2. *Should you tell the truth if it harms or destroys self-esteem?*
3. *Do we always know the truth? One philosopher said: "If it comes to being truthful or kind, I choose to be kind, I know what kindness is." Do you agree or disagree with that statement?*

Legality: Are the actions of the providers consistent with state and federal laws?

Discussion Questions

1. *Some patients feel admission to a hospital is a dehumanizing experience. Explain how hospitals strip patients of their personal identity. Can you think of examples not cited in the textbook/novel? Why is it important to treat patients as individuals, instead of numbers or diagnoses?*
2. *Traditionally, patients were not allowed to review the information in their medical records. Do you think this was for the benefit of the patient or the healthcare practitioner? Why do you think this policy was changed in the Patients' Bill of Rights?*
3. *Use a search engine on the Internet to find the American Hospital Association's Patients' Bill of Rights. Compare this to the Patients' Bill of Rights as written by the Administrative Council. Can you think of additional rights you might add to the list submitted by Elizabeth Flannigan?*

4. *Write a memo to a hospital supervisor about your concern that your hospital is not giving enough attention to preserving the dignity of their patients. Propose several programs the supervisor can adopt to create less dehumanizing hospital care?*

5. *Like it or not, sooner or later there will be rationing of healthcare resources. Otherwise, the United States will eventually spend 100% of its income on healthcare. A difficult question is how these resources will be rationed. For example: Assuming two people need a transplant, and there is only one organ available, what should be the rationing criteria? Possible criteria include:*

    a. *<u>How Important is the Person to Society</u>? The problem with this approach is deciding what we mean by "important." Who is more important, a 65-year old politician, or a 24-year-old mother of four?*

    b. *<u>Ability to Pay</u>: Do the rich have a greater right to life than the poor?*

    c. *<u>Age</u>: Should an organ be given to the person with the most years left to live?*

    d. *<u>Probability of the Best Outcome</u>: If one person has a 50% of living with the new organ, and the other a 75% chance, should the second person be given the organ?*

    e. *<u>Personal Responsibility for the Illness</u>: Two people need a lung transplant. One person developed cancer from smoking, the other developed cancer from a genetic defect. Should personal accountability be considered?*

    f. *<u>Some Other Rationing Criteria</u>*

<u>Required</u>: Assume you have been appointed Secretary of Health and Human Resources and have been asked to come up with criteria for the allocation of scarce healthcare resources. Write a three- to five-paragraph statement defining criteria you think would be fair. Remember, in the real world there is sometimes no "right answer." What this book tries to do is help you recognize the difficult decisions healthcare policy makers face, and provide experience in approaching difficult issues. The purpose of this question is to get you to think.

6. *Form the class into groups and, using the following form as a basis for discussion, review each of the actual case studies presented at the end of this chapter. Use the guidelines presented, and others you may think of to determine what the ethical issue is, who the stakeholders are, and whether the concerned parties acted ethically. Have a representative from each group report on their conclusions.*

Guidelines for Answering Bioethical Questions

Free Agency	Self-determination and freedom. The right of a rational person to self-rule and to generate personal decisions independently.
Questions to Ask:	***Answers from Group Discussion:***
1. Is the patient mentally and legally competent?	
2. Is there any evidence of incapacity?	
3. If competent, what is the patient stating about preference for treatment?	
4. If disabled, who is the patient's proper representative?	
5. Is the patient's representative using a suitable model for decision-making?	
6. Has the patient expressed prior preferences through advanced directives?	
7. Is the patient's right to choose respected?	
8. Has sufficient time been given for the patient to discuss and evaluate outcomes?	
Other questions the group may raise:	
9.	
10.	
11.	
12.	
Equality	The health care system must treat all patients equally.
Questions to Ask:	***Answers from Group Discussion:***
1. Are there biases that might prejudice the provider from giving a proper evaluation of the patient's quality of life?	
2. Are their family issues that might influence treatment decisions (exhausting the estate through medical bills)?	
3. Are there other financial factors that might influence a proper evaluation of the patient's quality	

of life?	
4. Are there conflicts of interest with the provider (doctor or hospital payment for example) that might influence the decision to withdraw life support?	
Other questions the group may raise:	
5.	
6.	
7.	

Kindness/Duty to do Good	Deeds of mercy, kindness, charity, and consideration for the welfare of other people.

Questions to Ask:	***Answers from Group Discussion:***
1. What are the prospects with or without treatment for a return to a normal life?	
2. What physical, mental, and social shortfalls is the patient likely to experience if the treatment succeeds?	
3. Are providers or others influencing decisions about treatment trying to see the situation through the patient's eyes?	
4. Is the provider giving the care that provides the most benefit to the patient?	
Other questions the group may raise:	
5.	
6.	
7.	
8.	
9.	

Obligation to do no Harm	Don't hurt the patient—the overriding principle for everyone that undertakes the treatment of patients

Questions to Ask:	***Answers from Group Discussion:***
1. Is there a plan with a justifiable reason to forgo treatment?	
2. If the treatment is experimental, has the patient been forewarned of the possible adverse effects?	
3. Are there plans for comfort and the relief of pain?	

Other questions the group may raise:	
4.	
5.	
6.	
Honesty	Is the health-care worker telling the truth?
Questions to Ask:	***Answers from Group Discussion:***
1. Has the patient been given a clear understanding of his or her diagnosis?	
2. Is the patient aware of the different treatment options?	
3. Does the patient know the potential benefits and dangers of each treatment option?	
4. Is there any reason the patient should not be told the truth about his or her condition?	
Other questions the group may raise:	
5.	
6.	
Legality	Are the actions of the health-care provider consistent with state and federal laws?
Questions to Ask:	***Answers from Group Discussion:***
1. Has the patient left a living will or health-care proxy?	
2. If there is a living will, do the instructions clearly cover treatments the patient does not wish to receive, such as his or her wish not to receive CPR, respiratory or chemotherapy? Are these directives being followed?	
3. Does the living will describe conditions (i.e. terminal illness, permanent coma) for which the patient would refuse treatment or interventions. Are these directives being followed?	
Other questions the group may raise:	
4.	
5.	

Ventilator. A mechanical device for artificial breathing.

Bioethical Case Studies

Healthcare Ethics Case Studies:

Use the model given in discussing the ethical issues involved in each of the following situations, and then present your conclusions to the class.

Case One:

A 47-year-old American Indian under treatment for depression attempted suicide by placing a shotgun under his chin and pulling the trigger. The blast blew off his chin, nose, eyes, and left him deaf. An ambulance was called and the paramedics provided lifesaving services. He was life-flighted to the nearest major medical center where heroic measures were taken which saved his life. He will be institutionalized for the rest of his life. Excluding legal issues, which may not always correlate with ethical issues, who were the stakeholders and what are the ethical issues?

Case Two:

An 86-year-old independent male was involved in an automobile accident that fractured the vertebrae of his neck. He suffers from severe neck pain but the doctors concluded that repairing the injury would cost him his life. A C-collar was placed on him, which he must wear for the rest of his life. He complains it is painful to wear. He has a tracheotomy, is vent dependent, is fed through a gastric tube, and (before the tracheotomy) had expressed a wish to die. His daughter, however, has power of attorney. Nurses report that he can no longer talk, but that when they hold his hand he cries. He has a two-point restraint because he tries to remove the ***ventilator*** *when his hands are free. Who were the stakeholders and what are the ethical issues?*

Case Three:

An individual with a similar situation to that portrayed in Case Two has been involuntarily ventilated. To conform to her wish not to have a tracheotomy, nurses have placed a mask on her face that forces high-pressure air into her lungs. The designers of the device admit that it is uncomfortable and should be used for short periods only. To conform to her previous request that she not have a gastric tube put into her body, which would have been relatively painless, she now has an NG nasogastric tube, which is considerably less comfortable. As she wishes to die, which is against the wish of her daughter who has her power of attorney, she has been placed under two-point restraint because she tries to remove her mask, gastric tube, and so on.

Narcotic. A drug, natural or synthetic, with effects similar to those of opium.

Before entering the hospital, the patient was taking Vicodin for nerve pain, and, on occasion, had taken Neurotin for arthritis. As her pain increased, the doctors ordered morphine. Her daughter recently instructed the nurses she didn't want her mother on pain medication as she "wanted her to be mentally alert" when she visited her. She requested that they give her no pain medication unless she was present to give permission. A nurse who felt the situation was a form of torture confronted her. "You mean that if your mother is in terrible pain you don't want us to give her pain medication unless you are present to give permission?" the nurse asked. The daughter reconsidered for a moment and then said: "I see your point, discontinue pain medication completely." The nurses report the woman's body is shutting down and she wishes to die. She has been put under restraint as she tries to remove the life sustaining equipment when not restrained. Who are the stakeholders and what are the ethical issues?

Case Four:

A 39-year-old woman in the Midwest allowed her 17-year-old daughter to use her car, even though the daughter had been drinking. The 17-year old was involved in a severe automobile accident. Her 14-year-old sister, who was in the automobile with her, suffered severe brain damage. The mother was advised by an attorney that, if the 14-year-old died, the 17-year-old daughter and perhaps the mother would face charges of manslaughter. When the 14-year-old daughter's system started shutting down, she was placed (at the direction of her mother) on dialysis, given a pacemaker, and placed on a vent. She soon became 100% vent dependent. Nurses report that, before her death, the young girl spent several years in severe pain. Who were the stakeholders and what are the ethical issues?

Case Five:

Nurses at an Alabama Hospital were instructed to give the charge nurse discontinued ***narcotics*** *with a sign-out sheet. Over a period of time, several nurses noticed the documentation was disappearing. There was some doubt as to whether the narcotics had actually been destroyed. The charge nurse's supervisor, a close friend, later reported that she fired her but did not note she had confessed to taking the narcotics as she "didn't want to destroy her career and her life."*

The charge nurse found a new job in an acute care hospital in an adjoining state. She worked in endoscopy where it was common to give IV Demerol routinely. Patients within the unit often complained that they were not receiving satisfactory pain relief. The nurse eventually overdosed and went into full cardiac arrest. She recovered and was subsequently arrested and now *faces the possibility of a prison term and a $10,000 fine. Who are the stakeholders, and what are the ethical issues?*

Case Six:

A 23-year-old woman overdosed on heroin. Her doctors reported that she was brain-dead and recommended taking her off the ventilator. Her mother believes that God will provide a miracle and the young woman will recover, marry, and have children and, therefore, has requested that everything be done to resuscitate her daughter in the event of cardiac arrest. The cost to Medicaid is over $30,000 a month. Who are the stakeholders and what are the ethical issues?

Case Seven:

A child under 18 years of age is brought in for a tonsillectomy. The child's parents have religious beliefs that preclude an individual from receiving blood. They tell the hospital that if the child bleeds there is to be no blood transfusion. Who are the stakeholders, and what are the ethical issues?

Case Eight:

A 37-year-old man is brought in for a tonsillectomy. He has religious beliefs that preclude him from receiving blood. He directs the hospital in writing that if there is bleeding, blood is not to be administered. How is this situation different from that reviewed above?

Case Nine:

A 21-year-old woman is 20 weeks pregnant and in need of radiation therapy because of a frontal brain tumor (anaplastic astrocytoma). The medical ethics committee found that: "The mother's life is in a medical crisis with such an aggressive tumor. The mother is critical to the life of the fetus." The committee recommended radiation treatment that will have the least effect on the fetus. The mother has refused radiation for fear it will harm the baby. Who are the stakeholders, and what are the ethical issues?

Case Ten:

A 25-year old woman had in vitro fertilization. She became pregnant, but all six embryos attached. She was encouraged to have doctors selectively remove some of the embryos to raise the chances of life without disability to the other infants and possible death to the mother. The mother's religious beliefs discourage her from abortion and she continues with the pregnancy. Who are the stakeholders, and what are the ethical issues?

AIDS. Acronym for autoimmune deficiency syndrome. A deficiency in immunity caused by an infection.

Business office manager. The hospital manager responsible for the creation, management, and collection of patient accounts receivable.

Chief nursing officer (CNO). The director of nurses.

Medicare. A federally funded program that pays the costs of healthcare for individuals sixty-five years and older.

Case Eleven:

A ***chief nursing officer (CNO)*** *is approached by the director of maintenance who is aware that she and her husband have been shopping for a contractor for a new patio at their home. The hospital has just poured a new sidewalk and has excess concrete. The director of maintenance offers to send his personnel to her home to pour the patio free. "There will be no additional cost to the hospital, as the workers are already on payroll," the director of maintenance assures. Who are the stakeholders, and what are the ethical issues?*

Case Twelve:

A CNO sits on the hospital equipment committee. She was instrumental in selecting Brand X heart monitors, an expensive capital acquisition. After the order has been placed, the seller offered to give her an expensive gift as a way of saying thanks for her influence. The gift was not discussed before the decision of the equipment committee. Who are the stakeholders, what are the ethical issues?

Case Thirteen:

A doctor had a member of his church congregation die, an individual held by high esteem in the community. The individual died of ***AIDS****, and had never received a blood transfusion. To protect his friend's reputation, the doctor changed the admitting diagnosis in the medical records after the death. Who are the stakeholders, and what are the ethical issues?*

Case Fourteen:

A 58-year-old woman was admitted to the hospital with a terminal injury. She had never applied for ***Medicare,*** *although she qualified, because her family had limited resources. The* ***business office manager*** *was finally able to get a verbal commitment that all costs would be covered retrospectively as of 2 p.m. At 1 p.m. she died and it appears, therefore, there will be no payment. A nurse suggests they change the hour of death to allow for payment. Who are the stakeholders and what are the ethical issues?*

Case Fifteen:

A baby formula seller offers to provide hospital administration free formula for babies within their family. Pharmaceutical reps offer the same program. Doctors are offered expensive vacations to exotic locations by pharmaceutical companies under the guise of educational conferences. Who are the stakeholders and what are the ethical issues?

Revenue. Funds that flow into an organization because of the sale of goods or services.

Case Sixteen:

A small rural hospital is on the verge of bankruptcy. The old administrator is fired and an interim administrator is appointed. In reviewing the accounting records, he finds that $125,000 of overpayments by patients have never been returned. If the hospital returns the money, it will be unable to meet payroll and will have to close. The hospital is old and will never be reopened, as it does not meet fire and safety code and is operating under a waiver. It is the only hospital within 50 miles of the community and is the largest employer in the community. If the hospital closes, 200 people will be thrown out of work. In addition, a new manufacturing company that is looking closely at the community will locate elsewhere. The new jobs from the plant, if it locates in the community, would raise the local population to the point where the hospital might be able to survive. The controller proposes to show the overpayments as ***revenue*** *and not return them to their rightful owners, the patients. Who are the stakeholders and what are the ethical issues?*

6

Quality Assurance—The Plan

Inferior vena cava filters. Filters placed in the inferior vena cava to prevent deep venous thrombosis and embolisms.

Internist. A specialist who focuses on diseases of adults.

Left renal vein. A vein running from a kidney.

Malpractice. An act of professional negligence that injures a patient.

Peer review. A review of a physician's hospital medical practice by a peer physician. Peer review is often conducted by committees who review medical records. The goal is to improve the quality of care provided by members of the medical staff.

Radiologist. A physician specializing in the field of radiology.

Residency. A training program following the internship that provides training in a specialized field of medicine. A medical school graduate who wants to be a radiologist, for example, will enroll in a radiology residency.

TOCA strips. A readout of a baby's heart rate and the mother's rate of contractions during delivery.

Dr. Thomas' breath exploded in a gale of rage. "You think the hospital's in financial trouble? You don't know what trouble is!" Dr. Thomas shouted, his eyes blazing with anger. He leaned forward in a threatening gesture. "You have a greater problem than money and I can summarize it in two words—quality assurance." He raised an eyebrow, "You need it simpler?" he said in an ugly tone, "how about malpractice?"

Dr. Thomas was a young internist. Two years earlier he finished his residency and moved to Heber City, Utah. Unhappy with the quality of care his patients were receiving, he was moving his practice to Salt Lake City.

"Tell me your concerns," Wes said calmly.

Thomas rolled his eyes, "Where do I begin?" he asked. "You have an 82 year-old doctor on the staff that still delivers babies. His hands shake. I don't think he's read a professional journal for 20 years. Last month we almost lost a mother because he won't (or can't) read **TOCA strips**.

"What's a TOCA strip?" Wes asked.

"A readout of the baby's heart rate and the mother's rate of contractions during delivery. The technology wasn't there when he came out of school and he either doesn't believe in it or doesn't know how to use it.

Thomas shook his head in genuine concern. "Anyone that's over 80 years of age needs a 100% **peer review** of all cases," he said.

"Other problems?" Wes asked.

Dr. Thomas took a breath. "You have doctors that are performing procedures for which they are not qualified. Dr. Kent shouldn't be inserting **inferior vena cava filters**. This should be done by a **radiologist** who can see what he's doing. "One of these days he's going to cover a **left renal vein** and clot it off."

Radiology is a problem," Latham continued. "Too many of our doctors have x-ray units in their office. It's a money maker but they aren't trained to read them.

Crash cart. A cart containing instruments and medication used in a cardiac arrest or Code Blue.

Defibrillator. Equipment used to restore a patient's heart from fibrillation to a normal heart beat.

Epinephrine. A stimulant used to increase heartbeat and the force of heart contractions.

Humerus bone. A bone of the arm.

JCAHO. Acronym for Joint Commission on Accreditation of Healthcare Organizations—an accreditation body.

Nursemaids elbow. A partial dislocation of the elbow, which occurs when the lower part of the forearm slips out of its normal position at the elbow joint. The injury is also called radial head dislocation.

Supra-condylar fracture. A fracture above the rounded articular surface at the extremity of a bone

Ulna nerve. A nerve running along the larger of the two bones of the forearm.

"Radiology is a problem," Latham continued. "Too many of our doctors have x-ray units in their office. It's a money maker but they aren't trained to read them.

"A couple of years ago a family practice doctor misread an x-ray of a 13-year old boy who fell out of a tree. Diagnosed it as a **nursemaids elbow** when in reality it was a **supra-condylar fracture** of the **humerus bone**. With a wrong diagnosis he applied a wrong treatment and damaged the kid's **ulnar nerve**."

"Are all of our quality problems medical-staff related?" Wes asked.

"No," Dr. Thomas continued. "Maintenance isn't running weekly tests on our **defibrillator** as required by state code."

"Central supply doesn't always restock the **crash cart** after a cardiac arrest." The lines around Thomas' mouth and eyes tightened. "Do you have any idea what it's like to be in the middle of a code only to find the cart is out of **epinephrine**?"

"And then there's our infection rate. Do you know if it compares with other hospitals in our area?" Dr. Thomas asked.

"No," said Wes.

"Neither does anybody else," the doctor said, throwing his hands in the air. "It's not monitored. Nor are needle sticks."

"Needle sticks?"

"Yeah," Thomas said sarcastically. "Did you ever hear about AIDS? Most hospitals have training and prevention programs to teach employees how to prevent needle sticks."

Thomas paused to catch his breath. "For the first time in its history, the hospital is applying for accreditation," he said. "Unless things change, the **JCAHO** visit will be a joke. If the newspaper gets a copy of their write-up, people won't even bring their pets here for treatment."

Thomas took a deep breath. "Since you arrived, all you have talked about is money. I understand you have to pay the bills, but before we kill any more people, I suggest you start paying attention to the quality of care we give our patients!"

Wes didn't sleep that night. Dr. Thomas' warning kept replaying in his mind: *Before we kill any more people, I suggest you start paying attention to the quality of care we give our patients!*

Lying in bed, he began to develop an outline of a plan. He would interview employees and doctors to gain a better understanding of the problem. Concurrently he would review accreditation standards to determine what JCAHO expected. Finally, he would visit with other hospitals to see what they were doing to improve the quality of their care.

Implementing a program of **total quality management** was more difficult than Wes imagined. Wes was unknown and his employees feared retaliation if they revealed internal problems. Employees were reluctant to talk to someone they didn't trust. To increase trust with employees, Wes began making daily rounds to all departments. He found these were of little use unless he knew the names of the people he was talking to. There's something about knowing an employee's name that increases rapport. He got a list of names with pictures from human resources and began memorizing the names of all employees.

Once a week he sponsored a "lunch with the administrator" session in the conference room off the cafeteria where employees could ask questions and voice complaints. He also set up a method for employees to send anonymous e-mails reporting problems within the hospital.

One nurse complained of several doctors who were unwilling to respond to nurses' phone calls once they left the hospital. "I had a patient who was failing last night," she said. "He was disoriented, his **blood pressure** was dropping through the floor, and he was going into **tachycardia**. I called the doctor. It was 2:00 a.m. and he blew up—didn't like getting phone calls that early in the morning. He told me he would handle the problem tomorrow. Problem was—it couldn't wait. It took two more calls from the nursing station and one from Dr. Flagg to get him to come in. When he did, he swore at the staff. Most of the nurses are afraid to call him and one of these days that fear is going to cost a patient his life."

"We have too many **medication errors**," a doctor reported. "Sometimes it's the fault of the doctor—illegible writing. Sometimes a nurse gives a wrong medication, or a wrong dosage of the correct medication. Abbreviations are a problem—some hospitals have outlawed them—it won't be popular with the medical staff but we should do the same."

"We have a doctor performing open-heart surgery at the hospital," the OR supervisor complained. "His **pump times** are twice what they are at the University Hospital. He's not **board certified**. One of our **anesthesiologists** refuses to work with him. The hospital never should have given him cardiac surgical privileges in the first place. You need to strengthen the credentials committee. Now it's nothing more than a good ole boys' club. The Rotary Club could do a better job of reviewing credentials than they're doing."

Wes even received an anonymous phone call from an emergency center nurse. "The people at our front desk aren't trained," he said. "Do you know that if you turn a patient away from the emergency center without a medical evaluation, the hospital can be fined tens of thousands of dollars?"

Wes didn't.

"Read up on it, it's called EMTALA. A violation happened last night. "We have an **alcohol rehab** program. A patient that has failed to finish the program four times came to the ER. They referred him to another hospital without an evaluation. That's called **patient dumping**. It's against the law.

Alcohol rehab. Short for alcohol rehabilitation. A unit or process of helping people with alcohol addiction.

Anesthesiologist. A physician who specializes in putting patients to sleep during surgery.

Blood pressure. The pressure of blood on the walls of veins and arteries.

Board certified. The process of having been examined and certified that one has at least the minimum level of knowledge and experience needed to practice within a medical specialty such as surgery, internal medicine, or obstetrics.

Medication error. The prescription or administration of the wrong drug.

Patient dumping. The practice of transferring patients that cannot pay their bills to other hospitals.

Pump time. The amount of time a patient undergoing cardiovascular surgery is on a bypass machine.

Tachycardia. Excessively fast heartbeat.

Total Quality Management (TQM). A management philosophy that focuses on the creation of continuous quality improvement to provide products that exceed the expectations of customers.

Acute myocardial infarction. A heart attack.

Adverse drug event. An unfavorable reaction to a drug. This can be caused by giving a patient the wrong drug, or a drug the patient is allergic to.

Central line infections. Catheter-associated blood stream infections.

Evidence-based care. Treatment approaches to a disease that has been verified through scientific studies.

Morbidity and Mortality Committee. A committee in some hospitals responsible for monitoring the quality of care provided to patients.

Pneumonia. An acute (brief) or chronic (long-term) disease characterized by inflammation of the lungs.

Rapid response team. A team assigned to respond to immediate emergencies such as a Code Blue.

Utah Health Care Association. An association that provides educational, lobbying and purchasing services to member healthcare organizations.

The emergency center of the receiving hospital reported us and we face a $35,000 fine.

Shortly after assuming the role of administrator, Wes received a phone call from Kirk Latham, the administrator of a 250-bed hospital in Provo. He was serving as president of the **Utah Health Care Association** and invited Wes to join that organization. "I know funds are limited in rural hospitals," he said. "There's never enough money to buy the expertise you need. If I can be of help, give me a call."

Two weeks later, Wes took him up on the offer. They met for lunch in a small hospital conference room in Provo. The topic of course was quality.

"I know you're an outsider," Latham began. "Has anyone ever told you who has the final legal responsibility for the quality of care given by the hospital?" Latham began.

"The medical staff?" Wes replied.

"Actually it's the Board of Trustees" Latham replied. "They have responsibility for admitting doctors to the medical staff and issuing privileges."

"My board doesn't have the technical knowledge," Wes replied.

"No, but they can be helped by a well-functioning medical staff, usually represented by the medical executive committee and other committees including the credentials committee and **morbidity and mortality committee**. For the next 30 minutes the two administrators discussed each committee and its role.

Latham concluded: "There is a national initiative called the 100k Lives Campaign, sponsored by the Institute for Health Improvement. They believe they can save 100,000 lives if half the hospitals in the country implement six initiatives." He pulled a card from his pocket and showed it to Wes.

1. *Prevention of* ***adverse drug events,***
2. *Prevention of* ***central line infections,***
3. *Prevention of surgical site infections,*
4. *Prevention of ventilator-associated* ***pneumonia,***
5. *The delivery of* ***evidence-based care*** *for* ***acute myocardial infarction****, and*
6. *The deployment of* ***rapid response teams****."*

Latham continued: "They have recruited 2,300 hospitals across the country to join with it in reducing unnecessary hospital deaths. The American Medical Association, American Nursing Association and Joint Commission on Accreditation of Healthcare Organization have all endorsed the campaign.

"I recommend you get the information, and implement the campaign," He said as the meeting concluded.

For the next two weeks Wes's primary focus was quality. Wes refocused the board on its most important job—quality assurance. This became less difficult once the board understood the legal **liability** of not doing their job.

The credentials committee was also strengthened. When a doctor applies for **medical staff membership**, a well-functioning committee should:

1. *Verify the applicant has graduated from an accredited medical school, served a proper internship and residency, and holds a valid state license.*
2. *Verify the doctor is board certified by the American Board of Medical Specialties, the American Board of Oral and Maxillofacial Surgery, or the American Board of Podiatric Surgery. If the doctor does not meet this requirement, he or she should be required to at least finish the educational and clinical requirements for an application for certification.*
3. *Perform a background check to verify references, and assure that the applicant has no history of criminal convictions or disciplinary action by any licensure board governmental agency or medical center.*

Wes directed the **infection committee** to collect data on **nosocomial infections**, and with the help of the nursing staff started new programs to cut infection rates.

His next task was to hire a **case manager**. The responsibility of this employee was to oversee the quality of care provided by doctors. Daily, she visited patient floors and reviewed medical records. Problems identified were forwarded to the **quality assurance committee**. During her first year, Dr. Emil Flagg asked her to focus on seven areas:

1. *The average time it takes for a hospital radiologist to read an x-ray and dictate the report to the doctor.*
2. *The time it takes to register a patient for admission to the hospital, or to register an* ***outpatient*** *for radiology or laboratory tests.*
3. *The average waiting time for a patient in the emergency room.*
4. *The time it takes a floor to get the results of a* ***stat*** *laboratory test.*
5. *The number of patient falls each quarter.*
6. *The number of medication errors and adverse drug events.*
7. *The number of employee needle sticks.*

Case manager. A person who continually monitors the quality of care provided to patients in the hospital. This is usually done by reviewing medical records to see that proper procedures have been followed and the right treatment has been given.

Infections committee. A hospital committee consisting of doctors, nurses, and other hospital employees responsible for monitoring hospital infections, finding their cause, and correcting these causes.

Liability. A legal obligation. A mortgage, for example, is a legal obligation to repay a sum of money loaned to purchase a building.

Medical staff membership. To practice medicine within a hospital, a doctor must apply for and be granted membership on the medical staff. Medical staff membership allows him or her to apply for privileges (the right to perform specific procedures), to attend medical staff meetings, and to participate on medical staff committees.

Nosocomial infection. An infection acquired in the hospital.

Outpatient. A patient diagnosed or treated at the hospital without being admitted to the hospital (or in some cases a patient admitted to the hospital for less than a twenty-four hour period).

Quality assurance committee. The committee assigned to monitor quality in the hospital.

Stat. Abbreviation for statim—meaning "at once, immediately."

Discussion Questions

1. *Some patients feel admission to a hospital is a dehumanizing experience.*

2. *Using the internet, define the term "quality assurance." How does the term apply to healthcare?*

3. *What is "peer review?" How does it work and in what ways is it an important component of quality assurance?*

4. *What is the Joint Commission on the Accreditation of Healthcare Organizations (JCAHO) and what are its objectives?*

5. *What is patient dumping, and what factors do you thing mandated legislators to make it illegal?*

6. *What steps should the Credentials Committee take when reviewing the application for admission to the medical staff from a physician?*

7. *What is a case manager and what is his or her responsibility within the hospital?*

7

Implementing Quality Assurance

Medical director. A doctor (often employed by the hospital) who has responsibility for representing the medical staff to the Board of Trustees and administration, and supervising the activities of the medical staff.

Emil Flagg sat quietly in the conference room off the cafeteria. In a few minutes, the quality assurance committee would begin. Reviewing the minutes of the previous meeting, he reflected with pride on the progress the committee made during its first two months of operation. Five years earlier, Dr. Flagg had ushered Dr. Marshall Kearl, a drunk physician, from the operating room. Connie Sieger, the O.R. supervisor, smelled alcohol on Dr. Kearl's breath when he came to check his schedule. Curious, she asked him what procedure he was there to perform. When he slurred the pronunciation, she called the **medical director**'s office.

Dr. Flagg took the incident to the medical executive committee. Since this was the third such instance, he recommended the committee permanently bar Dr. Kearl from the medical staff. In those days, however, physicians showed little interest in reviewing the care of other doctors. The committee suspended Kearl from the medical staff for two weeks.

It was a slap on the wrists for Dr. Kearl, and a slap in the face for Dr. Flagg. Flagg wasn't one to forgive easily. One month later when a patient sued Kearl for malpractice, Flagg testified against him and Kearl lost his license. Flagg smiled with satisfaction at the memory.

Things had indeed changed since the arrival of Wes Douglas. Wes recognized the hospital's credibility in the community depended on the quality of its care, which was dependent on quality of its medical staff. Wes's previous experience taught him the importance of Total Quality Management (TQM) in manufacturing, and he was eager to apply the principles to healthcare.

With Flagg's encouragement he replaced the chairperson of the quality assurance committee. The former chair was a pediatrician who hated confrontation. A good characteristic for a father or husband, but a poor one for a committee that had to review the competence of its medical staff. With Flagg's coaxing, Wes appointed Dr. Peter Slabbert, an aggressive surgeon totally committed to improving the quality of healthcare. Slabbert had the finesse of an assault rifle. "He's just the man for the job," Flagg reported.

Still, Flagg was not happy with the membership of the committee as a whole. He scowled as Dr. Henry Bozeman entered the room. Bozeman was an anesthesiologist. Flagg didn't trust Bozeman any more than he trusted Kearl.

ICU. Acronym for intensive care unit, the unit where patients in critical condition are treated.

Medical staff privileges. The procedures a doctor is approved to perform in the hospital.

Bozeman liked money. His practice depended on a good relationship with the hospital's surgeons. He was reluctant to find fault even the most negligent doctor behavior.

Then there was Dr. Tilich, seated directly across the table. At 300 pounds, he was a good candidate for a gastric bypass. Tilich was shoveling down a shrimp salad as Flagg eyed him with contempt.

Tilich earned several million dollars investing in Park City real estate in the 1990s. Five years ago, he retired from his practice. *Ten years after he retired mentally,* Flagg thought. Tilich rarely contributed anything to the committee. Flagg wondered why he even came to the meetings. *Maybe it's the free lunch,* he thought.

Wes Douglas arrived as Dr. Slabbert called the meeting to order. Slabbert reviewed the minutes of the previous meeting, then turned to the first item on the agenda—**medical staff privileges**. Dr. Slabbert presented the list of existing doctors forwarded from the credentials committee. He recommended approval for reappointment to the medical staff. The committee reviewed the names and approved them with a unanimous vote.

"We have an application for readmission to the medical staff from Dr. James Turley," Dr. Slabbert continued. He turned to Wes Douglas. "Dr. Turley was suspended from the staff three years ago for malpractice," Slabbert explained. "His primary problem was arrogance; he refused to take advice from his peers."

"Or even listen to my nurses," Elizabeth Flannigan interrupted.

Slabbert nodded. "Finally caught up with him. A nurse called his home about a patient in **ICU.** He wouldn't come in—the patient died. In June of 2005, we removed him from the medical staff.

"Where's he practicing now?" Wes asked.

"Snowline Medical Center." Slabbert scowled as he scanned Turley's file. "Got a letter from his partner—an unhappy camper. Wants him reinstated so he can provide coverage for the patients here." He glanced uneasily at the committee. "Discussion?" he asked.

"Does anyone know where the sour cream went?" Dr. Tilich asked.

Dr. Flagg scowled. "I visited with one of the doctors at Snowline last night." Turley intimidates most of the nurses—few are willing to stand up to him."

"Doesn't sound like he's changed much," Wes volunteered.

"He hasn't," Dr. Flagg said. "The credentials committee recommends his request be denied."

"There's never enough sour cream," Tilich mumbled. "Someone should talk to the dietary department."

Dr. Bozeman, spoke for the first time, his nasal voice lined with concern.

"Thought about the ramifications?" he asked.

Retractor. An instrument for holding or drawing aside structures beside a wound or operating field.

Scalpel. A surgical knife.

"Ramifications?" Slabbert asked.

"Yeah—what if he takes all his surgery to Snowline?"

Slabbert gave him a *"duh!"* look. "He already does," he said "Remember, he doesn't have privileges here."

"I mean his partner," Bozeman stuttered.

"Dr. Sampson?"

"Yeah—Henry Sampson. Does ten or eleven cases a week."

Slabbert shrugged. "His office is here in Park City. It would be really inconvenient to move his cases."

"It's a risk we'll have to take," Flagg chimed.

Bozeman, who was unhappy with most of the changes Wes Douglas had made, gave the young administrator a brass knuckles smile. "You're obviously worried about the hospital's uncertain financial position," he said. "Assuming Sampson takes his patients elsewhere, are you prepared to take the financial hit?"

"Probably cheaper than a malpractice suit," Wes said simply. "Besides, if he leaves, I'll recruit a replacement. Park City is a nice place to live; I think I can find a young surgeon coming out of a residency."

"This stinks!" Bozeman bellowed, pounding his fist on the table. "The whole nitpicking process stinks!"

Silence—

"Who're we trying to impress?" Bozeman continued, pointing his fork at Wes. "A two-bit administrator that doesn't know a **scalpel** from a **retractor**?"

"Don't get personal," Slabbert warned.

"We don't have money for this stupidity!" Bozeman continued. "T-Q-M," he said, drawing each letter out in contempt. "This isn't General Motors, it's *Brannan Community Hospital*!"

"The world's changing," Slabbert said, "so must the hospital."

Bozeman failed to decipher the calculus of Slabbert's logic. "Drive all the doctors away and there won't be a hospital!" Bozeman barked. "Since Hap left, everyone's acting like we're the University of Utah Medical Center."

"We can't go back to where we were six months ago," Slabbert said. "If we can't compete with the big boys on quality, we have to get out of the business." He pulled an envelope from a folder. "Remember, our own credentials committee supports the recommendation."

Bozeman's voice thickened with sarcasm. "Turley is gone, his partners may leave. I suppose if I don't shape up, I'll be next," he said sarcastically.

Silence—

"Maybe you will," Dr. Slabbert finally replied. For a moment their eyes locked, Bozeman blinked first.

"Do I have a motion?" Slabbert asked.

Dr. Flagg responded. "I move we recommend to the Board of Trustees that the application for membership and privileges of Dr. Turley be denied."

"All in favor?"

Douglas, Flagg, Flannigan, and Slabbert said aye. The committee turned to Dr. Bozeman, who was obviously rethinking his strategy. A week earlier Slabbert

Misdiagnosis. An incorrect diagnosis.

threatened to bring in his own nurse anesthetist. If Bozeman lost Slabbert and his partner Dick Hackley to a nurse anesthetist, his practice would be down to three days a week—and that was without the loss of Henry Sampson, Dr. Turley's partner. He cringed as he thought about the $900,000 mortgage on a new home he just built above the Stein Ericson Lodge.

"Your vote Dr. Bozeman?"

Silence—

Slabbert shelled him with an angry stare. "Are you with us, Henry?"

"I abstain," he growled.

Discussion One—Risk Management

Risk management is an issue for most hospitals. Some of the most common risk management issues are:

- *Misdiagnosis*
- *Failure to monitor the patient*
- *Failure to use the chain of command*
- *Falls and injuries*
- *Medication errors*
- *No response by hospital personnel to abnormal diagnostic testing values*
- *Misread radiology tests*
- *Infections*
- *Derogatory statements about nurses by doctors (or conversely) in front of patients*
- *Exposure to hazardous materials.*

Safety is another concern: Common safety problems include:

- *Blood and body fluid exposures (needle sticks, puncture wounds, broken glass vials)*
- *Lifting injuries*
- *Repetitive motion injuries*
- *Falls by employees or patients*

Discussion Two – Hospital Infections

Pathogen: *A microorganism that causes disease. Common pathogens include bacteria, viruses, and fungi.*

Bacteria: *These are classified according to:*

- *Shape:* ***Cocci*** *(spherical),* ***Bacilli*** *(rod shaped), and* ***Spirochetes*** *(corkscrew).*
- *Reaction to* ***gram stain****:*
    - ***Gram-positive bacteria*** *have thick walls that cannot be colorized, but are stained violet with a gram of cresyl violets stain.*
    - ***Gram-negative bacteria*** *can be decolorized with alcohol and are counterstained with* ***safranin*** *after decolorization, which gives a pink or a red color.*
        - *Whether a bacteria is gram positive or gram negative is important information for a doctor prescribing an antibiotic.*
        - *Some antibiotics work only with gram-positive bacteria, while* ***broad spectrum antibiotics*** *work against several classifications or groups of bacteria.*

Virus: *These are the smallest of the infection agents that, with few exceptions, can pass through fine filters that retain most bacteria. A virus is not visible through a light microscope, and is incapable of reproduction outside a living cell.*

Fungi: *These are plantlike pathogens (molds and yeasts).*

Bacilli. Rod shaped bacteria.

Bacteria. A one-celled microorganism.

Broad-spectrum antibiotics. Antibiotics that treat a broad spectrum of infections.

Cocci. Spherical shaped bacteria.

Fungi. Plantlike pathogens (molds and yeasts).

Gram stain. A process of staining bacteria that allows the classification of bacteria into two categories; those that take a gram stain from the application of cresyl violet and those that don't.

Gram-negative bacteria. A bacteria that does not take the cresyl violet stain.

Gram-positive bacteria. Bacteria that take a gram stain from the application of cresyl violet stain.

Pathogen. A microorganism that causes disease. Common pathogens include bacteria, viruses, and fungi.

Safranin. A red dye used as a microbiology stain.

Spirochetes. A corkscrew shaped bacteria.

Virus. The smallest of the infection agents, which, with few exceptions, can pass through fine filters that retain most bacteria. A virus is not visible through a light microscope, and is incapable of reproduction outside a living cell.

Infection Control Procedures

- *Wash hands:*
- *After patient contact*
- *Before and after eating*
    - *After using the rest room*
    - *After handling money*
    - *After removing gloves*
    - *Whenever cleanness of the hands is in question*
- *Try to keep soiled items from touching the skin and clothing.*
- *Wear a gown, a mask, and eye protection or eye shield when needed.*
- *Use care in handling equipment that may carry pathogens.*
    - *Verify that reusable equipment has been sterilized before using it on another patient.*
- *Transport soiled items in a manner that prevents exposure to pathogens.*
- *Never place soiled items on the floor.*
- *Avoid activities that raise dust when handling patients or equipment.*
- *Follow procedures when handling needles, scalpels, and other sharp instruments. Use biohazard containers to discard these used items.*
- *Avoid having the patient cough, sneeze, or breathe on others.*
- *Clean areas that are least soiled first, moving outward or forward.*
- *Dispose of soiled items into proper containers.*
- *When pouring liquids, such as mouth rinse and bathwater into the drain, avoid splattering.*
- *Clean and sterilize items suspected of having pathogens.*
- *Follow proper procedures for isolating infectious patients.*

Handling Sterile Forceps

- *Wash hands.*
- *Keep only one forceps in a container of clean germicidal solution.*

- *When removing forceps from a container, keep prongs together and facing downward; grasp handles and lift without touching the container above the solution line.*
- *Tap prongs together gently over the container to remove excess solution.*
- *When using forceps, keep them in a downward position to keep fluid from the prongs from running back to the handle. Use as needed to handle, transfer, or assemble sterile supplies and equipment.*
- *After the procedure has begun, never touch the tip of the forceps to a sterile field when placing supplies on a sterile field.*
- *After use, return the forceps to the container without touching the container.*
- *Sterilize the forceps and the container, and refill the container with fresh germicide weekly, or more often.*

Pouring Sterile Solutions

- *Always wash hands before pouring sterile solutions.*
- *Check the label before pouring sterile solutions.*
- *Unwrap the sterile container to be used for the sterile solution.*
- *When removing the cap of the sterile solution, place the cap on a surface that is level.*
- *When pouring, ensure the label is in the palm of your hand.*
- *When pouring a sterile solution, hold the sterile solution bottle about six inches above the container.*
- *If you are required to pour a solution onto a sponge, first pick up the sponge with the forceps, and then pour the solution on the sponge.*

Good website

Medical and surgical asepsis: http://www.cdc.gov/ncidod/hip/a_z.htm

See "Isolation Guidelines" and "Infection Guidelines."

Ergonomics. The study of work, more specifically the study of ways the workplace can be improved to lower employee injury and fatigue.

Discussion Three—Applying Principles of Body Mechanics And Ergonomics

- *Definition of body mechanics*
    - *Using the body's major movable parts (head, trunk, arms, and legs) efficiently to maintain balance, conserve energy, and avoid strain and injury while performing work*
- *Advantages of proper body mechanics*
    - *Prevention of injury*
    - *Reduction of energy consumption*
- *Ingredients of good body mechanics*
    - *Posture*
    - *Alignment of head, trunk, arms, and legs*
    - *Coordination of body movement*
- *Principles*
    - *Avoid unnecessary bending.*
    - *Avoid unnecessary lifting.*
    - *Avoid twisting when lifting. Face the object you are moving.*
    - *When changing direction of movement, turn your whole body.*
    - *Push, pull, roll or slide the object when possible.*
    - *Use your strongest muscles to do the work.*
    - *Use your thighs and hips by bending knees when lifting.*
    - *Use both arms to lift.*
    - *Move smoothly, avoid movements that are jerky.*
    - *Hold heavy objects close to the body or stand close to the person or object being moved.*
        - *If you hold the object away from the body, strain is placed on the muscles of the lower arms.*
    - *Get help if the person or object is too heavy.*
    - *Increase your base of support by placing your feet slightly apart (eight to ten inches works well for most people).*
    - *Avoid lifting heavy items above the head.*

Healthgrades.com. An organization that surveys hospitals and awards quality grades. Grades can be found on www.healthgrades.com.

Discussion Questions

1. *What is the Quality Assurance Committee, and what is its purpose?*
2. *Total Quality Management (TQM) has been used in manufacturing to improve the quality of products manufactured. Do you think that TQM is applicable to healthcare?*
3. *Go onto the Internet, pull up* **www.healthgrades.com**, *and list the ratings of two hospitals in your geographical area. How might this information be helpful to consumers?*
4. *What is the difference between medical staff membership and medical staff privileges? How often are both granted, and reviewed? By whom are they granted and later reviewed?*
5. *One of Brannan Community Hospital's doctors got in trouble for not listening to a nurse. What dangers are there to arrogant behavior in a hospital setting?*
6. *Does the Credentials Committee of the medical staff have the authority to grant medical staff membership or privileges to doctors?*
7. *Dr. Bozeman is concerned that tightening up qualifications for medical staff membership and privileges may cut admissions and hurt the hospital financially. What do you think of this argument?*
8. *What is a nosocomial infection?*
9. *What is the purpose of the Infections Committee?*
10. *What is a risk manager, and what is his or her responsibility?*
11. *Assume that you are the chief nursing officer (director of nurses) of a new hospital and have an interest in increasing patient safety. What data might you collect to help you in your job?*
12. *What are some of the top employee safety issues at Brannan Community Hospital?*
13. *What are two classification criteria for bacteria?*
14. *Explain how hospital employees can help cut hospital infections.*
15. *List five principles of body mechanics when moving a patient.*

8

Cultural Diversity

The Park City Rotarians met every Wednesday for lunch at the Prospector, a small café on Main Street. Wes joined the organization to meet civic leaders and increase his visibility in the community. The lunch routine was always the same. Introductions by the president and then "fines" for harmless transgressions like having your picture in the paper, or being bald. Opening exercises were followed by lunch. While club members ate, someone spoke. Wes slipped on a pair of sunglasses, and discreetly slept through a presentation on zoning.

Today the speaker finished early. After the obligatory applause, a waiter handed out desert—"death by chocolate." Wes calculated how many miles he would have to run to burn it off. Since becoming administrator, he had gained ten pounds. Across the table, a young professional made eye contact. He rose and extended his hand. "I am Rajendra Ramachandran," he said with a crisp English accent. "My friends call me Ray."

The table was too wide to shake hands from a sitting position. Wes snatched the napkin from his lap with his left hand, and rose, extending his right hand in greeting. "Wes Douglas," he replied. They shook hands, and Ray motioned for him to sit down. They returned to their seats.

When Wes joined the club, the president asked each member to stand and introduce himself. From the brief introduction, Wes remembered Ray. He was born in India, and educated in England. Two years ago, he joined a small law practice on Main Street.

"You are the new hospital administrator," Ray said in a tone that conveyed polite regret.

Wes responded with a curious nod.

"You have many problems at your hospital," Ray said. He shook his head with solemnity. "Many, many problems."

The conversation in the café quieted as several Rotarians turned to listen. Wes smiled. It was impossible to attend a public function without having someone attack him for a bad experience at the hospital. Being a hospital administrator; a friend told him, "is like being a fire hydrant in a pack of mad dogs."

Cultural sensitivity. An appreciation for the cultures and beliefs of others.

In-service director. A hospital employee responsible for the continuing education of the hospital's staff.

Personal space. The area surrounding a person that a person regards as his own—the distance from other people that a person needs to in order to feel secure or comfortable.

"I met my wife in England," Ray continued. "We have lived in the United States for ten years, in Park City for two." He nodded to himself. "We understand the culture, and we are comfortable with our new home."

Ray's face softened into deep sadness. "Recently, my father-in-law, a merchant in Kanpur, died. We returned to India for the funeral. Then, at my wife's insistence, we brought her mother to the United States. She will live with us until she joins her husband." His eyes narrowed speculatively. "Of course we do not know how long it will be, but she is not in good health.

"One month ago, she suffered a heart attack," he continued. We took her to the emergency center and our doctor admitted her to the intensive care unit." Ray shook his head. "I must report she had a bad experience."

"Park City is a small town," Ray said. The people are good, but isolated. My mother-in-law has not been exposed to other societies. Her religious and cultural beliefs are strong, but were violated—I'm sure more through ignorance than design." Ray studied his hands, folded in his lap, then looked directly at Wes. "You must do more to educate your employees on the beliefs and practices of patients from other cultures. If not, they will go to other hospitals."

For the next 30 minutes, Ray explained the culture of India. He discussed its dietary practices, beliefs about the origin and treatment of illness, and preferences on **personal space**. Their parting was cordial.

Concerned with what he learned, Wes returned to the hospital, curious to discuss what he had heard at Rotary with Ms. Flannigan, his director of nurses. He picked up the phone and punched in her extension.

"Ms. Flannigan? Wes Douglas here. What's your schedule this afternoon? There's something I need to discuss with you. Available now? Good, please come down." Two minutes later, she knocked, and then entered Wes's office. When she was seated, he spoke.

"What diversity training do we give our employees?" Wes began.

Flanagan was in a sour mood. Two nurses had quit. To meet staffing requirements she worked their shift, 11:00 PM to 7:00 a.m. She needed a bath, her feet hurt, and now Wes Douglas was asking her stupid questions.

"They're not trained on anything," she snapped. "Old Wycoff cut the heart out of our training budget. Our **in-service director** quit, and you've placed a cap on hiring new employees."

As a young man, Wes might have snapped back. Experience, however, had taught him that sarcasm or anger was always counterproductive. He started over.

"I received a complaint from a family member of one of our patients," he began. "He felt our staff lacked **cultural sensitivity**."

Flannigan shot him a skeptical look. "Who complained?" she demanded.

"A young attorney named . . ." Wes pulled the young man's card from his shirt pocket and read the name, "Ray Ramachandran."

Flannigan gave a curt nod. "Remember him," she snarled. "It was his mother-in-law wasn't it? Didn't speak English, we had to communicate through the family. Belonged to an Eastern religion—couldn't eat pork, had a lotta strange ideas." She smirked with intolerance. "I don't buy that stuff."

"You don't have to adopt the beliefs of the people we treat." Wes replied with as much patience as he could muster. "You do have to be respectful, however, and where possible, accommodate any cultural differences. The same is true of your staff."

Flannigan stiffened. "Foreigners—if they don't like it here, they can leave!"

Wes quietly studied the defiance on Flannigan's face. From the time he had first arrived, she had been a negative influence on the new atmosphere he was trying to create. He smiled grimly. *Unless her attitude improves, I'll eventually have to replace her.* This was not the time however. The nursing staff had seen enough disruption.

"The name Flannigan is Irish isn't it?" Wes asked, taking a different approach.

She looked up, startled. "Yes, I think I told you that once."

Wes nodded. "You also told me about how your great-grandfather emigrated from Ireland. He came in through the port of Albany, as I recall."

Flannigan smiled as she remembered the family stories about Patrick Flannigan. "Tough old codger," she said. "Never took guff from anyone."

"You told me when he first came to America, he had trouble finding work."

Flannigan nodded. "Lots of prejudice against the Irish then, some of it against Catholicism."

"You told me he finally found a job working for the railroad," Wes continued.

"That's how the family came west," Flannigan said. "He worked at the roundhouse in Montpelier, Idaho."

"You said the railroad supervisor gave him a rough time—he was Italian, if I remember correctly."

"Your memory's good," Flannigan replied. "The Italians and the Irish didn't get along. The railroad finally had to separate work crews to stop the fist fights."

"The conflict wasn't religious was it?" Wes asked. "Many Irish and most Italians of the era were Catholic."

Flannigan scowled. "No, it was about culture. The Irish and Italians had different languages, different customs, ate different foods . . . it created hostility." She smiled at the foolishness. "To his dying day, grandfather wouldn't sit at the same dinner table with an Italian."

"How *do you* feel about the Italians?" Wes asked.

"My son-in-law's Italian," Flannigan answered. "Good kid." She placed both hands on the desk and leaned forward with a hostile squinting. "You saying I'm prejudiced against Italians?"

Bias. A point of view that prevents unprejudiced consideration of an issue.

Culture. Social, artistic and religious belief structures distinguishing a specific society. Values and traditions handed down from one generation to another.

Ethnicity. The unity that comes from a common religion, belief, language, or culture.

Hispanic. An American of Spanish or Portuguese descent. The term is sometimes used as a demographic classification of those who speak Spanish.

Multiethnic. Being composed of members from more than one ethnic group.

Wes shook his head. "Obviously you're not. I'm just wondering why, given what you've told me about your grandfather."

Flannigan shrugged. "Guess as we got to know one another, the differences weren't all that important."

Wes was silent for a moment, hoping Flannigan was listening to her own words. "Then one difference between **bias** and acceptance is knowledge!" he said.

Flannigan nodded. "When people know more about each other, it breaks down some of the old hostilities." She shot him a knowing look. "I get your point," she said.

"We live in a **multiethnic** country," Wes continued. "Walk down Main Street. There are people from all over the world. If we are to serve them, we must understand their beliefs, especially as they relate to healthcare."

Flannigan was silent as she digested the message. "What do you want me to do?" she asked.

"I'd like you to have one of your nurses put a presentation together on cultural sensitivity. Find one who's interested in the topic. Before she presents it, run it past me."

A week later, Elizabeth Flannigan was back in Wes's office with Marie Juarez who had volunteered for the assignment. A dainty **Hispanic** woman, she emigrated from Mexico at age 7 with her parents. At 18, she entered college, graduating with a four-year degree in nursing. She was now pediatric supervisor.

As Flannigan and Juarez entered the office, Wes noticed the doubtful look on Marie's face. This was their first meeting and most employees were still suspicious about the new administrator.

Wes smiled reassuringly. "Thanks for coming," he said. "and for taking the assignment. The more we educate our staff, the better they will be at responding to the needs of our patients."

"Marie will present Thursday," Flannigan reported. "Would you like to hear the whole presentation, or just a summary?"

"A summary would be fine." Wes replied.

Marie moved to a whiteboard on the far wall. "I'll begin with a few definitions I copied from an old sociology textbook," she said. She wrote:

- ***Culture****—social, artistic, and religious belief structures distinguishing a specific society. Values and traditions handed down from one generation to the next.*
- ***Ethnicity****—the unity that comes from a common religion, belief, language, and culture.*

Cultural blindness. A situation where persons assume that cultural differences do not exist.

Pathogen. A microorganism that causes disease. Common pathogens include bacteria, viruses, and fungi.

Race. A classification system based on genetic characteristics such as color of skin, the structure of hair, and so on.

Therapeutic. Having the ability to benefit the patient medically.

Trauma. A mental or physical injury.

- ***Race****—a classification system based on genetic characteristics such as the color of skin, the structure of hair, and so on.*
- ***Cultural Blindness****—a situation where people assume cultural differences do not exist.*

As Wes studied the definitions, Marie explained race and ethnicity are not synonymous. "There are over 17 subcultures in the Hispanic group alone," she added. "My purpose will be to educate our staff on differences that must be considered when treating patients from different ethnic groups." She continued writing. "These differences include:"

Cultural Differences:

- *Food*
- *Gender roles*
- *Beliefs about personal illness*
- *Personal space*
- *Touching*
- *Communication*

Marie pointed to the first topic. "In healthcare, food has cultural as well as **therapeutic** significance," she said. "One has to consider not only what is eaten, but how it's prepared. For example, Puerto Ricans believe it's important to maintain a balance of hot, cool, and cold foods. By this, they mean spice, not temperature.

"Some of our patients are vegetarians," she continued. "Those of the Muslim, Jewish, and Seventh-day Adventist faiths have prohibitions against eating pork. If a patient isn't eating," Marie said, "the patient's culture could be the reason."

"Gender roles differ from culture to culture. In some cultures, the mother is the dominant decision maker. It is the mother, not the father the doctor should consult when seeking permission to treat a child.

"Culture also affects one's beliefs about the source of illness," Marie continued. "Our culture takes a scientific approach. We focus on **trauma**, **pathogens**, diet, and exercise. That's not true of all cultures. Some, for example, believe illness is a punishment from God."

"Personal space differs from culture to culture," Marie said.

"Define the term," Wes requested.

"Personal space is the area a person regards as his own—the distance from other people he or she needs to feel secure," Marie replied. "Arabs and

Africans stand closer when speaking than those of European descent. Violating personal space can cause discomfort, or worse—*anger*."

"Cultures have different beliefs about the parts of the body that can appropriately be touched by others. There are cultures, for example, that believe a person's head contains the spirit. To touch the head is a grave offense."

"How do you remove a bandage or clean a head wound on a patient with that belief?" Wes asked.

"By communicating what you are going to do, and the reason for it, before touching the head," she replied.

"Communication is a part of a treatment plan. In communicating with a person from any cultural group, a nurse or allied health professional should:" Marie wrote:

- *Speak clearly*
- *Show respect*
- *Never yell*
- *Verify the patient understands what is being said*
- *Use gestures*
- *Summarize*
- *Find an interpreter (maybe a family member) if the patient doesn't speak English*

"Aren't you going to say anything about body language?" Flannigan asked.

"I am," Marie affirmed. "Eye contact is considered impolite, even aggressive, by some groups including Native Americans, Asians, and Arabs. Hasidic Jewish males are taught to avoid eye contact with women. For Muslim-Arab women, it's considered immodest to look into a man's eyes."

Wes's brow furrowed. "Useful information."

"Questions?" Marie asked?

Wes shook his head. "Sounds good to me," he said.

Discussion One—Discrimination

Discrimination occurs when one person treats another differently because of some distinguishing characteristic such as religion or national origin. Discrimination because of race, sex, age, or disability is illegal.

Minority group. A member of a small group within a larger group.

Early discrimination laws focused on minorities. A ***minority group*** *is a cluster of people who differ from the majority in religion, race, speech, culture, appearance, and so on. The earliest legislation addressed discrimination against racial minorities. More recently, legislation has focused on groups who are not minorities, but differ in some important way from other populations. Women and the elderly are two examples.*

Racial Discrimination

Many countries have a history of racial discrimination, the United States being one. As the result of unfair practices, Congress passed a series of laws to end discriminating practices.

Amendments, Laws, and Court Rulings

Congress adopted the 13th Amendment in 1865. This abolished slavery but did not address citizenship. Three years later, the 14th Amendment corrected the problem. The 14th Amendment required states to grant all citizens "equal protection under the law." Even so, some states continued to prevent African-Americans from voting. In 1870, Congress passed the 15th Amendment that outlawed states from denying the right to vote because of race.

Although the 14th Amendment, guaranteed people "equal protection under the law," the meaning of the phrase changed slowly as courts successively interpreted its intent. In 1954, the Supreme Court heard the case Brown versus the Board of Education of Topeka, and ruled "separate but equal" education was not "equal."

Three years later, Congress passed the Civil Rights Act of 1957 that set up the Commission on Civil Rights, a government agency charged with investigating civil rights violations. To help with enforcement and compliance, Congress also set up the Civil Rights Division of the Department of Justice.

Congress followed this with the Civil Rights Act of 1960 that appointed referees to help blacks register to vote and barred poll taxes in federal elections.

Shortly after that, Congress passed the Civil Rights Act of 1964 that outlawed racial discrimination by employers and unions. It also set up the Equal Opportunity Commission to enforce the terms of the law.

Sexual Discrimination

Throughout their history, many societies have treated women unfairly. Before 1900, for example, few countries offered women the right to vote. It has only been recently that courts and legislatures have seriously considered equal rights for women.

Amendments, Laws, and Court Rulings

In 1920, Congress approved the 19th Amendment extending suffrage to women. In 1940 Congress, outlawed sex-based wage discrimination for firms with federal contracts.

With the Federal Equal Pay Act of 1963, the government required employees to pay men and women the same wage when they perform the same tasks. The following year, Congress outlawed job discrimination because of sex through Title VII of the Civil Rights Act of 1964. This legislation outlawed firms from firing women for pregnancy, when pregnancy did not affect job performance. It also outlawed the practice of reserving specific jobs for men, or for women.

Title IX of the Education Amendment of 1972 outlawed sexual discrimination by universities and colleges who receive federal funds.

The Supreme Court has ruled women must get the same fringe benefits as men, including social security, welfare, and workers compensation.

Age Discrimination

As people over 55 compose a major part of the workforce, legislatures have begun to focus on laws to remove age discrimination in the workplace.

Laws and Court Rulings

In the late 1960s, Congress passed The Age Discrimination in Employment Act of 1967. Congress cited the following reasons for passing this legislation:

- *Older workers were disadvantaged in their efforts to find and keep work.*
- *Employers were setting arbitrary age limits for some jobs.*
- *Long-term unemployment was up for older workers.*
- *Discrimination because of age was considered a burden on the economy.*

The purpose of the act was:

- *To promote employment of older people based on ability, rather than age.*
- *To forbid arbitrary age discrimination in employment.*
- *To help employers and workers find solutions to problems arising from old age.*

The act specifically forbids:

- *Discrimination in hiring or firing, because of age.*
- *Limiting, segregating, or classifying people in a way that deprives them of opportunity or status as employees.*
- *Cutting wages to comply with this legislation.*

Congress has mandated similar rules for unions.

Disability

Amendments, Laws, and Court Rulings

A disabled person is a person with a disability who is qualified to perform the essential tasks of the job with or without a reasonable accommodation by the employer.

In 1990, Congress passed the Americans with Disabilities Act outlawing employers with 15 or more employees from discriminating against qualified people who have disabilities, when an accommodation would not impose a hardship on the employer.

Discrimination under the ADA is outlawed in:

- *Recruitment*
- *Hiring*
- *Pay*
- *Promotion*
- *Selection for training*

The Americans with Disabilities Act has no affirmative action requirement. Employers are free to hire the most qualified applicant.

Discussion Questions

1. *Define the terms culture, ethnicity, race, and cultural blindness. How are they different and how are they the same?*
2. *Holistic medicine believes the whole is greater than the sum of the parts. It teaches that a health practitioner must not limit his or her attention to the biological expression of disease, but must look at the patient as a whole. Holistic medicine considers factors, including the patient's religious beliefs and emotional state. How does consideration of one's culture fit into holistic medicine?*
3. *List several guidelines for communicating with people from different cultural groups.*
4. *Review legislation and court rulings on gender-based discrimination.*
5. *What is the purpose of the Americans with Disabilities Act of 1990?*

9

High Noon

Accounts Receivable. An organization's record of bills that have not been paid for goods or services provided.

In-house collection agency. An agency owned by a firm (as opposed to an outside agency) that attempts to collect the firm's bad debts.

Loan committee. A bank committee that reviews loan applications and approves or denies these applications.

Arnold Wilson stood angrily. Placing both hands on his desk, he leaned forward, thrusting his jaw threateningly in the face of David Brannan. "Okay—I'll level with you, Dave. We've lost confidence in the hospital's ability to compete. Your controller can't even tell us where you're losing money!"

For 20 minutes, Wes Douglas watched a jousting match. On the offensive was Arnold Wilson, vice president of Park City State Bank, thrashing David Brannan for the hospital's poor financial performance. Wycoff, sitting in the corner, was uncharacteristically silent. Wes, the newcomer, said nothing. It was just as well—Wilson was doing his best to ignore him.

"Should've seen the response of the **loan committee**," Wilson said, throwing his hands up in disbelief, "when Selman told them the hospital doesn't even have accurate cost data on its products and procedures."

"Selman's your problem?" Brannan injected. "Selman's gone!"

"And who replaced him?" asked Wilson angrily.

"We don't have a replacement," Brannan admitted.

"No controller? And a new administrator who's never worked in a hospital?" Wilson hooted. "No wonder your employees lost confidence in the board. Do you expect the directors of my bank to react differently?"

"I expect them to work with us until we resolve our problems," Brannan said evenly. "For 30 years we've been a good account—a loyal customer even when other banks were offering us lines of credit at much lower rates."

Wilson's brows lifted in agonized expression. "David! We're not talking small amounts of money," he said throwing his hands in the air. "By your own projections, you're looking at a fourth quarter loss of $900,000."

Brannan was unimpressed. "If you call our line of credit, we won't be able to meet payroll. Then our revenue stops—and we won't be able to pay you the money we owe you."

"You owe us two million dollars," Wilson said, "*guaranteed* by three million in **accounts receivable**." He snatched a thick file from his desk and thumbed to the third page. "Here it is—your total accounts receivable at the end of August were $3,078,000. We have an **in-house collection agency**; if

Bankruptcy. A situation where a person or organization is unable to pay its bills. Often in bankruptcy, the court seizes the bankrupt person's or organization's assets and sells them to pay creditors (the people to whom debts are owed).

the hospital closes, we'll collect the accounts ourselves. The worst option would be to sell the receivable outright." Wilson slapped the file closed. "A group in Ogden has agreed to buy your accounts for 60 cents on the dollar—that's $1,800,000 in cash."

Brannan's lips sputtered in annoyance. "It's $150,000 less than you'll get if you stick with us," he countered.

"It's $1,800,000 more than we'll get if the hospital takes out **bankruptcy**," Wilson said. He dismissed the argument with a wave of his hand. "Besides, that's the worst case scenario."

Liam Russell, president of the bank, stuck his head in the door. Russell heard the commotion and came to see if he could help.

"May I join you?"

Brannan motioned for him to enter. A muscle twitched nervously in Wilson's jaw. Face reddened, he popped a pill. Russell started to close the door, and then noticed Wilson's agitation. He motioned for him to get a drink from the water cooler across the hall. Wilson left the room while Russell acknowledged Wycoff, and then crossed the room to shake hands with David Brannan.

"How are you, David?" Russell asked, pumping his hand firmly.

"I've been better," David said, clipping his words. He gestured to Wes. "This is Wes Douglas—new administrator."

Russell shook hands with Wes and motioned for Brannan to sit down as he seated himself in Wilson's chair. Interlocking his fingers, he leaned forward. "What seems to be the problem?" he asked with a frigid smile.

Brannan's eyes blazed—hot enough, Wes thought, to ignite the dried flower arrangement on the desk. "You know very well what the problem is!" Brannan barked angrily. "The bank's canceled our line of credit. Without it, we can't meet payroll. I want to know who's responsible!"

Wilson reentered the office, and Russell motioned for him to shut the door. Brannan's shouting was attracting the attention of customers in the lobby.

Russell arched his eyebrows. "I'm responsible," he said. "Some people think the money we loan is our own—they think they're borrowing the funds of a group of wealthy investors who own the bank. That's not the situation, David."

Russell made no attempt to hide the sarcasm in his voice. "The money we loan comes from depositors—school teachers saving for retirement, young couples planning for a home, small merchants trying to scratch out a living . . . we have a responsibility to those people, David. A responsibility to see their funds are wisely invested—that they aren't squandered on organizations unable to manage their own finances."

Call a loan. To demand that a loan be immediately repaid.

Collateral An asset held as security for a loan. Collateral has two purposes: (1) to provide an incentive for the borrower to repay the loan (if the loan is not repaid, the person who has loaned the money can sell the asset to recover the amount owed), and (2) to provide protection for the person making the loan.

Economics. The study of scarce resources.

Positive cash flow. When the amount of cash coming in exceeds the amount going out.

Secondary spending. When a person buys a pair of shoes within a community, the shoe seller can then use that money to buy groceries locally, and the grocer can then take those funds to pay for an automobile. The impact on the local community of the first dollar spent is therefore multiplied. This effect is called secondary spending.

Shareholder. An owner in a corporation.

"Don't give me that trash!" Brannan spat the words out contemptuously. "For 20 years, my father was a major **shareholder** in this bank. I know what banking's about."

Russell nodded, his face flushing with anger. "Your father's not a shareholder anymore," he said, his words short and biting. He picked up a copy of the bank's annual report and shook it in the air. "This committee calls the shots now," he said, slapping the picture of the new directors on the cover. He slammed the report down on the table. "We have a new loan committee, David. Would you like to know the committee's criteria for new loans?"

Before David could reply, Russell continued, his words coming out in staccato-like bursts. "Loans must have **collateral**," he said with scouring emphasis. "Loans can't exceed 70% *of collateral.* Borrowers must have **positive cash flows.** Borrowers must prove their ability to *pay their loans back!"*

"Why, David," Russell continued sarcastically, "your hospital doesn't meet a single criterion. We have *no choice* but to **call the loan**!"

The room was quiet as Brannan digested Russell's message. Wes was not aware David's father had been an owner in the bank. His withdrawal—for whatever reason—had caused a shift in power Brannan was just starting to understand.

From the corner, Wycoff appeared to enjoy the whipping Brannan was taking. Sitting next to him, Wilson, arms folded, stared at Russell approvingly. Brannan glanced at Wycoff, who gave no support, and then glared at Russell. Everyone expected Wycoff to speak, but he said nothing.

Sensing the meeting was about to end with disastrous results for the hospital, Wes injected himself for the first time. "I understand your commitment to your depositors," he said calmly. "That's why I find it hard to believe you're willing to see the community's only hospital go out of business."

"There are other hospitals in the area," Russell said defensively. "Some firm just built a new one in Midway—11 miles from here. It's not too far to go for healthcare."

"I'm not talking healthcare, I'm talking **economics**," Wes said, taking the offensive. "Brannan Community Hospital has about 350 employees. Surely you don't believe it's to the benefit of your depositors for the community to lose its largest employer."

A question shadowed Russell's eyes. "What do you mean?" he asked.

As Wes spoke, Wycoff's eyelids, veiled of any emotion, lifted slightly. He leaned forward to listen to the conversation. Wilson swallowed another pill.

"The hospital spends twelve million dollars a year on payroll. I have data showing 65% of the payroll dollars are spent locally. Every dollar of payroll creates another dollar in **secondary spending** in the community. In total, the hospital is responsible for sixteen million dollars a year in local spending."

Breakeven. A situation where an organization neither earns nor loses money; where revenues equal expenses.

Business plan. A written document explaining how a company will reach its goal of profitability.

Collateral. An asset held as security for a loan.

Lien. The right to keep another organization's property until a debt is paid.

Magnetic Resonance Imaging (MRI). A technology used by radiologists to create an image of internal body structures. MRI images are more clear than those produced by x-rays and do not expose the patient to radiation.

Net income. Revenue minus expense.

Wes paused for affect. "Are your directors willing to take this money from their depositors?"

Russell looked annoyed. "Who said anything about taking money from our depositors?"

"Who gets the sixteen million?" Wes asked. "Your customers, the local merchants. Many of those merchants have loans with your bank. With this decline in income, how many will be able to repay those loans?"

"Most of our employees are customers of the bank," Wes continued. "If the hospital closes, many will be forced to leave the community to find jobs. As they leave, so will their deposits. Most of these people own homes—mortgaged by your bank. As 200 homes hit the market, what will happen to the price of real estate in the community? What will be the effect on the bank as real estate values fall and your collateral in these homes dries up?"

The room was silent as Russell digested Wes's message. He bounced a questioning look off Wilson. "Is this the hospital's loan file?" he asked, pointing to the folder on Wilson's desk.

"It is," Wilson replied.

"Bring it with you. Let's meet in my office." Russell stood to leave and then turned to Wes. "Give us a few minutes—we'll see what we can do."

"Gentlemen, we have a proposition for you," Wilson said, when he and Russell returned. Russell delegated the meeting back to Wilson, who took a seat at his desk. Russell stood, arms folded, at the door.

"We'll continue to work with the hospital for 90 days, at which time we'll reevaluate our financial relationship," Wilson announced. "Our conditions are as follows: In 30 days you'll have a **business plan** showing how you'll compete profitably. In 90 days, you'll be at **breakeven**. In 120 days, you will reach a **net income** of at least 3% of total revenue. We assume you won't be able to reach these goals without layoffs and a restructuring of your entire operation," he concluded, looking up from the notes taken in Russell's office.

"The accounting system . . . you forgot the accounting system," interrupted Russell.

"Oh, yes. In 60 days, you must have an accounting system in place able to report product cost. We expect these costs will be shown in your updated business plan."

"I think we can do that," Wes said.

Wilson paused for a moment to look at Russell, who nodded for him to continue. "There's one last requirement," Wilson added. "Unless you're willing to meet this final requirement, the deal's off. We want a **lien** on the new **MRI** you bought last January, and on the land you own north of town as **collateral**."

Brannan sat up. "That's a little stiff," he complained. "The MRI was bought with a grant from the Mike and Sara Brannan **Foundation**. We were hoping to hold the land **lien free**—even if we can't build a new hospital at this time, there's a partially completed doctors' office building on the property."

"Those are our requirements," Wilson stated with finality.

Edward Wycoff, who was taking notes, looked up. "I have an alternate suggestion," he said, choosing his words carefully. "I don't know how the Brannan family would feel about a lien on the MRI the foundation gave the hospital. They've contributed significantly over the years—it would be a shame to turn our backs on that support."

David Brannan gave Wycoff a look of disbelief mixed with gratitude—it was the first time David could remember Wycoff speaking favorably of the Brannan family.

Wycoff continued, addressing Russell directly. "Your last requirement closes the door on several options our new administrator might need to turn the hospital around. I think there's a better way."

"I'm listening," Russell said cautiously.

"What if I were willing to **guarantee the line of credit** up to two million dollars? The bank would still have the loan—collateralized by the accounts receivable. All the requirements you stipulated would remain, *except the liens on the equipment and the property.*"

"I think the loan committee might approve something like that," Russell responded. "What do you think, David?"

"I think it's a gracious offer," Brannan responded. "I'll have the hospital's attorney draw the **note** up."

"My attorney insists on doing that," Wycoff interrupted.

"What?" Brannan asked.

"The note would be guaranteed by stock I've set up in a **living trust**—for the benefit of my children," he added. "My attorney is a careful businessperson. I've discussed it with him, and he has insisted the trust own the liens.

"The trust doesn't want to own an MRI or 100 acres of land," Wycoff continued assuringly. "But an arrangement of this kind would give an incentive for management to take the actions needed to put Brannan Community Hospital **in the black**."

Brannan was silent, the gratitude dissolving from his eyes. Wycoff was the smarter of the two, and he knew it. His father never trusted Wycoff. Still, David Brannan was unable to guarantee the note himself; and for his family's sake, he didn't want to see the hospital close. He considered the situation momentarily and then nodded his agreement.

Russell grinned broadly. "Good! I'll arrange for the bank's attorney to meet with your trustee," he said, holding his hand out to Wycoff. "I hope we've happened on an agreement that will assure the hospital's continued operation while protecting the bank."

"I'm sure it will be to our common benefit," Wycoff replied.

Foundation. A charitable organization that dispenses money or services for the good of the community.

Guarantee the line of credit. A line of credit is an agreement that allows a customer, at his or her discretion, to borrow funds from a bank for operations. Lines of credit are often secured by assets that may be sold if the loan is not repaid.

In the black. Financial slang for operating an organization with a profit.

Lien free. Without a **lien.**

Living trust. A legal document that holds title or ownership to a person's assets. In some ways it is like a will in that it includes instructions on the disposition of that person's property on his or her death, many times to charitable organizations.

Note. A document showing the existence of a loan.

Although the weatherwoman forecast rain, the sun was shining through scattered clouds as Wes left the bank, grateful for the help offered by Edward Wycoff. *I misjudged Wycoff,* he thought. *Few board members would be willing to risk their own money to save a community hospital. There's more at stake than I thought. This is a great guy—I mustn't let him down.*

Alone in the bank's conference room, Wycoff placed a long-distance call. "Mr. Devecchi, please," he said when a secretary answered. She put the call through immediately.

"Devecchi," he said. "This is Wycoff—they bought it! Yeah, I gave Wes Douglas just enough rope to hang himself. No, I don't think Brannan suspects anything. Yes, we've got the liens. They have 90 days . . . and then we've got 'em."

Discussion One—Consequences of Bankruptcy

This chapter reviews an important meeting with the directors of Park City State Bank. The bank has decided to call the hospital's line of credit. This means money loaned to the hospital to pay salaries and buy direct materials must be immediately repaid. The hospital does not have the funds to repay the loan. Without a line of credit, the hospital will have to stop operations and will probably face bankruptcy.

When a business goes into bankruptcy, assets are usually sold at a small percentage of market value, creditors are only partially repaid, employees are fired, and the local economy suffers.

Discussion Questions

1. *Place yourself in the position of Wes Douglas, administrator of Brannan Community Hospital. If the bank cancels the hospital's line of credit, the hospital will close. Assume you are preparing for the meeting. Write a brief statement of your goals for the meeting, and what your approach will be.*

2. *Place yourself in the position of Arnold Wilson, vice president of Park City State Bank. Assume you are preparing for the meeting. Write a brief statement of your goals for the meeting, and what your approach will be.*

3. *Sometimes people criticize banks for not loaning money to organizations with bad credit. Where does the money they loan come from? Do banks have responsibilities beyond profits?*

4. *Why was it important to the bank that the hospital install an accounting system?*

5. *Does Edward Wycoff have the interests of the hospital employees in mind with his offer? Is it ethical for Wycoff to profit from the death of the hospital?*

10

Never Give Up

Wes thought often about his grandfather, Admiral Wesley Miller Douglas, a naval engineer with degrees from Annapolis and the Massachusetts Institute of Technology. As much as anyone, grandfather shaped the beliefs and attitudes Wes carried into adulthood.

In 1983, Grandfather encouraged Wes to join a local Boy Scout troop. He realized 14 year-old Wes needed a better outlet for adolescent energy than girls and skateboarding. Wes quickly climbed to the rank of life scout. At 16, he was ready to tackle the rank of eagle.

This required an Eagle project. As Wes was interested in the environment, grandfather proposed Wes restore a nature trail in a state park not far from his home. He would clear the trail of weeds and rubbish. In addition, he would build a park bench every quarter mile, and a small pavilion at the three-mile mark.

Grandfather Douglas, an engineer by training, reviewed Wes's proposal. He thought it was too large. Wes knew better, or so he thought, and presented the proposal as written. In later years, Wes would learn to take counsel from those older and wiser.

Wes started the project June 1st. He planned to finish by July 1st. By the middle of July, however, he had only reached the halfway mark. Part of the problem was the park ranger. Ranger Morris believed in quality. If Wes didn't do the job right the first time, he made him repeat it. While Wes's friends spent their summer swimming, earning money, or chasing girls, Wes spent his clearing weeds, hauling rocks, and building benches. By August 1st, he was ready to quit.

Wes complained bitterly to his father, who encouraged him to see the project to completion. Looking for an ally, he rode his bicycle to grandfather's home. Grandfather Douglas listened patiently as Wes explained the difficulty of the project. When the boy finished, the retired admiral spoke. "You made a commitment that's going to be difficult to fill," he admitted. "Before you back out, however, you need to think about the consequences."

Wes's body stiffened. "Consequences?" he asked.

Managed care. An approach to cost control that includes preauthorization for expensive procedures, incentive reimbursement, retrospective (after-the-fact) quality audits, and second opinions.

Grandfather nodded sympathetically. "Consequences. As unhappy as you are with the park ranger, he has invested much time in planning and supervising your project. Because of your promise, he persuaded the Parks Department to buy lumber for the benches and pavilion."

Wes shook his head in denial. "The project's too much work," he protested.

"Maybe . . . but you're the one who designed it."

"Grandfather. It's ruining my summer!"

"Better your summer than your reputation."

"I don't care what others think," Wes replied flippantly.

"I do—you share my name."

Wes was silent, shamed by the clarity of his grandfather's logic.

"A reputation is an important commodity," Grandfather continued. "It is based on character. Character is formed by habits, and habits are formed by actions." The admiral's gray eyes softened as he placed a hand on the boy's shoulder.

"This isn't the last time you'll face a task that's bigger than you," Wes. "Quit now, and you'll set a precedent. The next time you bump up against a problem, it will be all the easier to retreat. Give up a couple of times, and you'll form a habit. Habits are hard to break. Reinforce it, and soon you'll lose the strength to complete anything that challenges you."

For the rest of the summer, grandfather drove him to the state park. They finished the project just as school started. In later years, Wes would reflect it was one of the turning points of his adolescent years. It taught him the meaning of perseverance.

Twelve years after the death of his grandfather, Wes returned to the trailhead at the top of the park. With permission from the Parks Department, he placed a small plaque where the trail ended. On it was a quotation by Winston Churchill—one his grandfather branded into the soul of young Wes Douglas.

"Never give up," the plaque said, *"Never, never, never give up!"*

After Wes's meeting with the bank, he met with the hospital's supervisors to draft a plan to make the hospital profitable in 90 days. "What obstacles do you face in running your departments?" he asked as the meeting started.

Jeff Lee, director of the laboratory, spoke first. "Our biggest problems are our losses. For many years, the hospital made money. Some departments were profitable on less volume than they're running now." Lee shook his head in confusion. "I've heard the problem is **managed care**. I don't know what it means. Wycoff tells us managed care has created a new environment—one requiring us to manage our departments differently. No one has told us how."

Wes wrote on the board:

Managed care—training and management

Elizabeth Flannigan, director of nursing, spoke next. Flannigan was famous for her skirmishes with the medical staff. She was not the kind to take guff from anybody. "Our budgeting system stinks," she said bluntly. "The forms we're asked to fill out each year are impossible to understand, and there's no one to answer questions."

Barry Lindeman, the laundry manager, agreed. "Some of us spend days preparing forecasts and budgets. When they come back, management has cut them without our input or consent. It's stupid to hold us accountable for budgets we didn't prepare," he said, his face flushing red.

"This isn't a recent event," Flannigan added. "The controller's office has never listened to our complaints or been open to our needs. They think we work for them, while in reality, they should be working for us." Wes nodded, writing on the board:

Poor budgeting system
Unresponsive controller's office

"Most of the time we can't understand what they're talkin' about," Barry chimed in. "They have their own language—they do. Why . . . they're harder to understand than the docs."

Flannigan spoke: "We don't get reports useful for making decisions," she said.

"Financial reports aren't timely," complained June Hammer. "What good are January's reports in May?"

Turning to the board, Wes wrote:

No service orientation
Poor communication
Reports—unacceptable format and untimely

"Other problems?" Wes asked.

The room was silent. "Those are the big ones," Flannigan said finally. "Give us the tools we need to run our departments and we'll fix our own problems."

"You'll get 'em," Wes replied.

Discussion One—Overcoming Discouragement

Anyone who goes into business will face times of discouragement, even failure. Studies done by business schools on the lives of successful executives show that one of the most important characteristics of successful professionals is a willingness to keep trying, even in the face of defeat.

> *"I am not judged by the number of times I fail, but by the number of times I succeed; and the number of times I succeed is in direct proportion to the number of times I fail and keep on trying." Tom Hopkins*

Many people are not willing to give failure a second opportunity. The experience is so unpleasant, they never try again. A person is only a failure when he or she stops trying, a lesson Wes Douglas learned at an early age from his grandfather.

In this chapter, Wes has begun a plan to put the hospital at breakeven in 90 days. His first step was to meet with his department heads. His goal was twofold: (a) understand the problems, and (b) obtain the support of department heads in solving them.

Discussion Two—Deciding Priorities

If Wes Douglas is to be successful, he must win the confidence of his supervisors. To do that, he must build rapport. Early in his administration, Wes met with his department heads to learn their problems, and to find out how he could help. The department heads were responsive, and gave him a long list of problems they were having with administration, accounting, and so on. As his time was short, Wes set priorities according to importance.

Dwight Eisenhower hired a consultant shortly after being elected President of the United States, to help him set priorities and manage his time. The consultant told the president to prepare a list of the activities that had to be completed each day, and not leave his office until they were finished.

The president called the consultant in a week later and fired him. "The system is useless," he said. "The issues that are pressing are not always important, and the issues that are important, aren't always pressing."

Every CEO must struggle between spending time on those issues that are pressing, and those issues that are truly important.

Discussion Three–Participative Management

One misguided practice of some hospital administrators is to prepare department budgets without department head input. This is a mistake for two reasons: (1) supervisors understand their own departments better than the administrator and are in a better position to know what is fair and reasonable, and (2) a supervisor will have more commitment to a budget he or she participated in preparing.

Discussion Questions

1. *Are the problems raised by the hospital department heads problems, or merely symptoms of a larger problem? If they are symptoms, what might the larger problem be?*

2. *Wes has received a long list of complaints from his first line supervisors. He can't solve them all immediately. Assume you are the interim administrator. Set priorities for the problems presented according to your opinion of their importance. Write a brief justification of your priorities.*

3. *Communication is of limited value if the receiver doesn't understand it. One of Wes's department heads complained accountants use technical terms the non-accountants have trouble understanding. Is accounting the only department in the hospital where this is a problem? How can hospital employees be more sensitive in the way they communicate with patients and non-technical employees?*

4. *Several departments complained the accounting department was not helpful. The department didn't have a service orientation. Who are the customers of the accounting department? Is accounting there only to crunch numbers, or does it have other obligations?*

5. *If you were the supervisor of a department, and your employees didn't have a service orientation, how might you train them to be more sensitive to their mission?*

Writing Exercise

6. *All of the following quotes by successful leaders follow one central theme. Taking these ideas, write a one-page paper on failure as a stepping-stone to success.*

"Don't be afraid to fail. Don't waste energy trying to cover up failure. Learn from your failures and move on to the next challenge. It's okay to fail. If you're not failing, you're not growing." H. Stanley Judd

"Forget about the consequences of failure. Failure is only a temporary change in direction to set you straight for your next success." Denis E. Waitley

"Never walk away from failure. On the contrary, study it carefully – and imaginatively – for its hidden assets." Michael Korda

"The credit belongs to the man who is actually in the arena; whose face is marred by dust and sweat and blood; who strives valiantly; who errs and comes short again and again; who knows the great enthusiasms, the great devotions, and spends himself in a worthy cause; who at the best knows in the end the triumph of high achievement; and who at the worst, if he fails, fails while daring greatly . . ." Theodore Roosevelt

"We learn wisdom from failure much more than from success. We often discover what will do, by finding out what will not do; and probably he who never made a mistake never made a discovery." Samuel Smiles

"What is defeat? Nothing but education. Nothing but the first step to something better." Wendell Phillips

"When defeat comes, accept it as a signal your plans are not sound, rebuild the plans, and set sail once more towards your coveted goal." Napoleon Hill

"Would you like me to give you a formula for success? It's quite simple, really. Double your rate of failure. You're thinking of failure as the enemy of success. But it isn't at all. You can be disgraced by failure – or you can learn from it. So go ahead and make mistakes. Make all you can. Because, remember, that's where you'll find success. On the far side of failure." Thomas J. Watson

11

A Dynasty Falls

Loggias. A roofed outdoor gallery attached on one side to a building and with an entry on the other side.

Venetian. In this textbook/novel, relating to the architecture of Venice, Italy.

Vestibule. An enclosed space between the outer and inner doors of a building.

Victoria Gothic. An ornate 19th century architectural style equated with a romantic view of the world and nostalgia for England.

Perched high on a hill overlooking the small resort town of Park City is the Brannan Mansion. Built in 1896 in a **Victoria Gothic** style, its high **Venetian** tower reflects the arrogance and energy of its builder, Mike Brannan—an Irishman who struck it rich in the silver mines of Park City in the late 1880s.

Ornate wrought iron doors—added more for decoration than protection—guard an outdoor **vestibule**. Beyond those gates stand large double doors of carved oak and beveled glass; beyond those doors lie waterfall staircases and paneled nooks, warmly lit by stained glass.

Deep within the bowels of the mansion is the library. Roughly 30 feet square, the room is interlaced with **loggias** and balconies, its formal design contrasting sharply with the Gothic asymmetry of the other rooms of the 19th-century mansion.

David Brannan hadn't been in this room since he left for college—he preferred his condominium high above the Stein Erickson Ski Lodge overlooking Park City. Today, however, he had come to sign documents that would dissolve a financial empire built by three generations of the Brannan family.

It was 3:30 in the afternoon, and David poured another drink. Replacing the bottle on the heavily carved walnut desk his great-grandfather imported from Italy, he toasted a portrait of the old goat that hung high above the hand-carved marble fireplace.

Michael James Brannan immigrated to the United States in 1882 from Monahan, Ireland. Arriving through the Port of New York, he and his brother Patrick remained long enough to visit family and buy supplies before heading west for the goldfields of California. They never reached their destination. Stopping in Salt Lake City for supplies, Mike fell in love with a Mormon girl, married, and never left Utah.

For a time, Mike and his brother tried farming. They failed miserably. Mike wasn't a Mormon, and wasn't a farmer. Rumors of the discovery of silver on a spur not far from Dayton Peak soon drew him to the ledges and peaks of the Rocky Mountains east of Salt Lake City.

Liquidity. A measure of the ability of a company to pay its short-term debt (debt that must be repaid within a year).

Speculative venture. A business proposition with high risk.

The American Lode was the first mining claim in the district. It was not until the discovery of the Ontario mine in 1879, however, that Park City started to flourish. Purchased in 1872 by George Hearst, father of William Randolph Hearst, the Ontario Mine would produce fifty million dollars in silver ore. Later mines—the Pinion, the Walker, the Webster, the Flagstaff, the McHenry and the Buckeye—would create a dozen or so family fortunes, including the Brannans'.

As David studied the portrait, his eyes shimmered with genuine curiosity. He wondered what the old boy would think if he could see the family today. Gone were the silver and coalmines, the bank, the newspaper, and the hotel. All that was left was the stock in a small software firm, which would provide enough money to fund a small trust for David's mother. He took another drink, wiping his mouth with the back of his hand, and set the tumbler back on the table.

Part of the family's financial disaster might have been avoided if his father, James Brannan, had not insisted on running the business late into his eighties. Much of the family income came from coal mines in Carbon County—the silver mines closed long ago.

David's father resisted modernization, pumping money into highly **speculative ventures**, including the software company. These required huge amounts of cash, risking the family's **liquidity**. Facing the possible loss of his investment, he flipped 180 degrees, spending six million dollars on improvements and mining equipment. The market for coal was depressed, however. Strapped for cash, Brannan Inc. collapsed like a house of cards. Unable to cope with failure, James suffered a massive stroke in February, dying early in March. David Brannan inherited the family business, along with some of the blame for its collapse.

David's eyes flashed with anger as he studied the photograph of his father on the desk. With a violent sweep of his arm, he knocked it off, the glass shattering as the sterling silver frame smashed into the stone mantle of the ornate fireplace and bounced onto the marble floor. He studied it for a moment—broken at his feet—and then poured another drink.

David was not like his father—or his father's father, or his father before him. He hated the family business as much as he hated his father. Given a choice, he would have chosen a professorship in history or literature at some small Ivy League college.

He wasn't given a choice, however. Free agency wasn't a part of the Brannan family vocabulary—not where children were concerned. Jim enrolled his son in engineering at the Colorado School of Mines believing one day David would take over the family's operations. David took two quarters of math and flunked out. Later, with financial help from his mother, he finished a degree in American Studies from a small college in the East. He taught at a college in Minnesota before returning home to settle his father's estate.

David was grateful to his mother—she was the only buffer between him and the unpredictable wrath of his father. For his mother's sake, he did his best to save what remained of the family's fortune. There wasn't much left to save, however, and he didn't know how to save it anyway.

His thoughts were interrupted by voices in the parlor. His mother hosted the women's' auxiliary of the hospital the last Wednesday of every month. She was not fully aware of the family situation. Her home was paid for, and David hoped to get enough money from the sale of the remaining businesses to maintain her in a reasonable way for the rest of her life. At 82 years of age, she deserved better than this.

David's shoulders rose and fell as he sighed deeply. Studying the documents on the desk, he slowly picked up a pen and signed the declaration of bankruptcy. The hospital wasn't the only organization in the community with financial difficulties.

12

Why Are Costs So High?

Managing partner (CPA firm). The senior partner in a public accounting firm.

The first snow of the season was blanketing the foothills as a blue Taurus broke out of Parley's Canyon east of Salt Lake City on Interstate 80. Wes Douglas caught a glimpse of the valley. He first visited Salt Lake City with his parents in the 1980s. On returning six months ago, he was surprised by the changes that had taken place.

In the distance, a cluster of skyscrapers, majestic and tall like the lofty mountains, surrounded the granite towers of the Mormon Temple—a landmark that dominated the skyline for many years. To the north, high on a hill, the State Capitol stood guard over the valley, its copper dome reflecting a history of mining and mineral exploration—an important counterpoint to the ecclesiastical history of the state. Originally settled by Mormon pioneers in 1847, later joined by prospectors and soldiers, and home of the 2002 Winter Olympics, Utah had become as diverse as its scenery.

The purpose of Wes's trip was a meeting with the hospital's auditors in Salt Lake City. With a 90-day commitment to reach breakeven, he needed to understand more about hospital accounting and finance. The public accounting firm that prepared the hospital's financial statements was a good place to start. Wes took the Sixth South Street exit downtown. Parking in the basement of the Utah One Building, he caught an elevator to the tenth floor where he introduced himself to the firm's receptionist, then took a seat.

In less than a minute, Karisa Holyoak, **managing partner**, appeared. She was tall and slender and had a bewitching smile that faintly reminded him of Kathryn. Her eyes sparkled with enthusiasm and intelligence.

Karisa led him to a small conference room. "You have been on the job fewer than three months," she said, taking a seat directly across from Wes at the conference table. She looked at him with wide and curious eyes. "Usually it takes me longer than that to get in trouble with a new client. How can I help you?"

"I'm the one in trouble," Wes murmured, mirroring her expression. "I'm trying to understand how a hospital that charges $3,500 a day can run at a loss."

Health economics. Economics is the study of scarce resources—the study of how resources are produced and distributed. Health economics is an area of economics that focuses on the healthcare industry.

Karisa smiled—she'd considered the question. "Our firm's had the hospital account for 20 years," she told him. She opened the audit file and laid it on the table. "For many years, the hospital was one of our most stable clients."

Karisa thumbed through several reports, opening the most recent audit. "About three years ago, the hospital's financial position started a downward spiral," she continued, reading from her notes. Although volume went up, revenue went down. We concluded the problem was managed care."

"What's that?" Wes asked.

"An approach to cost control. It's changed the way administrators have to manage. Brannan Community Hospital is having more difficulty than others. We tried to do an analysis to determine where you're losing money, but the data simply isn't available—lousy information system."

Wes nodded in agreement. "I need better data to run the hospital. I feel like a pilot flying without instruments."

"Good analogy," replied Karisa. "You're also running out of fuel. Unless the situation changes, you'll be out of cash in two to three months."

Wes sighed. "It might not take that long. Any suggestions on how to proceed?"

Raising her eyebrows, Karisa leaned forward. "May I be candid?" she asked.

"Please," Wes nodded.

"You're a nice guy, Wes, but you're out of your league. You're an accountant. You don't know the first thing about hospitals.

Wes agreed. Three months on the job convinced him hospital administration was different from anything he previously experienced. The assumptions were different, even the terminology was new. The departments in the hospital were like separate kingdoms—each with its own language and customs.

"What do you suggest?" he asked.

"Find another job . . . or find a mentor."

"I can't quit," he said. "There's too much at stake."

"For you or the hospital?"

"Both."

Karisa nodded knowingly.

"Can you suggest a mentor?" he asked.

"I don't know anyone with all the answers, but I can put you in contact with someone who might get you started. We occasionally use the services of a health economist at the University Hospital—a fellow named Herb Krimmel," Karisa said, retrieving his address from her computer. "Dr. Krimmel has an interesting background—he's a doctor with a degree in **health economics**. He teaches at the University Hospital. Coincidentally, he lives in Park City."

Opening her day planner, Karisa wrote a note. "Let me give him a call," she said. "I think he'll be willing to talk to you. You might ask him to introduce you to the Controller. He has an impressive system for controlling costs. Maybe you can borrow some of his ideas."

Karisa gave him a dazzling smile, stood, and held out her hand. "Hope I've been helpful," she said.

Wes took her hand and shook it warmly. "Thanks. I'll be in touch."

Thursday evening, Wes got a phone call from Karisa telling him she had spoken with Krimmel. "As it works out, his car's in for service," she said. "Since he's a neighbor, he wondered if he could catch a ride to the hospital with you tomorrow morning. He promised to set you up with the people who can explain what's happening in the industry." She paused. "You'll find him a little eccentric, but I think you'll like him."

After hanging up, Wes called Krimmel, and arranged to pick him up at his home the next morning.

Discussion One—The Impact of High Healthcare Costs on the Economy

Healthcare costs have grown at an unprecedented rate over the past three decades. Costs have risen to the point that they are threatening the competitiveness of American manufacturers in global markets. American automobiles, for example, have more money invested in each car for employee health costs than they do for steel—a difference of about $1,800 a car—when compared to cars made in Japan. The next three chapters discuss the reasons for high healthcare costs and present several approaches to cost control.

13

A Lesson in Medical Economics

Dr. Krimmel's home, a two-story farmhouse, was three miles north of Park City. The doctor was waiting for him at the curb. "I'm Herb Krimmel," he said as he opened the door. Climbing in, he brushed the residue of what looked like cornmeal from his tweed coat onto the floor. "Breakfast is always a mess." Wes looked at him oddly. "Yours?"

"No, the chickens!" Krimmel replied. "Run a small farm. The wife would like me to sell 'em, but I wake up early—old age you know. It gives me something to do before she gets up." His eyes twinkled. "Besides, the chickens are the only ones around here who listen to me."

Krimmel laughed. Wes couldn't help but laugh too as he studied his odd traveling companion. Short and chubby, Krimmel had curly red hair, a large Roman nose, and round horn-rimmed glasses that looked like small fishbowls, as they magnified his eyes in a peculiar sort of way. Wes turned onto the highway.

"You're new on the job?"

"Quite."

"And no experience?"

"Not in hospitals."

Krimmel raised one eyebrow "You've chosen an exciting time to enter the field. How's it going?"

Wes nodded his head up and down, and then left to right as though he couldn't agree with himself. "Good . . . well, not so good," he confessed somberly.

Krimmel didn't say anything, but studied the cornmeal at his feet. "Ought to vacuum your car more often," he mumbled.

"I'm told our medical director's an old friend of yours." Wes said.

"Who's that?" Krimmel asked.

"Dr. Emil Flagg."

Krimmel chuckled. "An old friend? Wouldn't go that far. We were classmates in medical school. Courted the same girl. I won of course." He smiled, obviously pleased with himself. "Always felt he was a bad sport," Krimmel said with a grin. "How do you get along with him?"

Bigger-is-better syndrome. The perception of some physicians and patients that larger hospitals provide better quality than smaller hospitals.

Cost-per-patient-day. Total hospital costs divided by the number of hospital patient days.

Patient day. One day spent by a patient in the hospital.

Room rate. A daily charge by the hospital designed to cover nursing and hotel (meals, Housekeeping and so on) services. Total per-diem (per-day) charges are found by adding the room rate to ancillary (x-ray, laboratory, pharmacy, and so on) charges.

A look of uncertainty settled on Wes's face. "Don't know—only talked with him once. Didn't go well—more a confrontation than a meeting. Flagg thinks medicine's too commercial; he thinks there's too much emphasis on the bottom line. Blames business people like Edward Wycoff."

"Who's Wycoff?"

"Our finance committee chair, a retired banker. He thinks I'm his ally."

"Are you?" Krimmel asked.

"Not sure," Wes looked hopefully at Krimmel. "That's part of the reason I came to see you."

"Emil and I were in the same class in medical school—the class of 1964," Krimmel said. "It was a different era—one in which healthcare workers stressed quality but paid little attention to cost. One reason was costs were low. When Emil and I graduated the **room rate** at the University Hospital was $35 a day—total costs including x-ray, lab, and pharmacy were about $70."

"What is the average **cost-per-patient-day** today?" Wes asked.

"About $3,500."

Wes whistled softly. "That's a big increase," he said. "What caused it?"

"Technology. Construction costs for new hospitals can exceed one million dollars a bed, including the investment in medical equipment."

"Is there anything hospital administrators can do?"

"They can try not to overbuild," Krimmel replied. "Duplication's expensive. When I was a medical student at the University of Colorado Medical School in Denver, there were 22 hospitals in town. All were operating at 60% occupancy, and most of them were building."

"Why build, if you aren't full?" Wes asked.

"Several reasons," Krimmel replied. "Prestige, salary, a desire to give the medical staff the latest technology, and job security. Physicians and patients alike seemed to share the ***"bigger-is-better"*** **syndrome**. Patients equate size with quality."

"What's size got to do with salary?" Wes asked.

"Hospital administrators' salaries usually correlate with number of beds. The larger the hospital, the larger the paycheck."

"What about job security?"

"It's difficult to fire an administrator in the middle of a building project," Krimmel replied. "A three-year building project provides three years of added security for an administrator in trouble with the board."

"You sound cynical," Wes said.

"A little." Krimmel's face softened. "In all fairness, however, that's probably the least important reason. The biggest issue is technology."

"Isn't technology good?"

"Yeah, but we have to use it efficiently. After graduating, I did my residency at St. Joseph's Hospital in Denver—a fine hospital. While I was there, Presbyterian Hospital, which was directly across the street, installed a two-million dollar piece of equipment for use in their cancer treatment

Arms-length purchase price. A negotiated price between two unrelated individuals.

Demand. As used in economics, the amount of goods bought by customers at each level of pricing.

Free market. An economic system where persons are allowed to decide what is produced, who produces it, and for whom it is produced. Prices in a free market are usually established by the interaction of supply and demand.

Price competition. Competition between sellers based on price.

Supply. In economic terms, the amount of a good or service a provider will manufacture at a given price level.

program. Shortly after that, the Board of Trustees at St. Joseph's announced they planned to buy a similar unit."

Krimmel shook his head in disbelief as he remembered the experience. "One afternoon, we confronted St. Joseph's administrator in the hall. We asked her if she thought about the impact this would have on cost. One community would be paying for two machines, each worth two million dollars, and each operating at 30% of capacity. It doesn't take a rocket scientist to realize duplication raises costs, and someone has to pay the bill."

"I'll never forget her answer! *Young man*, she said, *when it comes to patient care, cost is not an issue. At St. Joseph's we don't compete on cost, we compete on quality!*'"

Krimmel swore under his breath. "It was a bunch of bull. Presbyterian was St. Joseph's main competitor. If their doctors went to a competing hospital, they might like it better and not come back. The administrator's concern was loss of volume.

"In 1964," Krimmel continued, "there were few incentives for hospitals to control costs. Specifically, there was no **price competition."**

"They didn't compete on price?"

"Right."

"Why?

"Know anything about economics?" Krimmel asked.

"Took a course in graduate school—didn't like it much."

"You're typical," Krimmel quipped. I teach the subject. Majored in economics before medical school.

"When you took the course," he continued, "you probably learned to have price competition you need a **free market**. Remember what that is?"

"I think so, but why don't you explain it."

"A free market," Krimmel explained, "exists where private individuals (as opposed to the government) decide what products will be made, how many will be made, who will make them, and for whom they will be made. Prices in a free market are usually established by the interaction of **demand** and **supply**."

"It's starting to come back," Wes said.

"Your professor probably taught you the conditions for a free market to exist," Krimmel said. "Do you remember what those are?"

"I think so. A free market requires a consumer . . . who makes the decision to buy . . . shops on quality and price . . . and negotiates an **arms-length purchase price**."

Impressed, Krimmel raised his eyebrows. "That's pretty good," he said. "I'll have to invite you to speak to my class."

Wes looked at Dr. Krimmel warily but said nothing.

"Let's talk about how market forces work in most industries. Then let's compare that with what happens in healthcare."

Cholecystectomy. An operation to remove the gall bladder.

Palpate. To examine by pressing with the fingers or palms.

Price elasticity. When price influences the volume of sales of a product. When there is price elasticity, as prices go up, the number of goods bought decreases. When prices go down, the number of goods bought increases. There is little price elasticity for life-saving healthcare services.

From the animated expression on Krimmel's face, it was obvious he enjoyed this topic. Despite a couple of kinks in his personality, Wes suspected he was a pretty good teacher.

"You're driving a new car," Krimmel said.

"A new Taurus," Wes said proudly.

"Fine . . . let's talk about how the market works in the auto industry. Who decided you needed a new car?"

"I did."

"How did you decide that?" Krimmel pressed.

"The second transmission fell out of my Yugo."

"Okay, you're a consumer who can identify a need for transportation."

"That's right," Wes said, "I met the first requirement for a free market."

"What did you tell me was the second?"

"The consumer must shop on quality and price," Wes answered.

"Did you do that?" Krimmel asked.

"Yes."

"How?"

"I read the automobile reviews in *Consumer Reports.* I also talked to people who owned models I was interested in."

"Was price a consideration?"

"Yes."

"Did you negotiate?"

"Yes."

"How?"

"Visited a couple of dealers—bargained with the salespeople."

"You're sure price was important to you?"

"Absolutely," Wes said.

"Let's say the price for a new car was $50,000. Would you have bought one?"

"Probably not."

"What if the price was $5,000?"

"I might have bought two—a car for work, and a light truck for the mountains."

"As price goes up, demand goes down," Krimmel said. "We call it **price elasticity."**

Wes was starting to catch on. "Car manufacturers compete on price. This gives them an incentive to keep their costs as low as possible. Therefore, market forces work well in the auto industry."

"You're good," Krimmel said in mock amazement. Wes grimaced.

"Now let's talk about the traditional healthcare industry," Krimmel continued. "Assume you wake up one morning with a pain in your belly." Krimmel poked him in the stomach. "You **palpate** your abdomen, run a few tests, and decide you need a **cholecystectomy**—right?"

"What's a cholecystectomy?"

"A gallbladder operation. You don't know much about medicine," Krimmel noted.

"Right."

Krimmel studied Wes thoughtfully. "So we've identified we're missing the first requirement of a free market."

"An informed consumer," Wes confirmed.

"Right. So who decides if you'll purchase a lab test or an operation?"

"My doctor."

"And who provides the product?"

"My doctor."

"Who prices the product?"

"My doctor."

"You're repeating yourself . . ."

"I noticed," Wes said.

"Why delegate all that to your doctor?" Krimmel asked skeptically.

"He understands medicine—I don't."

"That's right. The doctor has information you don't have. This puts you at a disadvantage."

Wes nodded.

"Do you think the lack of consumer knowledge is a greater problem in healthcare than say in the car business?" Krimmel asked.

"Probably."

"What if the system was set up so it was the auto salespeople who decided when their customers bought new cars?"

"Good deal for the salesperson, maybe not so for the consumer." Wes speculated.

"Why?"

"Salespeople earn money by selling products. They'd have an incentive to sell them something they don't need."

"Maybe that's the situation in healthcare," Krimmel said.

Wes's eyes widened with recognition. He was starting to understand the economic power the doctor has over the consumer.

"Okay," Krimmel continued, "we've determined the healthcare industry fails the first test of a free market—the consumer doesn't make the decision to purchase. Now, once the decision to buy has been made, does the consumer shop on the basis of quality?"

"It's hard for patients to judge quality," Wes said. "They don't have the background."

"That's right," Krimmel affirmed. "Studies show patients judge the quality of a hospital's care by its *hotel services*—the cleanness of the room, the friendliness of the personnel, and the quality of the food.

"How about price. Do you think a patient who needs open-heart surgery shops on the basis of price?"

"Nope."

"Why?"

"Prices aren't usually available," Wes said. "I've never seen a price list on the wall in a doctor's office."

"Neither have I," Krimmel volunteered. "Let's say prices were available . . . do you think it would make a difference?"

"Not much. I can't imagine someone asking a friend *'Do you know where I can get a cheap heart operation?'"*

"Doesn't happen," Krimmel said. He cocked his head to one side. "Why?"

Wes turned the question in his mind. "People equate low price with low quality. No one wants a shoddy operation."

"And . . . ?" Krimmel prodded.

Wes grinned. "Who wants to drive a hard bargain with a doctor who's going to cut you open tomorrow?"

Krimmel laughed. "I never thought about that," he remarked slapping himself on the knee. "Very good! Seriously though, let's talk about price elasticity. If you were perfectly healthy, and the surgeon ran a special on cholecystectomies—a complete operation for $1,225—how many would you buy?"

"None."

"What if we lower the price to $200?" Krimmel asked.

"If I were healthy, I wouldn't buy one," Wes responded.

"What if your daughter developed a brain tumor and the cost of the life-saving surgery was $125. How many brain operations would you buy?"

"One, of course."

"What if the price was $10,000?"

"I would still just buy one operation."

"A million dollars?"

"For my little girl—I'd try to find a way."

"Ha!" said Krimmel. "So price *doesn't* influence the quantity of life-saving healthcare goods and services purchased—there's little or no price elasticity."

"For many products and services, that's probably true," Wes responded grimly.

Krimmel was silent as he collected his thoughts. "When consumers fail to shop on price, incentives for cost control by suppliers disappear," he said. "That's one reason healthcare costs are so high.

"While we're on the subject of cost incentives," Dr. Krimmel continued, "there's one other reason I should mention. Patients usually aren't the ones who select the hospital—it's the doctor. Because of that, many hospitals view the doctor, and not the patient, as their primary customer.

"When I was doing my residency at St. Joseph's, I moonlighted in the emergency center at Presbyterian. One day, Presbyterian hired a new administrator, a woman who felt she needed to do something to cut the cost of healthcare.

Fee-for-service. A traditional doctor payment system. The doctor would bill for his or her services, and the patient or insurance would pay the amount billed. Fee-for-service was a retrospective payment system, one where the price of a product or service was set after the care was delivered and usually not subject to negotiation.

"Since doctors control about 70% of hospital costs," Krimmel continued, "she decided to focus on the medical staff first. Her first action was to tell her medical staff they were no longer going to purchase excess medical equipment. If one group of doctors wanted Sony heart monitors for surgery and another wanted Sylvania, the two groups would have to get together and agree on one brand. They would no longer duplicate equipment just to keep people happy. The hospital also looked at the 'freebies' the doctors were getting—free meals in the cafeteria, free laundry, free treatment and drug prescriptions for family illnesses, and so on. Cost control was the new administrator's focus.

"St. Joseph's hospital administrator took a different approach," Krimmel continued. "He told me it was his philosophy to keep the medical staff happy. *Give the doctors what they want* was his motto."

Dr. Krimmel gave Wes a searching look. "Guess who got most of the patients?"

"Probably St. Joseph's," Wes replied. "They gave the doctors what they wanted."

Krimmel gave him a thumbs-up. "You've got it," he crowed. "A study conducted in 1975 showed many hospitals were operated to maximize doctor income."

Krimmel continued. "One way to do that is to provide excess capacity. Under **fee-for-service**, a doctor's income is a function of the time he or she spends treating patients. A doctor waiting in line for an operating room or piece of equipment isn't earning money."

Krimmel looked directly at Wes. "When I first joined the staff of University Hospital, most of our surgeons were screaming for more operating rooms. Operating rooms are expensive to build. The administrator looked at the surgical schedule and found our surgeons were only using the operating rooms 60% of the time. Couldn't figure it out. What he failed to realize, however, was despite the low use, there were still times when more than one doctor needed the same working suite. When an emergency arose, someone was bumped from the schedule or had to wait to get into surgery. Downtime is costly for the doctor."

"Then the ideal situation from the doctor's standpoint would be to have one operating room staffed and equipped at all times for every surgeon?" Wes asked.

"Yes. Remember, the doctor didn't earn any more money if the hospital was operated efficiently than if there was excess capacity. The doctor didn't share in the costs of inefficiency.

"Please don't misunderstand me," he continued, "I'm not saying medical people are dishonest—some of the finest people I know are doctors. It's just people respond to financial incentives—and the incentives of the old system were wrong."

"Interesting," Wes responded. "I've never had it explained that way before. Are there other causes influencing costs I should be aware of?"

"There are," Krimmel replied. "I've set up appointments later in the week with other members of the faculty and staff I think can best explain them to you."

Wes was elated as he drove back to Park City. He was starting to understand how healthcare differed from other industries. Hard work was good therapy. There were periods of up to a week now that Wes didn't think of Kathryn. That too was a good sign.

He built a special room in his heart only she would ever occupy, carefully walled off from all else. From time to time, she would knock, and he would open the door to see if she was still there. In his mind, she smiled on those occasions, giving a reassurance all would be fine.

His new job, difficult as it was, was giving him a new sense of purpose. Even the back injury was improving. He was seeing an orthopedist in Salt Lake City. The doctor gave him a set of exercises to strengthen the muscles in his back, and they were working. The pain was notably less. The healing had begun.

Discussion One—Unreimbursed Care

Another reason for increasing health care costs for the paying consumer is unreimbursed care. A hospital the author recently consulted with h hospital that bills $190 million a year but collects only $100 million. Which groups fail to pay the full cost of hospital services received?

- *Federal and state governments through Medicare and Medicaid programs. While promising healthcare benefits for an increasing aging and indigent population, politicians have been unwilling to provide the funding to cover the total costs of their promises.*
- *Insurance companies who, because of their volume, are able to demand significant discounts.*
- *The uninsured. Many uninsured people with life-threatening illnesses are unable or unwilling to pay for the hospital services they have received.*
- *Insured patients whose insurance companies send their checks directly to the patient will often use the money to buy new furniture or automobiles while leaving the hospital unpaid.*

Diagnostic tests. Tests performed to diagnose an illness.

Discussion Questions

1. *One reason healthcare costs have risen dramatically over the past three decades is the cost of technology. Name one action health professionals can take to help contain technology costs.*

2. *According to Dr. Herb Krimmel, why did the administrator of St. Joseph's Hospital build a cancer treatment unit when there was an identical one right across the street from her hospital? What impact did her decision have on the costs of healthcare in her community?*

3. *What is a free market and what are the conditions for its survival? Does the healthcare industry compete in a free market?*

4. *When you are shopping for a new pair of running shoes, how do you compare the quality of the various brands you are considering? Do quality and price influence your decision? Why is it healthcare consumers have difficulty judging the need for, and the quality of, the services they receive?*

5. *According to Dr. Herb Krimmel, some hospitals don't think the patient is their primary customer. Who do they think the customer is, and why?*

6. *In 1972, health professionals could order* **diagnostic tests**, *laboratory tests, x-ray studies, and so on without significant review by insurance companies, employees, employers, the government, and so on. The emphasis was on quality. Today the emphasis is on quality and cost. What caused the change in emphasis to occur?*

7. *Accessibility to healthcare for all people has become an important discussion topic in the United States. Is there a fallacy in focusing solely on quality, if no one can afford the product offered by the hospital?*

14

Gaming the System

Actuary. An individual who calculates insurance premiums

Dean of the school of medicine. The chief academic administrator in a school of medicine.

Diagnostic services. Tests and procedures performed to diagnose an illness.

Director of reimbursement. A hospital manager responsible for negotiating contracts with insurance companies, training hospital managers how to make money on these contracts, and managing the contracts.

Oncologist. A cancer specialist.

It was 9:00 a.m. as Wes Douglas's automobile turned onto Medical Drive. As Dr. Krimmel had a meeting, the doctor asked Wes to drop him at the main entrance. Before leaving the car, he directed Wes to the office of Dr. Allison Lindberg, **dean of the school of medicine**. Dr. Lindberg, an **oncologist** by training, was waiting for Wes in her office. Wes guessed she was in her mid-fifties. She had shortly tapered silver hair, and wore a white lab coat over a finely cut pantsuit of gray wool.

"You're here to learn about healthcare cost," she affirmed, as she motioned for Wes to take a seat.

Wes took a chair next to a large window overlooking the Huntsman Cancer Center. "Yes," he replied. "I'm especially interested in incentives, or the lack thereof, for cost control."

"It's interesting you should mention that," Lindberg said. Her eyes narrowed as she focused on a report on her desk. "Got a memo this morning from our **director of reimbursement**—it's an interest of his as well."

Lindberg thumbed to the second page. "One of the fastest growing components of healthcare costs is **diagnostic services**," she said. "Things like lab and x-ray tests. When properly used, they're great. There's concern, however, that a few doctors may be using them to raise income.

"An **actuary** in Salt Lake City," she continued, "did a study on doctors who own lab and x-ray units. They use twice the tests per patient visit of doctors who don't. Her findings are consistent with studies conducted in parts of the country where there are a surplus of doctors. Contrary to what economists project, increased competition doesn't reduce doctor income."

"I think I know the reason," Wes said. "Doctors can create demand. They decide what tests are ordered. Lab and x-ray tests can be a good source of additional income."

"I think you're right," Dr. Lindberg said. "An Eastern economist studied the phenomenon. Concerned with the variation he found in the number of laboratory tests ordered by doctors of the same specialty in the same hospital, he was able to isolate only one variable that statistically accounted for the **variance**."

"What was that?" asked Wes.

"Volume—the lower the doctor's patient volume, the greater the tendency to order unnecessary tests. The root of the problem is consumer ignorance. The patient can't judge if they need a particular test or not."

She continued, "Lab and x-ray tests are not the only areas where consumer ignorance provides an incentive for doctors to give excessive or inappropriate services." "Several years ago, there was evidence we were performing too many **elective surgeries**. In addition, for many years, there were places in the country where the hospital length of stay was longer than necessary. Ideally, the number of days a patient stays in the hospital should be solely dependent on the patient's medical condition.

"For many years, insurance companies paid hospitals **cost reimbursement**. Whatever their costs, they received full payment from Medicare, Medicaid, and most insurance companies. Some **payers** added a small markup for profit."

"Why would a **nonprofit organization** need a profit?" Wes asked.

"To pay for inflation. If you buy a piece of equipment for $10,000, chances are it will cost more when the time comes to replace it."

Dr. Lindberg continued. "Under cost reimbursement, factors other than the patient's medical condition influenced how long the patient stayed in the hospital."

"Such as . . . ?" Wes asked.

"Hospital occupancy," Lindberg replied. "I did my residency at Community Hospital in St. Louis. Whenever **occupancy rate**s dipped, our hospital administrator would catch doctors in the hall as they did their morning rounds. He'd say something like 'Doctor Smith, remember the new piece of equipment you've been after me to order for the lab? It's in! It cost $360,000.'

"The doctor, of course would express appreciation. Then our administrator would mention today's occupancy rate was 53%. 'It's hard to justify expensive equipment, with half your beds empty,' he'd say as they parted."

Lindberg smiled conspiratorially. "Guess what? In a few hours, the hospital's census would mysteriously start climbing. Patients scheduled to go home would be kept another day. Some patients who could safely be treated in outpatient settings would be admitted to the hospital."

Reimbursement. Synonym for payment.

Variance. Also known as cost variance. The difference between what something should cost and what it actually costs. If the cost to remove an appendix is budgeted at $3,000 (the standard cost), and the actual cost is $3200, then the variance is $200.

Cost reimbursement. A payment system where the provider (doctor or hospital) gets paid total billed costs as payment. Often an additional mark-up is added to pay for inflation. Since the doctor or hospital gets paid for all costs, regardless of inefficiency, there are few incentives for cost control. Cost reimbursement was the dominant payment system for many years for Medicare, Medicaid and Blue Cross.

Elective surgery. Surgery that is not essential for the life or good health of the patient. A facelift is an example of an elective surgery.

Nonprofit organization. An organization formed to provide services often not available through the private sector. Surpluses of nonprofit organizations cannot be kept or given for the benefit of specific persons but are used for the mission of the organization.

Occupancy rate. The percent of hospital beds occupied.

Payer. The person or organization that pays the healthcare bill. Private insurance companies such as Blue Cross, and governmental insurance programs such as Medicare and Medicaid are payers.

Incentive payment. A payment system designed to decrease cost by penalizing hospitals and doctors for poor efficiency, and rewarding them for high efficiency. A synonym for incentive reimbursement.

'There weren't many incentives for cost control," Wes affirmed. "So what's the answer?"

"Some think it's **incentive payment**," responded Lindberg."

"What's that?"

"An incentive payment is a payment that gives a doctor or hospital an incentive to control costs," Lindberg replied.

"How does it work?"

"The answer to that question can best be given by Larry Ortega, our director of reimbursement," she said.

Discussion Questions

1. *Why would the ownership of a laboratory or x-ray unit by a doctor influence how many lab or x-ray tests he or she orders? Should doctors own laboratories and x-ray units?*
2. *What is a director of reimbursement? Why is this person an important part of the administrative team? What do you think the training requirements should be for a director of reimbursement?*

15

Adverse Incentives

The director of reimbursement's office was in the basement not far from the hospital laundry. The director, Larry Ortega was not there when Wes arrived. His secretary explained he was in negotiations with a health insurance company downtown. He called, she said, to say he'd be late. Wes took a seat and, for the next 15 minutes, thumbed through a copy of *Healthcare Financial Management.* Ortega arrived shortly after 10:00 a.m. The Weather Channel forecast a heavy midmorning storm. From Ortega's appearance, the storm had arrived.

Ortega was 56 years old, had a lean frame, wore a crew cut, and had a no-nonsense way about him reminiscent of his military training.

"Sorry to be late," he said, shaking the rain from his umbrella. He unbuttoned his coat, unwrapped his muffler, and motioned for Wes to follow him into a small office maintenance had built from a laundry linen room. The hospital was full and office space was at a premium.

He motioned for Wes to take a seat. He checked his phone pad for messages and then looked Wes squarely in the eyes.

"Herb Krimmel said you wanted to talk to me about hospital reimbursement systems," he began.

Wes nodded. "I've learned that many incentives to control costs in other industries don't exist in the healthcare industry. Some have suggested incentive payment can help. I'm told you're an expert on the subject."

Ortega scowled as he considered the question. "How much do you know about the history of hospital payment systems?" he asked.

"A little."

Ortega rose from his desk and retrieved a coffeepot from a hot plate on the small credenza behind his desk.

"Coffee?" he asked.

"No thanks."

Ortega poured a cup and returned to his desk. "During the 1970s," he said, "when hospital inflation was taking off, many legislators felt the best approach to cost control was regulation. Consistent with that view, they passed laws setting up agencies to review requests to build new hospitals or purchase expensive hospital equipment. Without prior approval, hospitals would not be

Comorbidity. The existence of two or more unrelated diseases in one person.

Director of purchasing. The person responsible for purchasing supplies, materials, and contract services for the hospital. Synonym for director of materials management.

Severity of illness. A measure of how sick a patient is.

Vendor. A person or company that sells products or services to a hospital. A medical supply company is a vendor.

reimbursed for the cost of the building or equipment. He paused to fan his coffee. "Some states even established governmental agencies to approve hospital charges."

"It sounds like the model the government uses to regulate utilities," Wes remarked.

"I think that's what they had in mind," Ortega replied.

"It works for electric companies; how well did it work for hospitals?"

"Not well," admitted Ortega. "Utility companies have one product—natural gas for example. Hospitals have thousands. There are over 60,000 products and services at University Hospital.

'Two patients with the same diagnosis can require different care depending on their age, the **severity of illness**, and other illnesses the patients might have."

"That's called **comorbidity**," Wes offered.

"Right. The number and complexity of services offered by most hospitals is mind boggling—too complex for any regulatory body to understand."

"You're telling me central planning didn't work for healthcare for the same reason it didn't work for Eastern Europe and the former Soviet Union," Wes volunteered. "The economy's too complex for one central body to manage."

"That's right," replied Ortega. "There's little evidence regulation did anything to control costs. If anything, it raised them by creating a new bureaucracy."

Ortega shook his head. "When it didn't work, some decided the answer was incentive payment–a payment system that would encourage doctors and hospitals to consider cost when considering a treatment plan."

"How? Wes asked, taking notes.

"By making the doctor and hospital share the cost of inefficiency. Before 1984, many insurance plans paid hospitals and doctors cost reimbursement. Do you know what that is?"

Wes nodded. "Just learned about it," he said. "Hospitals were reimbursed costs, with a small markup for profit."

Ortega smiled cynically as he placed his coffee mug on his desk. "It doesn't take a rocket scientist to find the easiest way to raise profits when you are being reimbursed costs plus a 3% profit."

"Raise cost!" Wes said.

"That's right. Although I don't think anyone purposely raised cost with the sole objectives of increasing profits, strong incentives to control cost didn't exist." Ortega leaned back in his chair and stared out the window. "When I retired from the military in 1980, I was hired as **director of purchasing** at Long Beach Memorial Hospital in California. I wish I had a nickel for every time an equipment **vendor** said: Don't worry about the price—it's cost reimbursable under Medicare."

Blue Cross. A health insurance company.

Premium. An amount paid to buy insurance coverage.

Wes's eyes reflected bewilderment. "Cost reimbursement is not a common payment system," he said. "About the only other place I've seen it is in the defense industry—it's also used in some segments of the construction industry. Why was cost reimbursement the payment system of choice in healthcare?"

"The answer lies in the history of the health industry," Ortega responded. "The first insurance company in the United States was **Blue Cross** founded by Justin Ford Kimball. Kimball was a university administrator serving on the Board of Trustees of Baylor Hospital. Concerned that professors weren't paying their hospital bills, he started the first health insurance company in the 1930s. The **premium** was something like $3.50 per month.

In the 1930s, most hospitals were nonprofit corporations. These were run by charitable organizations—groups Kimball thought should be protected from financial risk. When the time came to select a payment method, he chose cost reimbursement.

As other insurance companies entered the healthcare market, they followed suit. That decision cost consumers billions of dollars over the next several decades."

"You're telling me the nonprofit status of early day hospitals influenced the selection of a payment system," Wes stated.

"That's right."

"Then I guess my next question is—why were hospitals nonprofit?"

"Because they evolved from poorhouses," Ortega said. "In the early part of the twentieth century, people who had family or money died at home. The paupers died in charitable institutions. These poorhouses were the forbearers to hospitals.

"Early hospitals were not the high-tech organizations we have today," he continued. "The Sisters of Holy Cross started the first hospital in Salt Lake City to care for the large number of silver miners in Park City who were dying of lead-poisoning. It was an epidemic of significant proportions. Want to know how they solved the problem?" he asked.

Wes shrugged. "Scientific breakthrough?" he guessed.

"It was a breakthrough, all right—although I'm afraid it wasn't scientific," Ortega answered, a smile lighting his dark blue eyes. "They got the miners to wash! Doctors finally discovered if miners would bathe more than two or three times a year, they wouldn't absorb lead from silver ore through their skin."

Ortega smiled sympathetically. "I tell the story simply to show how far medicine has come. In the early part of the twentieth century, patients had a better chance of dying if they were admitted to the hospital, than if they stayed home."

Wes processed Ortega's message. Hospitals were different in history and incentive from the manufacturers he had worked with. He understood now why Karisa Holyoak felt he needed a better understanding of healthcare if he were to succeed in his new job.

"Okay," said Wes. "I understand why most hospitals were nonprofit organizations, and how this influenced insurance companies to adopt cost reimbursement. I also understand how reimbursement destroyed incentives for cost control—incentives that exist in other industries. My next question is—what's the alternative?"

"Some think it's incentive payment," replied Ortega.

"Is this the same as prospective payment?" Wes asked.

"That's one form of incentive payment." Ortega replied. "A **prospective payment system** is one where an insurance company negotiates with a doctor or hospital a **fixed price** before the time the patient is treated. Using construction terms—it's a **fixed-price contract**."

Wes nodded. "I understand the terms. When I was in college, I worked part time as an accountant for a building contractor. Some of his projects were built under fixed-price contracts; others he built on a cost reimbursement basis."

"Do you think he managed them the same?" asked Ortega.

"Probably not. There is more incentive to control cost under a fixed-price contract than under a **cost reimbursement contract**."

"Why?" Ortega asked.

"Fixed-price contracts place the contractor at risk; cost reimbursement contracts don't."

"That's right," replied Ortega. "Most people are less careful when spending other people's money than they are when spending their own. The same principle holds true for healthcare," he continued. "Doctors had little to lose if hospital supplies or staff were used inefficiently, and since hospitals were reimbursed for inefficient care, hospitals didn't have much to lose either."

Ortega leaned back in his chair as he studied Wes Douglas. *Wes is a bright enough fellow, but he still has a lot to learn*, he thought. "I think the best person to explain how prospective payment systems can change doctor

Cost reimbursement contract. A contract where the price of a product or service is not finalized until after the work is done. The customer pays full cost, even if there is a cost overrun from what the contractor originally estimated. Hospitals were originally paid under cost reimbursement contracts by insurance companies. Regardless of how efficiently or inefficiently care was provided, full costs were reimbursed by patients and insurance companies. Cost reimbursement contracts sometimes include an additional amount for inflation, new technology and so on. This amount is sometimes called a fee to differentiate it from the profit earned by for-profit hospitals.

Fixed price. A price fixed in advance that is not adjustable regardless of the actual price of the product or service finally delivered.

Fixed-price contract. A contract where a price is set before the work to produce the product is carried out. Many homes are built under fixed-price contracts. If there are cost overruns, then the building contractor must absorb the loss. DRG and capitation payment systems for doctors and hospitals are examples of fixed-price contracts.

Health Maintenance Organization (HMO). An organization that delivers healthcare. Originally, HMOs tried to control health care costs by: (1) paying physicians and hospitals capitation instead of billed charge payments, (2) requiring patients to use specific doctors and hospitals, (3) providing financial incentives for patients to adopt healthy lifestyles, and (4) requiring second opinions or preapproval for expensive procedures that are often abused.

Prospective payment system. A payment system for doctors and hospitals. In a prospective payment system, the bill is calculated before services are given. A prospective payment system is a fixed-price contract. If the cost of the services provided exceeds the prearranged amount, the healthcare provider must absorb the loss. Prospective payment systems shift the risk of cost inefficiency from the patient or doctor to the hospital.

Health Maintenance Organization (HMO). An organization that delivers healthcare. Originally, HMOs tried to control health care costs by: (1) paying physicians and hospitals capitation instead of billed charge payments, (2) requiring patients to use specific doctors and hospitals, (3) providing financial incentives for patients to adopt healthy lifestyles, and (4) requiring second opinions or prior for expensive procedures that are often abused.

System. An orderly and complex arrangement of parts.

behavior is Charles Stoker, the director of our new **health maintenance organization**. He's out of town today, but he'll be back later this week."

Discussion One—Systems

*A **system** is an orderly and complex arrangement of parts. There are many types of systems including:*

- *Physiological systems—the digestive system, the neurological system, and the circulatory system.*
- *Economic Systems—capitalism and socialism.*
- *Computer systems—network mainframe, and PC computer systems.*

Systems have the following elements:

- *Input—resources entering the system*
- *Throughput—the processes and resources used to create a product*
- *Output—the final product*
- *Feedback—information taken from the output to control or correct errors in throughput*

Backwards thinking. A system of analysis that starts with the final goal in mind, then works backwards analyzing how each activity contributes to the goal.

Systems analysis. Analysis of a system which is an orderly collection of parts.

Systems thinking or systems analysis. An approach to problem solving that focuses on the system as a whole, and the relationship of its interconnected parts.

Exhibit 1—Basic Components of a Generic System

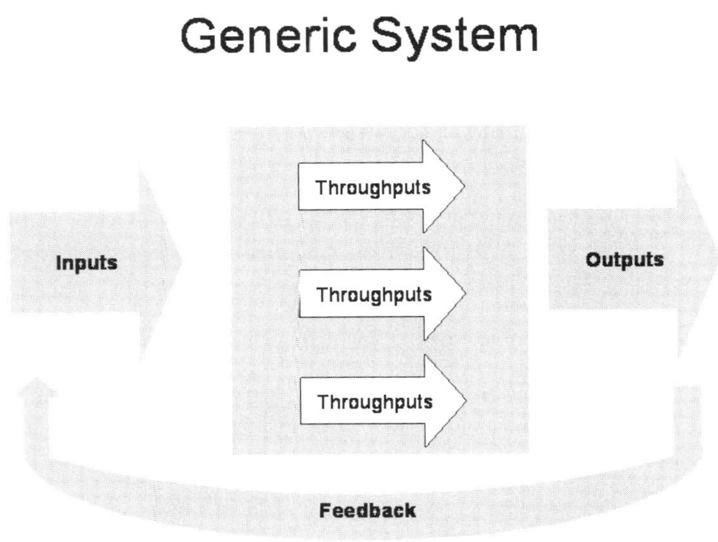

*One approach to problem solving is **systems thinking** or **systems analysis.** Systems thinking is a way of solving problems by looking at a problem from a broad perspective, looking not only at the individual parts of the system, but the way these parts relate to each other. Systems thinking recognizes the whole is greater than the sum of its parts, and often results in different conclusions than those reached by traditional problem solving models.*

The American health care industry is a system. System components include doctors, hospitals, insurance companies, and so on. In addressing a problem, it is important to look at the system as a whole and not just focus on one or two components.

*Systems thinking involves **backwards thinking**. It begins with the final goal and works backwards, analyzing the relationship of each part or activity to the goal. For example, if the goal of a team is to produce a low cost, but high quality medical product, then backwards thinking starts with the final product and evaluates each input and activity involved in producing the product to see if:*

1. *It was needed for the manufacture of the product*
2. *It raised quality*
3. *It cut cost*

If the answer to (1) is no, the team might evaluate stopping the input or process. If the answer to (2) or (3) is no, then the team might redesign the input or throughput to achieve that goal.

Advantages of Systems Thinking

In a world of complex organizations, systems thinking offers the following advantages:

- ***Global Approach to Problem Solving**: Systems thinking helps employees "see the forest for the trees." It enables team members to understand the big picture.*
- ***Focus**: Systems thinking allows problem solvers to identify cause and effect relationships. It focuses on the activities needed for change.*
- ***Teambuilding**: Systems thinking helps team members identify the goal of the team, and understand how their individual activities contribute to that goal.*

Discussion Two—The American Healthcare Delivery System

The American healthcare delivery system is one of the largest and most complex systems in the world. We model it by adapting the generic system in Exhibit 1 (shown earlier in this chapter).

Exhibit 2—American Healthcare System

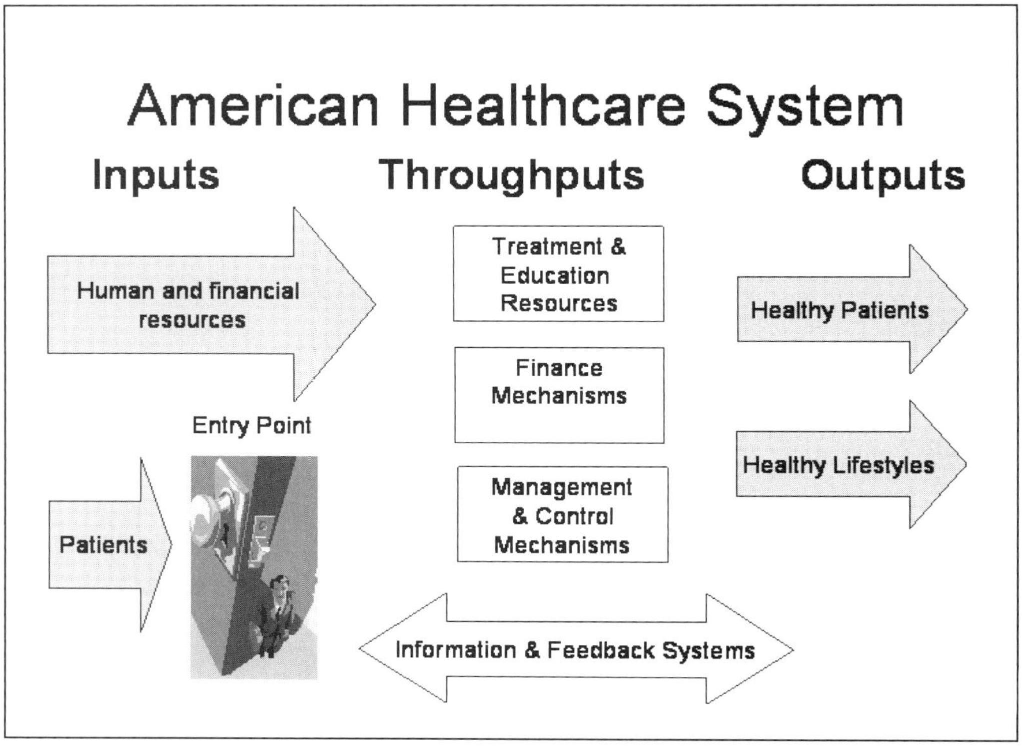

As with the generic model, the American healthcare system has inputs, throughput, output, and a feedback loop.

Inputs

Inputs include:

- *Human and financial resources*
- *Patients*

Human and Financial Resources

Human resources are the professionals who diagnose and treat patients, also the personnel who provide ***support services*** *such as Housekeeping. Human resources consist of the doctors, nurses, respiratory therapists, certified nurse* *assistants, administrators,* ***dieticians****, housekeepers, and accountants who work in the healthcare system.*

Financial resources *are the funds used to pay the salaries of healthcare personnel, the buildings and equipment used to treat patients, and the financial institutions that loan or disperse these funds.*

Patients

Patients are the people who enter the system for preventive, diagnostic, or ***treatment healthcare services****.*

One of the best ways to cut healthcare costs is to prevent illness. It is less costly, for example, to prevent a heart attack through proper diet and exercise, than it is to perform a quadruple bypass. With healthcare costs increasing, ***preventive medicine*** *is an essential component of the healthcare delivery system.*

An important part of preventive medicine is education. Education can take place in schools, through public service announcements (for example, antismoking campaigns), or through various other activities.

Employers recognize a healthy employee produces more and costs less than a sick employee. Healthcare actuaries report the monthly healthcare cost for an employee who smokes is $60 higher than for the employee who does not. Employees who are overweight or fail to exercise also have higher costs.

Therefore, many companies offer various on-site health prevention programs for employees, including exercise gyms, diet counseling, and smoking cessation.

Patients entering the healthcare delivery system need a well-defined ***entry point****. How does a 55-year old male with* ***vertigo*** *know where to enter the system? Should his first contact with the system be:*

- *An ambulance?*
- *A general practice doctor?*
- *A* ***neurologist****?*
- *A* ***psychiatrist?***
- *The emergency center?*
- *Alternatively, some other individual or institution?*

Dietician. A person trained in the practical application of diet in the treatment of illness.

Entry point. The place where a patient enters the health care delivery system.

Financial resources. Funds used to pay the salaries of healthcare personnel, the buildings, equipment, and supplies used to treat patients and the financial institutions that loan or disperse these funds.

Neurologist. A specialist in the diagnosis and treatment of diseases of the neurological system.

Preventive medicine. Services designed to prevent, rather than treat illness. Examples of preventive medicine include annual physicals, good nutrition, exercise, and the discontinuance of unhealthy habits such as smoking and over eating. Also called preventive healthcare services.

Psychiatrist. A physician who treats mental illness, often through the prescription of drugs.

Treatment healthcare services. Procedures designed to restore the patient to a state of health. Medication, surgery, and physical therapy are examples of treatment healthcare services.

Vertigo. A sensation of spinning or whirling.

Home health agency. An organization that provides healthcare services to patients in their home.

Taxonomy. A classification system

Triage. Medical screening of patients to decide priority for treatment.

Work-in-process. Goods being manufactured for sale that are not yet finished.

An effective entry point provides:

- ***Triage****—medical screening of patients to determine their relative priority for treatment.*
- *Timely entry into the system—entry soon enough to prevent further damage from the trauma or illness.*
- *Access to resources—proper and cost effective resources to diagnose and treat the patient (an emergency center is not a proper or cost effective way to treat an ingrown toenail or pediatric sore throat).*

Throughput

In manufacturing, throughput is known as ***work-in-process****—goods being manufactured. In the healthcare delivery system, throughput is the patient.*

A ***taxonomy*** *is a classification system. There are many ways to classify the resources used during throughput. Examples include:*

- *Education and treatment resources*
- *A financing mechanism*
- *Management and control mechanisms*
- *Information and feedback system*

Education and Treatment Resources

Education and treatment resources include:

- *Hospitals*
- *Physician offices*
- *Outpatient clinics*
- *Outpatient surgical centers*
- ***Home health agencies***
- *Medical and nursing schools*
- *Long-term-care hospitals*
- *Public health organizations*

Co-payment. An amount not covered by insurance and paid by a patient at the time of treatment. Co-payments are designed to prevent unnecessary care.

Diagnostic healthcare services. Tests and procedures performed to diagnose an illness.

Finance mechanism. The system used to pay the cost of healthcare.

Insurance premium. A payment paid by an employer or enrollee for health insurance.

Physical therapy. The treatment of musculoskeletal disease, injury, and so on through massage, infrared or ultraviolet light, electrotherapy, hydrotherapy, heat, and exercise.

Preventive healthcare services. Services designed to prevent, rather than treat illness. Examples of preventive medicine include annual physicals, good nutrition, exercise, and the discontinuance of unhealthy habits such as smoking and over eating.

Treatment healthcare services. Procedures designed to restore the patient to a state of health. Medication, surgery, and physical therapy are examples of treatment healthcare services.

Throughput services provided by these organizations include:

- ***Preventive healthcare services****—services designed to keep the patient well. Education and immunization are two examples of preventive services.*
- ***Diagnostic healthcare services****—tests and procedures to determine the patient's diagnosis.*
- ***Treatment healthcare services****—procedures designed to restore the patient to a state of health. Medication, surgery, and* ***physical therapy*** *are examples of treatment healthcare services.*

Finance Mechanisms

A second important component of the American healthcare delivery system is the ***finance mechanism****—someone must pay the bill. America lacks one mechanism for financing healthcare. Instead, it relies on various mechanisms. This results in complexity and some duplication. In addition, some segments of the population are not covered.*

How does America finance healthcare?

- *Self-pay: Some patients pay for their own healthcare. These are the self-employed, uninsured employed, and the unemployed.*
- *Employers: Many companies provide employee health insurance. The benefits vary widely. Most firms require the employee to pay a part of the premium. Almost all firms require cost sharing through* ***co-payments*** *at the time of service. As healthcare costs continue to rise, it appears certain the employee will pay a larger and larger percentage of the health* ***insurance premium****.*
- *Private Insurance: Some people buy individual or family policies from health insurance carriers. These are usually more costly than the group insurance contracts bought by employers. In addition, coverage is often limited, and some people are unable to qualify for coverage.*
- *Medicaid: Medicaid consists of state-run programs that pay for some healthcare services for the poor or indigent.*
- *Medicare: Medicare is a federally funded program that pays for some healthcare products and services for those 65 years of age and older.*
- *The healthcare industry****:*** *Many healthcare providers, most specifically hospitals, are*

Bad debt. A bill that will not be paid.

expected to provide charity care in return for nonprofit exemption from income and property taxes. Most hospitals also have a large ***bad debt****. Many hospital emergency centers, for example, collect less than 50% of billings. In the end, the consumer pays these costs.*

In future years, it is possible the government will replace the many programs used to pay for healthcare with some type of universal financing. What form this program will take remains to be seen.

Management and Control Mechanisms

The American healthcare system has many management and control mechanisms. These include planning and regulatory agencies, licensure bodies, and legislative mandates.

Information and Feedback Systems

Control is ineffective without feedback. Information systems include the financial and cost accounting systems used by hospitals and other healthcare organizations. Feedback systems also include quality review mechanisms, such as accreditation and peer review.

A free market cannot exist without information. The Security and Exchange Commission (SEC), for example, works to assure buyers of stocks and bonds have as much information about the companies they are investing in as the sellers of those securities. There is no effective feedback mechanism for health consumers. Patients lack feedback on the need, cost, and quality of most services they receive.

Output

Output is the product of the system. Often, it is difficult for a service industry to define its product. In healthcare, for example, what is the ultimate product?

- *A patient?*
- *A hospital admission?*
- *A patient day?*
- *An illness?*
- *A personal service such as an x-ray or appendectomy?*
- *A healthy community?*
- *Some other definition?*

For illustration purposes, in Exhibit 2 we have chosen healthy patients and healthy lifestyles as the output or product of the American healthcare delivery system.

The Healthcare Delivery System is Like a Mobile

The healthcare delivery system is like a mobile. Movement or pressure exerted on one component exerts pressure on others. For example:

- *Successful pressure to cut costs (one barrier to entry) will affect the volume of patients entering the system (input) and the number seen by the system (throughput).*
- *Greater volumes of patients entering the system (input) and seen by the system (throughput) could cause the finance mechanism (another component of throughput) to flounder or fail.*
- *Pressure to cut the cost of throughput, might raise the number of people entering the system (input).*
- *Changes in the financing mechanism (one component of throughput) through redesign of reimbursement, might affect cost, quality, and access to care.*
- *More resources spent preventing illness will cut resources needed for diagnosis and treatment, both components of throughput.*
- *Restrictions on human and financial resources through licensing, education, or inadequate funding can influence the volume of throughput. Staff shortages, for example, can raise wages, which can bring pressure to bear on financing mechanisms.*

Summary

The healthcare industry is a complex system of many parts. It is impossible to change one part of the system without influencing others. Historically, some people have attempted to fix the system by focusing on one or more "broken parts." By failing to consider the "big picture," however, they often reap unintended consequences. Those wishing to address quality, cost, and accessibility must adopt a systems approach to problem solving.

Discussion Three—The Patient Protection and Affordable Care Act

A Brief History of Universal Healthcare Legislation in the United States

A significant attempt to enact **universal health insurance** *began in the 19th century with the "Bill for Benefits of the Indigent and Insane" which would have provided free healthcare for the indigent and the insane. President Franklin Pierce proposed it, but Congress failed to pass it.*

Not quite a century later, President Franklin Roosevelt drafted a proposal to amend **Social Security** *legislation to include a governmentally funded healthcare program. This was a time period when private health insurance was growing rapidly, and Congress felt this need could be better served by private industry. The legislation failed.*

In 1974, President Richard Nixon proposed in his State of the Union Address the enactment of universal health insurance. His plan was known as the "Comprehensive Health Insurance Act of 1974." It was popular with lawmakers on both sides of the isle (Republicans and Democrats). Some feel that the legislation was killed by Senator Ted Kennedy who felt the act did not go far enough. In later years he expressed his regret at having opposed this legislation.

Two decades later Hillary Clinton, the wife of President William Clinton campaigned for universal healthcare coverage. An extended debate ensued, but once again this legislation failed to pass.

It was not until 2010 that a United States president, President Barack Obama, successfully led Congress in the passage of universal health insurance. The legislation was the Patient Protection and Affordable Care Act. For brevity we will use this name in the remainder of this section.

Old Problems—A New Proposal

Whether or not the Patient Protection and Affordable Care Act is the answer to the nation's healthcare problems, few argue that something needed to be done. A significant portion of the population was without insurance coverage, and costs were increasing at a rate that if unchecked could eventually have bankrupted the country.

Professor Richard McDermott, the author of Code Blue became a hospital administrator in 1971. At that time, the room rate for his hospital was $35 per day. Employers, unions, and patients labeled those charges as "outrageous!" "How can a hospital spend $35 a day for hospital care?" they asked.

Accountable Care Organization (ACO). A coordinated group of hospitals, physicians, and other healthcare providers that seek to provide high quality in a cost effective manner. Payment is based on quality as measured by health outcomes, and includes fee-for service and capitation .

Capitation Payment: A payment program where a hospital or physician receives a fixed monthly payment to provide a specified set of medical services to a person covered for specified healthcare benefits.

Clinical Episode. A medical event that is a part of a larger series of medical events.

Gross Domestic Product. The value of all the goods and services provided by a country in a year.

Prospective Payment System. A payment system where the price of a service is set before the service is delivered.

Stakeholder. An individual or institution that has an interest in a policy, program, or institution. Someone who influences or is influenced by the actions of a program or institution.

The "per diem rate," which is calculated by taking all the revenues of the hospital and dividing them by total patient days, was $75.

In 2008, when the author stepped down as the chair of the board of trustees of a similar community hospital, the per diem rate was $3,500 a day. By 2013, there is evidence that this figure may have doubled.

In 2011, total health care expenditures in the United States totaled $2.7 trillion, approximately 20% of the ***Gross Domestic Product****. At currently levels of escalation, the country could eventually consume its entire output healthcare, of course, an impossible situation.*

HOW WILL THE PATIENT PROTECTION AND AFFORDABLE CARE ACT AFFECT HEALTHCARE STAKEHOLDERS?

This section explores the goals of the Patient Protection and Affordable Care Act, its intended consequences, and some possible unintended consequences. It will do so by examining the impact the Patient Protection and Affordable Care Act will have on is stakeholders. A ***stakeholder*** *is an individual who has something to gain or lose by this legislation. For or the purpose of brevity, we classify stakeholders into three categories: (1) those who provide healthcare services, (2) those who receive healthcare services, and (3) those who pay for healthcare services.*

THOSE WHO PROVIDE HEALTHCARE PRODUCTS AND SERVICES

Physicians and Other Healthcare Professionals.

A primary objective of the Patient Protection and Affordable Care Act is to change the way that health services are provided through a variety of actions including the formation of the ***Accountable Care Organization (ACO).*** *An ACO is group of physicians who come together to provide coordinated care.*

The government will pay some ACOs a fee for service. Most organizations, however, will be paid under a prospective reimbursement payment system. This may include a fixed payment per ***clinical episode*** *or a* ***capitation payment****.*

Although some fee-for-service may still exist, a primary emphasis will be given to ***prospective payment*** *designed to influence the doctor to control cost while providing a high level of care. Some doctors will be paid on a defined* ***clinical episode*** *while others may receive* ***capitation payment.***

Patient Centered Outcomes Research Institute. A non-profit federally funded organization charged with monitoring the products and services provided under the Patient Protection and Affordable Care Act, and identifying physicians and hospitals that provide substandard

The objectives of prospective payment will be to: (1) Provide incentives for physicians to use resources most effectively while treating and hopefully curing the patient, (2) Encourage physicians to use those treatments show to be most effective in curing specific disease, and (3) Encourage doctors to provide preventive medicine

The Patient Protection and Affordable Care Act provides for extensive monitoring of physician decisions. Electronic medical records are mandated.

The act creates a nonprofit ***Patient Centered Outcomes Research Institute*** *to examine the effectiveness of procedures, drugs, medical devices, and medical treatments. The act will also seek to identify high-risk providers, those who practices do not meet a high standard of care.*

Physicians identified through medical audit as having substandard care will be educated. Those who still fail to perform will lose their ability to practice medicine.

Possible Unintended Consequences

Opponents of the Patient Protection and Affordable Care Act believe that lower compensation, shrinking independence, greater regulation and increased paperwork will lead to physician shortages. Some physicians have already announced retirement due to the Patient Protection and Affordable Care Act.

Students Entering the Healthcare Field

The legislation will fund scholarships and loan repayment programs students entering the healthcare field. It will seek to increase the workforce by funding expanded community health programs.

Hospitals

One primary objective of the Patient Protection and Affordable Care Act is to reduce costs what some politicians view as hospital inefficiencies. Whether or not the government has demonstrated a talent to reduce inefficiencies in its own hospitals, (Veterans Administration and Military Hospitals) is open to debate. It plans to do this through prospective reimbursement, greater oversight and greater regulation.

Medicare will still reimburse hospitals under the Diagnostic Related Group (DRG) payment and in some cases through Capitation Payment, both of which are discussed in this book.

Hospitals are mandated to install comprehensive computer information systems. Proponents of the Patient Protection and Affordable Care Act believe that he cost of regulation, new information systems, and so on will be made up by a decrease in the uninsured population who in many situations pay only a portion of their hospital bill, or in some cases pay nothing at all.

Even after the full implementation of the Patient Protection and Affordable Care Act, there will still be uninsured segments of the population such as those who will opt for paying a penalty rather than purchasing health insurance and illegal immigrants who are currently excluded from the program, but nevertheless receive healthcare, often through more expensive emergency centers.

The Pharmaceutical and Medical Device Industry

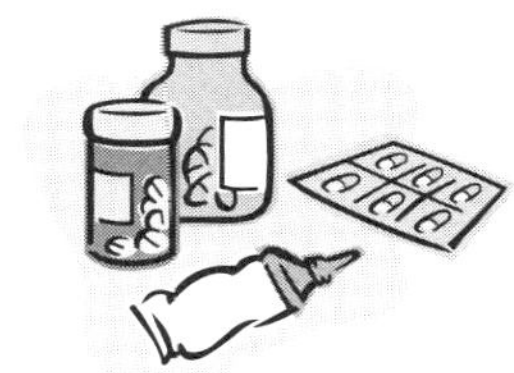

Support for the Patient Protection and Affordable Care Act from the pharmaceutical and medical device industries has been divided. Supporters believe that the legislation will bring to these industries as many as 50 million people who cannot afford pharmaceuticals. Opponents point out that in return for increased volume, the industry has agreed to a $100 billion drug discount upon implementation of the legislation.

THOSE WHO PAY FOR HEALTHCARE SERVICES

The Insurance Industry

For reasons unknown to the author the proponents of the Patient Protection and Affordable Care Act and demonize the insurance industry, portraying them as a major player in the escalation of healthcare costs the country is currently experiencing. The thesis is that the insurance industry refuses to control costs in an effort to increase profits. In reality there is not a lot that insurance companies can do to decrease costs. Most of the cost decisions are made by providers, who as the book reports, may at times have incentives not to act in the best interest of the patients.

The insurance industry is also a low profit industry. Profits over the past decade have averaged 4% as opposed to 20% profit seen by the pharmaceutical industry.

As mentioned above, there are over 50 million people uninsured in 2011. Some of these were uninsured due to an inability to pay premiums. Others have the income that would allow them to purchase insurance policies but elect to use their money's elsewhere.

The Patient Protection and Affordable Care Act would address this problem by mandating insurance for those who can afford premiums by providing government assistance to those who cannot. Insurance companies will no longer be able to establish yearly or lifetime caps on healthcare spending, and will not be able deny patients coverage based on current illness or pre-existing conditions.

Exchanges. Under the Patient Protection and Affordable Care Act these are marketplaces where patients shop for health insurance.

Independent Payment Advisory Board (IPAB). A federally funded program charged with developing programs to reduce healthcare spending.

Medicare. A federally funded program to provide healthcare benefits to those sixty-five years of age and older, and certain under-age-65 disabled individuals.

Medicaid. A government program funded with state and federal funds to provide healthcare to the poor.

Possible Unintended Consequences

Of all the provisions of the Patient Protection and Affordable Care Act, the mandate prohibiting denial of insurance based on illness is the most problematical. For this provision to work well patients as well as sick patients must enroll in insurance plans. Insurance is based on the concept of distributing risk over broad populations.

The Patient Protection and Affordable Care Act mandates a penalty for those who do not purchase health insurance, however the penalty is significantly lower than the premiums that would be paid by individuals.

Beginning in 2014, those without insurance will pay a tax that is the greater of a flat fee, or a percentage of family income. The flat fee will be phased in over several years. In 2014, the penalty will be $95 per adult in an uninsured household, increasing to $325 in 2015, then to $695 in 2016, after which it will increase annually in line with consumer inflation. For employers the fee will be $2,000 per year per employee excluding the first 30 employees.

The concern is that since both the employee and employer penalties are significantly lower than the cost of a health insurance policy, and since pre-existing illnesses cannot be used to deny coverage, that many people will opt to pay the penalty, waiting to enroll in insurance they are hit with a major illness. If this occurs, only the ill will enter the insurance pool, driving the costs higher or bankrupting private insurance companies.

Federal State and Local Governments, Agencies and Programs

Medicare and Medicaid

There are, of course, programs that provided insurance coverage to segments of the population prior to the Patient Protection and Affordable Care Act. These include ***Medicare*** *and* ***Medicaid****.*

Medicaid is a state administered program, subsidized by the federal government that pays for the health costs of the poor. Medicare is a federal program for those 65 years of age and older.

The Patient Protection and Affordable Care Act will "extend benefits" for Medicare patients while cutting funding by approximate $716 billion. The Medicare program will be regulated by an ***Independent Payment Advisory***

Board (IPAB). *The objective of the IPAB will be to recommend programs to reduce Medicare spending "if Congress fails to act." The IPAB is given the ability to make significant changes to Medicare and Medicaid without normal political process.*

Past Projections of the Costs of Federal Healthcare Insurance Programs by the Office of Management and Budget (OMB). The OMB has not had a good record of forecasting federal expenditures for new federal insurance programs. In 1967 it estimated that Medicare would cost approximately $12 billion by 1990. Actual coats were more than $98 billion. Costs currently exceed $500 billion.

Exchanges

The Patient Protection and Affordable Care Act creates ***Exchanges*** *which are "marketplaces" where Americans can compare and purchase insurance plans. By 2014, these will be the only places where individuals who receive federal subsidies for insurance can buy their insurance. Proponents of the legislation fee these exchanges will make it easier for individuals to compare policies and that price competition will drive insurance premiums down.*

Detractors argue the Patient Protection and Affordable Care Act will cost rather than save money, that projected reductions in future federal deficits caused by the implementation of Medicare are flawed, and that increased costs will eventually lead to health care rationing.

Employers

Employers will bear a significant burden under provisions of the Patient Protection and Affordable Care Act. Firms with more than 50 workers will be required to provide coverage for their employees or face a fine of $2,000 for each worker (excluding the first 30 employees). As mentioned above, one concern is that since the fine is significantly less than the cost of insuring an employee that many employers will drop their existing coverage and pay the fine.

Taxpayers

Under the mandates of this legislation, families will receive tax credits for the purchase of health coverage. Families who earn more than $250,000 per year will pay an additional .09% hospital insurance tax on unearned income. There will also be taxes on dividends, annuities, royalties, rents, branded prescriptions, medical devices, insurance companies, and indoor tanning services

Those Who Receive Healthcare Products and Services—The Patients

One of the largest questions concerning the Patient Protection and Affordable Care Act is what will be the impact on patients. The objective of the legislation is to increase coverage by mandating that employees and employers purchase insurance coverage or pay a penalty.

The population of uninsured patients can be divided into two categories: (1) those who are too poor to purchase healthcare insurance, and (2) those who have the money to purchase insurance but would prefer to spend their money elsewhere.

Pay for Performance. A payment system that attempts to improve quality and decrease cost by paying on the basis of patient outcomes.

Treatment Protocols. Recommended or mandated procedures for the treatment of disease.

The poor will receive subsidies based on income to purchase insurance. The more affluent will either purchase insurance or pay the penalty discussed above.

THE ECONOMY

A discussion on the possible impacts on the economy of the United States, detailing both arguments of those who believe Obama care will reduce and those who believe it will increase total healthcare expenditures is beyond the scope of this textbook/novel. It is sufficient to say, however, that in either event the legislation will have a profound impact on the United States economy.

Discussion Four—Pay for Performance

This chapter has discussed several types of incentive payment systems including capitation payment and DRG reimbursement. Another form that has been tried ***is pay for performance,*** *which is being experimented with on a limited basis.*

Like other forms of incentive reimbursement, pay for performance does not pay doctors and hospitals according to the number and types of services provided as, is done under fee-for service. Unlike capitation payment and DRG reimbursement, however, pay for performance pays doctors based on ***clinical outcomes*** *such as "did the patient get better?"*

Pay for performance requires physicians to use specific ***treatment protocols*** *to receive payment. Put another way, it rewards hospitals and doctors for using those diagnostic tests and treatments statistically shown to cure disease. Where medical errors can be shown, or where it can be determined that physicians have used unnecessary treatments, payment is denied.*

Pay for performance has received the endorsement of numerous professional organizations such as the American Academy of Family Physicians. Their support is based on the condition that pay-for-performance will:

- *Involve practicing physicians in the design of the program*
- *Support the physician-patient relationship*

- *Focus on improvement in quality of care*
- *Use only scientifically validated data that been shown to improve healthcare outcomes*
- *Make participation in the program voluntary*

Comorbidity. The existence of two or more unrelated diseases in one person.

As with all proposals that involve public policy, pay for performance has its detractors. Their concerns include:

- *The cost of auditing the treatments provided by physicians and hospitals. Also of concern is the question of who would do the auditing—physicians who might better be employed treating patients, or paraprofessionals armed with checklists second guessing the actions of better trained professionals?*
- *Concern that focusing on a few specific elements in the treatment of disease might lead to the neglect of treatment of other elements such as when there are **comorbidities** (i.e. the patient has more than one illness).*
- *Concern that population groups with limited financial resources to purchase expensive medical treatments might not be accepted by physicians wishing to improve their performance scores.*
- *Concern that mandatory treatment protocols will provide a disincentive for physicians to experiment with new and improved treatments.*
- *And finally, concern that it will be difficult to get everyone to agree on a specific set of treatment guidelines.*

What does the data show? Several studies have been conducted to see if pay-for-performance improves clinical outcomes. These studies have been financed by both public and private organizations. The findings to date are mixed.

Discussion Questions

1. *Before 1984, how did most insurance companies pay hospitals for the services they provided to patients?*
2. *If you were the administrator of a hospital that received full costs plus a profit of 3% for the services your hospital provided, what is one way you*

could raise profits? How strong are the incentives under cost reimbursement for the hospital to be efficient?

3. *Give a one-paragraph history of Blue Cross. Why did Justin Ford Kimball, the founder of Blue Cross, feel hospitals should be paid under a cost reimbursement system?*
4. *Why were most hospitals formed as nonprofit organizations? Did this influence the type of payment received?*
5. *Define cost reimbursement and prospective payment. Are the incentives to control costs the same under each of these systems? Why?*
6. *Before setting up prospective payment, the federal government tried to control the rise in healthcare costs through regulation. They reasoned they could control costs by forcing hospitals to seek approval for all rate increases, similar to the practices used at that time to regulate utilities. Why didn't this work?*
7. *Define the word "system" and give several examples of systems.*
8. *What are the four components of a system?*
9. *Explain what "backwards thinking" is, as it relates to systems.*
10. *The healthcare delivery system is like a mobile. Pressure or movement exerted on one component exerts pressure others. Give an example.*
11. *Briefly review the attempts by governmental agencies to implement a form of universal healthcare.*
12. *What is an Accountable Health Organization (ACO) and what are its objectives?*
13. *Who are the stakeholders in the Patient Protection and Affordable Care Act?*
14. *List the objectives and possible adverse consequences of the Patient Protection and Affordable Care Act.*
15. *How does pay for performance differ from other forms of incentive payment?*

16

Is There a Solution?

HMO. Abbreviation for Health Maintenance Organization.

Over-utilization of healthcare services. Using more healthcare resources than needed to treat the patient.

Charles Stoker stood five-foot-eight and had a salt and pepper Van Dyke beard. His full head of wavy hair, silver with a few black highlights, bestowed a patrician-like appearance. A former hospital administrator, Stoker was hired to organize the hospital's first health maintenance organization, more commonly called an **HMO**. It was Wes Douglas's second day at University Hospital, and he was back to learn more about hospital cost control.

"I've seen three revolutions in the healthcare industry in my lifetime," said Stoker. "The first one occurred in the 1970s when hospitals started grouping together to form hospital chains. It was a difficult time for many hospital administrators who were accustomed to the independence and lack of accountability of the old system." Wes took notes.

"The second revolution," Stoker continued, "took place in the 1980s with the introduction of prospective payment systems. Cost reimbursement placed little risk on healthcare providers and encouraged waste and **over-utilization**. It was difficult for administrators who grew up in a no-risk environment to change the way they did business.

"The third revolution occurred in the 1990s as more providers assumed an insurance role, bypassing insurance companies and contracting directly with employers to provide health services. Some hospital chains even formed their own insurance companies."

Wes shot Stoker a questioning look. "Why would a provider willingly assume the risk of starting an insurance company?"

"Two reasons," Stoker replied. "Market share is the first. Prospective payment limited the growth of hospital revenue. It capped payments and cut length of stay. The only way for hospitals to increase revenue was to capture more patients," he explained.

Capitation payment. A payment system where a hospital or doctor gets a fixed monthly payment to provide medical services to a person covered under a health insurance program. Capitation payment is a form of prospective reimbursement. Prospective reimbursement means that the cost of the medical treatment is negotiated in advance.

Captive health plans. A health plan, often owned by a hospital corporation, that dictates to its enrollees what hospitals and doctors patients must use.

Inpatient. A patient admitted to the hospital for diagnosis or treatment. To be classified as an inpatient, many insurance companies require that a patient stay in the hospital twenty-four hours or more.

Obstetrician. A specialist concerned with the care of women during pregnancy.

"**Captive health plans** allow hospitals to do that by telling employees what doctors they must use to get maximum discounts," Stoker continued, "and by controlling where participating doctors admit their patients."

"And the second?" Wes queried.

"Cost control."

"Are health-maintenance organizations a recent development?" Wes asked.

"Yes and no," Stoker replied. "The first HMO was formed in the 1940s by an industrialist named Henry Kaiser. Kaiser negotiated a contract to build ships for the war effort. To recruit employees without violating wage controls, he offered his employees health benefits. His program used a prospective payment system called capitation payment."

"What's that?" Wes asked.

"A **capitation payment** is a fixed payment a doctor or hospital receives each month to give healthcare to a specific group. The provider receives the same amount per month, whether the patients use the system or not. For example an employer might pay a group of doctors and hospitals who have banned together $250 per employee to take care of all their healthcare needs, **inpatient** and outpatient."

"How does that control costs?" asked Wes.

"It provides an incentive to keep the patient well," Stoker said. "And if the patient becomes ill, it encourages the doctor or hospital to use the most cost-effective treatments to get him or her better. There is still an incentive to get the patient well; the threat of malpractice is an important one. Also, HMO's compete in the marketplace. If employers are unhappy, they can always go elsewhere.

Stoker studied Wes. It was obvious he wasn't following. "Let me give you an example I often share with employers when I'm marketing our plan," Stoker continued. "Role play with me. Assume you are an **obstetrician** at Brannan Community Hospital. Last Friday, one of your patients came in, and you delivered her baby. It's Monday morning, and you're up on the floor doing rounds. As you are writing her discharge orders, she says something like this:

Dr. Douglas, we appreciate the way you run your practice. We have used you to deliver all three of our children. In addition, we have referred several of our neighbors to you.

"You smile appreciatively—it's nice to have satisfied patients—and continue writing the discharge summary. Then she hits you with a request."

Dr. Douglas, I have a problem. As you know, I have two preschoolers at home. For the next few days, it's going to be hard to take care of them and a new baby. My husband works full time.

Indemnity insurance plan. A traditional insurance program design that provides few incentives for cost control. Indemnity policies usually: (1) pay billed charges, (2) allow patients to select their own doctor and hospital, and (3) provide little peer review.

Intermediary. See third-party payer.

Utilization review. An audit or review, sometimes by an insurance company, to find out if specific services are being over-used by doctors or patients.

My mother is flying in from Seattle to help, but she works and can't get off until Wednesday.

How about letting me stay in the hospital until then? My husband works at the steel plant where he's insured by Blue Cross's traditional health insurance indemnity plan—it will pay all the added cost.

Wes wrinkled his brow. "What's a traditional health insurance indemnity plan?" he asked.

"An **indemnity insurance plan** is one that places no limit on hospital length of stay, has no **utilization review**, and pays the hospital under cost reimbursement."

Stoker stroked his beard philosophically. "You're the doctor, Wes. If you say no to her request, what do you have to lose?"

"Her goodwill," Wes replied. "She might change doctors. Worse still, she might bad-mouth me to her neighbors or friends, which would cause me to lose more patients."

Stoker nodded in agreement, "That's right," he said. "What if you say yes, what do you have to lose?"

"Not much, I'm not paying the bill."

"Okay," Stoker replied. "What about the other stakeholders in your decision. Let's start with the hospital. Remember, this is a traditional insurance program—hospitals are still under cost reimbursement."

"Well—the hospital administrator will probably be happy," Wes said. "A longer length of stay will raise costs which will raise revenues and profits."

"That's right," said Stoker, his eyes flashing with approval. "How about the insurance company?"

"I'm not sure . . ." said Wes.

"In the 1970s, they didn't care," said Stoker. "Most health insurers felt their role was that of **intermediary**, or bill payer. Insurance companies simply passed the added cost to the employer in the form of raised premiums. Rarely did they question what types of services were provided or how much they cost."

"What about the employer?" asked Wes. "He certainly wouldn't be happy about the doctor's decision to leave a patient in the hospital two days longer than necessary. Eventually that would lead to higher premiums"

"That's true," said Stoker, "but he was so far removed from the decision, he had little to say in the matter."

"Cost reimbursement didn't do much to control costs," Wes observed.

"That's what I'm saying," said Stoker. "Now let's talk about economic incentives under a capitation payment system. Let's assume now that you're a doctor who has been hired by an organization that receives a capitation payment." Stoker paused as he formulated his thoughts.

Enrollee. A person covered by a health benefit plan.

Expense. A cost recorded on the income statement.

"I'm the medical director again, it's your first day on the job, and I call you into the office and say something like this:

> *Dr. Douglas, welcome aboard! Your references are excellent and we're happy you accepted our job offer. I think you'll find this a good place to work.*
>
> *Before you begin seeing patients, however, there are a few things you should know. You are not paid fee-for-service, as other doctors, you get a salary plus a bonus. Your bonus is paid in December, and may run anywhere from zero to two-hundred percent of your salary, depending on how much money our HMO has left at the end of the year from the premiums we collect from employers.*
>
> *We receive $250 a month for every **enrollee** in our HMO. For this $250, we provide all the health services the patient requires, including office visits, laboratory and x-ray tests, prescriptions, physical therapy, and hospitalization. If the patient uses no services during the month, we get $250 from his or her employer. If the patient uses $100,000 of healthcare services, we still get $250.*
>
> *Bonuses come from the premium pool left after **expenses** are paid. Our doctors get 80% of these profits; the remainder is kept by the HMO to buy equipment, provide working capital, and so on.*

Stoker continued. "Now let's go back to that maternity patient. This time let's assume she's insured by our HMO." Stoker smiled menacingly. "Now, tell me how you'd react."

Wes's eyes narrowed. "I'd be reluctant to grant her request," he said. "If not medically needed, I'd want her out of the hospital."

"Why?"

"Two added days of hospitalization would cut year-end profits."

"What else would it cut?" Stoker asked.

"My year-end bonus."

"That's right! What about the hospital administrator—how would he or she feel about the decision to leave the patient in the hospital longer than medically needed?"

"If the hospital's being paid under capitation payment, there is no incentive to raise patient days—to the contrary, there's an incentive to get the patient out. More days mean more costs, which results in less profit."

"Why?"

"Because the hospital gets the same payment, whether the patient stays two days or twenty."

"And the insurance company?" Stoker asked.

Wes shrugged. "You tell me."

"As health costs have risen, employers have become more price conscious. Insurance companies quote rates once a year. If their rates are higher than competition, they lose business. Today insurance companies are aggressive in overseeing hospital costs."

"Okay," Wes said. "Then the insurance company wouldn't be happy with an extended stay either."

"What about the employer?" Stoker asked.

"He would be happy. For the first time there would be an incentive for the healthcare provider to make cost-effective decisions."

"True."

Wes shot Stoker a skeptical look. "Sounds good in theory—but are HMOs more cost-effective than traditional insurance programs?"

"There's evidence they are," said Stoker. "One of the main components of healthcare cost is hospitalization. Local studies show participants in indemnity plans produce 300 to 400 patient days a year per 1,000 enrollees. HMOs produce 220. Some companies estimate they've cut employee healthcare cost by as much as 25% since enrolling in an HMO."

"If HMOs work so well, why didn't they take off back in the 1940s when Henry Kaiser invented the model? Before 1985, I'd never heard of an HMO," Wes added.

"For many years, medical associations were effective in shutting them down," said Stoker. "When I was a healthcare administration student in Seattle, there was a doctor in the inner city who started charging his patients on a capitation basis. The Washington Medical Association tried to get him thrown in jail for violating state insurance laws—laws they helped draft; laws designed to keep HMOs out of the state.

"One of the most aggressive medical associations in the country was the Oregon Medical Association," Stoker continued. "It persuaded the legislature to pass a law stating HMOs could keep none of their profits while having to absorb all of their losses. It was a law designed to force HMOs into bankruptcy—which it did.

"In other parts of the country, medical associations prohibited doctors who worked for HMOs from joining state medical associations. These same organizations then changed hospital bylaws to forbid doctors who were not members of local medical associations from joining hospital medical staffs. It worked great. HMO doctors couldn't admit patients to hospitals. They were effectively stopped from practicing medicine."

"What changed?" Wes asked. "They obviously practice in hospitals today."

Diagnosis related group. A disease grouping developed by the administrators of Medicare for payment to hospitals.

DRG reimbursement. See diagnosis related group reimbursement in glossary.

"In the early 1980s, the federal government passed legislation overriding the anti-HMO laws state legislatures passed through the years. The impact was astounding. Hundreds of HMOs were formed throughout the country."

"Are HMOs the wave of the future?" Wes asked.

"For a while we thought they were. Patients don't like the controls HMOS place on their selection of doctors, however, and medical associations and the news media have created the impression HMOs give substandard care. Many cost control features of HMOs are being overridden by legislatures. For better or worse, enrollment in HMOs is on the decline."

"Does anyone else use prospective payment?" Wes asked.

"Medicare has developed a system called **DRG reimbursement**. It has been copied by some Medicaid and Blue Cross groups."

"What's a DRG?" Wes asked.

"It stands for **diagnosis related group**."

"A mouthful," said Wes.

"Sure is," replied Stoker. "DRG payment is a form of prospective payment. Under capitation payment, the hospital receives a fixed payment for every enrollee every month, regardless of the services given. Under DRG reimbursement, it receives a fixed payment per *diagnosis related group*."

"So what's a *diagnosis related group?"* Wes asked.

"It's a disease classification. When a patient is discharged from Brannan Community Hospital, he or she is assigned a DRG, which is determined by the doctor's discharge diagnosis.

"In 1984," Stoker continued, "Medicare classified all diseases into 380 or so *diagnosis related groups.* The classification was done according to anatomical system, and the cost needed to cure the illness. In theory, all diseases in DRG 200, for example, cost about the same to treat.

"In explaining their new system to hospital administrators, Medicare administrators said something like this:

> *In the old days, we paid you under cost reimbursement. Whatever you spent in treating the patient, we reimbursed. Now we are going to pay you under a fixed price system. Every DRG has a fixed price. For example, every time you admit a patient with a DRG of 386, we will pay you $3,850. We will pay you that amount whether you keep the patient in the hospital three days, or thirty. We will pay you $3,850 whether you feed him steak or bread and water; whether you give him anesthetic or hit him with a rubber hammer. We expect you to get our patients well, but we don't care how much you spend—you'll only receive $3,850 in reimbursement.*

Average length of stay. The average number of days spent by a patient in a specific hospital. It is calculated by dividing total patient days by the number of admissions.

Stoker gave Wes a quizzical look. "What do you think that did to hospital length of stay?" he asked.

"It probably reduced it."

"It did," replied Stoker. "Before introducing DRG reimbursement, the national **average length of stay** was about thirteen days. In one year it dropped to seven. In Utah, it dropped from seven days to about three and one-half. We have a younger population and had fewer unnecessary hospital beds."

"Thirty percent of the admissions at Brannan Community Hospital are Medicare patients," Wes said. "With that restriction on revenue, how does a hospital survive under DRG reimbursement?"

"By controlling costs," Stoker replied.

"What keeps the hospital from providing less care than needed to get the patient well?" Wes asked.

"I'm not sure I have an answer to that," Stoker replied. "The threat of a malpractice suit plays a role. In addition, if discharged patients are readmitted within a short period, the hospital receives no reimbursement for the second admission. There's an incentive to do it right the first time."

"It sounds like it's a new era for hospital management," Wes said. "I feel sorry for those who can't adapt."

"So do I," said Stoker. "Shortly after managed care was introduced, 30% of the hospital administrators in the country lost their jobs. Many couldn't adjust."

"Let's see if I understand," Wes said in summary. "Under cost reimbursement, hospitals made money by admitting many patients, and giving them many services."

"True," Stoker replied.

"Under DRG reimbursement, they earn money by admitting patients, but giving them fewer services."

"That's right."

"But under capitation payment, they earn money by not admitting the patient at all."

"You've got it. Capitation payment provides a strong incentive to keep the patient well, or to get him well as soon as possible, once admitted."

Stoker continued. "Hap Castleton and his medical staff were still operating on cost reimbursement assumptions, and it almost killed the hospital. If Brannan Community Hospital is to survive, it will have to change the way it does business. Your task will be to pull it off, without getting canned."

Driving back to his apartment that evening, Wes reflected on what he learned about healthcare costs, and the steps being taken by government and industry to stem the tide of inflation. His conversation with Stoker on

Obstetrics. A medical specialty concerned with the care of women during pregnancy.

prospective payment systems clarified the issues discussed in his first meeting with the board.

Hap and his administrative team had not anticipated the dramatic way prospective payment would influence the operation of their hospital. Wes now understood why doctors like Dr. Flagg felt threatened by the changes taking place in the healthcare industry. Under cost reimbursement, doctors who admitted many patients, kept them in the hospital for long periods of time, and used high quantities of ancillary services, were heroes to the hospital administrator.

With the adoption of prospective payment, however, high cost doctors became the villains. Retraining doctors in the new model would be difficult.

In many ways, the economics of incentive payment made sense to Wes. Still, there was an issue that bothered him—quality. *"Under capitation payment, what's to prevent doctors from providing too little care or too few services?"* Dr. Flagg had told him of instances where **obstetric** patients were being discharged on the same day as delivery. He was uncomfortable with that practice, and so was Wes.

There were other quality issues that bothered Flagg as well. He was concerned that prospective payment had caused hospitals to cut staffing to the point that patient safety was jeopardized. With the pressure the board was putting on Wes to meet budget, he understood how this could happen.

Maybe Flagg's behavior is understandable. He was raised in an era that rewarded independent thought and action. That wasn't all bad. HMOs with their pre-certification, utilization review panels, and salaried doctors have changed the equation.

Wes heard rumors of hospital systems that were bullying doctors into selling their practices. "*Sell your practice and join us as an employee or we'll build a clinic across the street and put you out of business*," they reportedly told doctors. In the old days, private-practice doctors were the hospital's valued customers. In a staff-model HMO environment, they became *the competition*.

Wes shook his head as he thought about the conflicting forces he would have to contend with as the new administrator of Brannan Community Hospital—doctors who wanted more equipment, a board that wanted lower costs, and patients who expected the hospital to save them *"at any cost,"* but not bill them. It was easier being a CPA.

Discussion One—Have We Got What We Asked For?

When the author received his master's degree in healthcare administration in 1971, hospitals were being criticized by business, unions, consumers, and the government for not being more businesslike. An article in Fortune Magazine called the healthcare industry an industry of pushcart vendors in an age of supermarkets. Many felt if administrators ran hospitals like for-profit businesses, healthcare costs would decrease.

Hospitals responded to this public pressure by setting-up new information systems, merging into corporate hospital chains, and discontinuing services that were not cost-effective. Insurance companies designed incentive payment systems to encourage providers to be more cost conscious when treating patients. The industry moved from a charitable model, where hospitals cooperated, to a competitive model.

Having received the response they wanted, businesses, unions, consumers, and the government reacted with horror. "They are running hospitals like businesses!" they screamed. Before we return to the previous model, it is good to understand the inefficiencies that drove the initial change.

Discussion Two—Listening Skills for the Healthcare Professional

Listening may seem like an inborn ability, but active listening requires practice and skill. Have you ever had a conversation with someone who is distracted? Being a good listener is an important part of successful communication.

Characteristics of good listeners include:

- *An interest in the subject*
- *The ability to focus*
- *A desire to know, versus a desire to be known*
- *The ability to set aside prejudice*
- *The ability to read body language*
- *Patience—a willingness to give the speaker time*
- *A willingness to put oneself into another's situation*

If you want to raise your listening skills, you should:

- *Talk less, listen more. Pay attention to what the speaker is saying, instead of thinking about what you are going to say next.*
- *Give feedback—paraphrase or restate what the other person is saying. Offer a tentative interpretation.*
- *Reflect on what is being said.*
- *Ask questions—probe.*

Discussion Questions

1. *Charles Stoker has seen three healthcare revolutions in his lifetime. List these, and tell what impact each had on the delivery of healthcare in the United States.*
2. *What factors have encouraged some hospitals to develop their own insurance-based managed care programs?*
3. *If the first health maintenance organization was formed in the 1940s by Henry Kaiser, why did it take so long for HMOs to develop in other parts of the country?*
4. *Why might a fee-for-service doctor have more incentive to provide unnecessary services than a doctor paid under capitation payment?*
5. *From an incentive payment standpoint, why might there be a greater incentive for a doctor to provide preventive health care in a health maintenance organization than in a fee-for-service private practice?*
6. *Most Blue Cross organizations were established by hospital administrators to assure hospital bills would be paid. Before the 1970s, the Board of Trustees of most Blue Cross plans was mainly composed of hospital administrators. How might this arrangement have discouraged programs like Blue Cross from challenging hospital costs?*
7. *What incentives are there for a health maintenance organization doctor to provide adequate healthcare services? What is to keep the doctor from withholding needed treatment?*
8. *What impact did the introduction of DRG reimbursement have on the average length of hospital stay nationally? Explain why DRG reimbursement provides an incentive to get the patient out of the hospital as quickly as possible.*
9. *Under a DRG reimbursement system, the hospital must admit a patient to receive payment. The incentive is to get the patient out of the hospital as quickly as possible. What is the incentive with regard to hospitalization under a capitation payment system?*
10. *As a hospital administrator paid under a cost reimbursement system, how happy would you be with a doctor who used a greater than average number*

of hospital resources in treating his or her patients (i.e. more lab tests, longer hospital length of stays, and so on). Assume your hospital was suddenly put under DRG reimbursement. How happy would you now be with the same doctor?

11. *What is the downside to providing incentives for healthcare workers to cut healthcare costs? Is it possible to control costs, while still providing a high quality of healthcare?*

12. *One of the healthcare revolutions Stoker mentioned was the consolidation of independent hospitals into large corporate-style hospital chains. What do you think might be the advantages and disadvantages of this consolidation?*

17

The Robbery

Health Occupation Student Association (HOSA). An organization for high school and college students interested in the healthcare field. HOSA provides information and activities designed to help students decide on a proper healthcare career.

"Whoever broke in must have known what they were after," said Sergeant Peter James O'Malley, rubbing the scruff of his morning beard with the back of his hand. O'Malley hadn't shaved yet—the call from hospital security came as he was getting into the shower.

O'Malley was an old-time cop—one who made an effort to know everyone on his beat. Park City was a safer and friendlier place because of Sergeant Peter O'Malley. With his red curly hair and large beer belly, he looked like a character from a Norman Rockwell painting.

O'Malley's eyes, a curious shade of green, swept the room for more clues. "Whatever they wanted, it wasn't money," he said. "The cash drawer's intact—the safe wasn't even touched." He shook his head as he studied an old desk in the corner next to a large window. "What they wanted was here," he said with a generous sweep of his arm.

Moving to the desk, he removed a small magnifying glass from his shirt pocket and examined the broken lock on the file drawer. The surface had been dusted for fingerprints—none were found. Finished, he tucked the magnifier back into his pocket. "Prints were wiped clean," he sniffed. "Who does the desk belong to?"

Kayla Elmore, a student volunteer with the ***Health Occupation Student Association (HOSA),*** stepped forward. "It's Del Cluff's desk," she said, her eyes wide with wonder. This was the most exciting thing that had happened since Emil Flagg forgot to set the parking brake in his 1989 pickup truck, and it careened through the hospital lobby.

"Did it have any valuables in it?" O'Malley asked.

"I doubt it," she said softly, "Cluff didn't have any valuables." Several employees laughed. Mr. Cluff came to work looking like a Bavarian peasant—the ill-fitting suits covering his lumpy body were "Goodwill Industry specials." He lived in a rented room two blocks from Main Street and drove a battered Volkswagen bus.

Incident report. A document used to report an incident that harmed or had the potential to harm a patient, employee, or visitor. Incident reports include medication errors, falls, patient refusal of treatment, safety violations and patient complaints. Incident reports are an important part of a risk management program, a program designed to cut the risk of injury to those entering the hospital (patients, visitors, doctors, employees and so on).

Kayla's smoky blue eyes sobered as she studied the battered desk. "It hasn't been opened since the accident," she continued looking up at O'Malley. "Mr. Cluff's still in a coma at the University Hospital—he has the only key."

O'Malley looked at the desk. It certainly was open *now.* Someone had used a crowbar to pry the lock off the file drawer. The contents were scattered on the gray linoleum floor. O'Malley was silent as he completed an **incident report** attached to his clipboard.

"With no suspects, and no idea of what—if anything—was taken, there's not much more I can do," he said. He signed the report with a flourish and handed it to Emma Chandler, the acting controller. "Initial here and I'll file a report with the department."

Emma signed the form and handed it back to O'Malley. She examined the desk once more, shot a glance at Wes Douglas, who had come for his 9:00 a.m. appointment, and shrugged.

"This is the first time you've had a burglary—and to think all they got were some old files," O'Malley said. His stern expression relaxed into a smile. "At least they didn't get the payroll—that's all this new Douglas fellow would have needed." There was a ripple of laughter. By now, the entire community was aware of the administrator's precarious situation.

Satisfied the investigation was over; Emma Chandler retrieved an armful of folders from the floor and dumped them on Del Cluff's desk. Others followed suit. While the employees straightened the room, Emma grabbed Wes by the arm and led him into the hall. Wes and Emma had been scheduled to review the hospital's financial reports. "If you still want to meet," she said, "we can use the conference room."

"Got a better idea," said Wes. "I need your signature on a note at the bank. Let's take care of that. While we're out, you can show me the property Wycoff wants the lien on. Any other agenda items can be covered as we drive."

The paperwork took less than five minutes to finish. The bank president was so happy to have Wycoff assume financial responsibility for the hospital's two million dollar line of credit; he almost offered Wes free checking on his personal account. Instead, he gave him a plastic ballpoint pen with the bank's name and a picture of him on the side.

Five minutes later, Wes's Taurus was turning north on the old highway leaving Park City. "What happened to Selman?" Wes asked as they merged with traffic.

"He got caught in the middle," Emma replied. "Hap didn't like him because he was too conservative with the hospital's finances. Edward Wycoff didn't trust him because he wasn't conservative enough. The issue came to a head during negotiations for the new hospital.

Bottom-line. Synonym for profit (found on the bottom-line of the income statement).

Fully-insured. In a fully-insured health insurance program, the insurance company assumes full risk for the difference between the health premiums paid by the employer and the actual cost paid to doctors and hospitals.

Mutual insurance company. An insurance company owned by its enrollees.

Self-insured health insurance plan. An insurance plan where the employer pays the insurance company for the actual costs of employee care. Compare with fully-insured plan.

"Hap realized the competition would eventually capture his market if he didn't replace his outdated hospital. He was too ambitious, however. He wanted to build too many beds—to grow the business too fast. Wycoff recognized prospective payment would limit the hospital's ability to pay for a large new building. He was unwilling to approve the blueprints without a clear understanding of how the debt would be repaid. Either view, taken to an extreme, could have spelled disaster. Selman tried to play the middle ground and alienated both sides."

"Old Chinese saying—*Man who walks in middle of road gets hit by cars going both ways,*" Wes said.

Emma smiled and nodded. "Good observation. Hap didn't value Selman's judgment. Hap was an optimist and didn't like what his controller was telling him. Nevertheless, Selman remained loyal to Hap, even when it hurt his relationship with Wycoff."

"Why?" Wes asked.

"Three years ago, Selman's wife was diagnosed with cancer. Selman was so upset he didn't pay attention to business. It was the end of the fiscal year, and the hospital was changing how it paid for the employee health insurance plan, converting from a **fully-insured** to a **self-insured plan**. Over ten years it amassed $600,000 of savings, held in a special fund by the company."

"Since it was a **mutual insurance company**, the hospital was technically entitled to 80% of the fund. In the new contract, the insurance company cancelled the hospital's right to the money. Selman signed without noticing the clause. It cost the hospital almost $500,000."

Wes whistled. "Painful mistake."

Emma nodded. "Wycoff found out about it and went through the ceiling. He stormed to the board and demanded Selman be fired. Hap, aware of Selman's personal turmoil, stepped in and took blame for the mistake.

"Hap was more popular with the board back then," Emma continued. "Wycoff didn't have the political power to oust him. Roger Selman kept his job—Roger Selman never forgot the favor."

Wes's eyes darkened. "That explains why Wycoff moved so quickly in firing Selman after Hap died," he said. "He was settling an old score."

Emma gave Wes a side look. "You're probably right. You have to understand Wycoff did many right things, though often for the wrong reasons. He was brilliant, but ruthless—people didn't mean anything to him."

"Hap, on the other hand, did many things that didn't seem sensible from a business standpoint. However, there was never a doubt about his loyalty to the patients, or his employees. He was stubborn, sometimes even prideful—but he cared about people, and the employees loved him for it. Even in a managed care environment, he believed hospitals should act like charitable institutions."

A shadow of irritation crossed Wes's face. "When the public started demanding a **bottom-line** approach to hospital management," he said, "the industry lost some of the characteristics that made it special."

Emma sighed. "It's a different game today. In the old days, the goal was to heal the patient, regardless of cost or the patient's ability to pay. Hospitals were often inefficient and sometimes outright wasteful, but they cooperated with one another in achieving their goals. Today, the goal for many administrators is to cut costs and save money, even when doctors, employees, and patients are treated less than honorably."

"Let's hope they reach a balance between efficiency and empathy," Wes said.

"Some are there already. For others, it will take longer."

Less than a mile north of Highway 40, Emma motioned for her boss to stop his car. Wes pulled off the road. About 600 yards up a hill, a chain-link fence enclosed the abandoned site. The construction equipment was gone. All that remained were the footings, a pile of bricks, and two stacks of rebar.

"That's all there is?" Wes asked in surprise.

Emma nodded. They left the car, climbing the hill in long lumbering steps.

"Our property runs from the fence to the top of the hill," Emma reported, pointing east. "One hundred acres in all, bought in 1993. There were to be three construction phases. Phase 1 was the doctors' office building; phase two the outpatient building, phase 3 patient rooms and support departments.

"The building project was to be financed by bonds guaranteed by Park City State Bank. Back then, the bank was owned by the Brannan family. The Mike and Sara Brannan Foundation pledged an additional one million dollars."

"Neat package, too bad it didn't work," Wes said.

"When the Brannan empire unraveled, so did the new hospital," Emma replied.

Wes was impressed. The property was easily accessible from the freeway and already had power and water. "How much of the land was needed for the hospital?" he asked.

"The three phases would have occupied 35 acres," Emma responded. "The rest was for future development. Rumor has it a group from Chicago would like to buy the property for a hotel complex. If we sold it, we could get triple what we paid for it. A better alternative, however, would be to build a new hospital."

A black Lincoln Continental crested the hill and stopped. Two men exited. One of them pointed to a barbed wire fence that bordered the property on the north. "Looks like Wycoff's car," Emma said.

Wes opened his car door and retrieved a set of binoculars from under the seat. "It is," he said. "Who's with him?"

Wes passed the glasses to Emma. Emma was silent as she adjusted the focus. "Tony Devecchi," she said. "Wycoff brought him to Kiwanis last week. He's a retired businessman from Arizona. Owns a chain of nursing homes. He's been kicking around town for a couple of weeks. Probably looking for a place to retire."

Philanthropy. To increase human wellbeing, often through charitable donations.

"What's he doing with Wycoff?" Wes asked.

"Want to ask him?"

Wes considered the question. "No, it's time to get back to the hospital. If he's got money, Wycoff's probably hitting him up for a contribution."

Wes was quiet on the drive back to the hospital. The discussion about Edward Wycoff and his relationship with Roger Selman reminded him of the power struggle within the board. Wes was aware of the conflict when he accepted the job. Then he believed the issues were black and white. Now he was starting to see shades of gray.

Although Hap Castleton was gone, Wycoff, Brannan, and the medical staff were still at war. At first, Wes thought the battle was over efficiency—the good guys were for lower cost and higher quality care; the bad guys were for inefficiency and the status quo. Wes now saw the stakes involved more than money and power. Issues of quality, compassion, and even integrity had muddied the waters. The more he learned, the more difficult it was to identify exclusively with either side.

Wycoff understood finance, but was insensible that healthcare was about people. Hap was well intentioned, but his hostility to accountants and efficiency experts hampered his ability to control costs.

What value is high-quality care if no one can afford it? Wes didn't blame Hap for not cutting costs in areas that would reduce accessibility or quality. He did blame him, however, for refusing to adopt efficiencies that could have avoided the crisis Brannan Community Hospital faced.

Wes frowned. *Then there's Wycoff—what's he up to? Is he trying to help a hospital nurtured for a generation by the* ***philanthropy*** *of the Brannan family, or does he have other motives?* Wes believed the former, but the skepticism from the medical staff made him wonder.

When Wes returned to the hospital that afternoon, there was a note on his desk that Kayla Elmore, the HOSA volunteer assigned to the business office, wanted to see him. He called and asked that she come down.

Kayla smiled satisfaction as she entered his office. "I think I know what the robber took," she said handing him a folder. "This was on the floor along with all the other things from Cluff's desk. It's empty now; it wasn't when Cluff had me type the label."

Internal audit. An audit conducted by hospital personnel (as opposed to an external audit conducted by outside auditors—often certified public accountants).

Wes took the folder, the label read: ***Internal Audit****—Pharmacy.*

"Did you read what was inside?"

"Nope, just typed the label. When I saw it on the floor, empty and all, I thought it might be important."

"Might be," Wes affirmed.

Discussion Questions

1. *In her conversation with Wes Douglas, Emma Chandler, Acting Controller, had this to say:*

   > *"It's a different game today. In the old days, the purpose was to heal the patient, regardless of the cost or the patient's ability to pay. Hospitals were often inefficient and sometimes outright wasteful, but they cooperated with each other in achieving their goals. Today the goal for many administrators is to cut costs and save money, even when doctors, employees, and patients are treated less than honorably."*

   Assuming her observations are correct: (1) what contributed to this change in attitude, and (2) do you think it is possible for the healthcare industry to find a middle ground?

2. *As he becomes more familiar with the issues facing Brannan Community Hospital, Wes Douglas is less inclined to view many issues in black-and-white terms. Castleton, Wycoff, Brannan, and the medical staff are at war. One group wants cost control and efficiency, the other wants quality and compassion. What viewpoint do you agree with, or like Wes Douglas, do you find some merit in each argument? Explain your position.*

3. *Refer to question 2 above. How might each viewpoint, taken to an extreme, violate ethical standards?*

18

The Hospital Bazaar

Pink shop. A gift shop operated by hospital volunteers (in some hospitals called 'pink ladies'). Profits from sales in the pink shop are given to the hospital for nursing scholarships or to buy medical equipment.

It was 10:00 a.m. Saturday. *Time for a break*, Wes thought as he stretched the knots out of his back. Inhaling deeply, he pushed the chair away from his desk, piled high with reports. Crossing his office, he locked the doors. He was exiting to the lobby when he heard a familiar voice. Turning, he saw Amy Castleton.

"A little higher, Niels, and to the right," she said, motioning with both hands. Three feet above on a metal ladder, 61-year-old Niels Svendsen, senior custodian, obediently rehung a poster on the freshly painted wall.

Wrinkling her brow, she studied the new location and then smiled with satisfaction. "That'll do it!" She said brightly.

"Finally," Niels gasped good-naturedly. Removing a roll of tape from his worn coveralls, he attached the poster securely. It advertised the auxiliary bazaar to be held early that afternoon in Canyon Park.

Petite and flower-like, Amy wore a pink cotton volunteer's uniform that defined the narrowness of her waist. As Niels teased her, she laughed, tossing her head to the side so her thick, auburn hair bounced on her shoulders. Turning to take another poster down the hall, she ran headlong into Wes. "Excuse me!" she gasped. "Didn't know you were there."

She stepped back embarrassed; he struggled not to blush. It was not every day a beautiful young woman ran into his arms. Tongue-tied, he pointed at the poster. "Must be the hospital bazaar today?" He was immediately embarrassed by the stupidity of his statement. *Of course, the hospital bazaar is today,* he thought, *it's been advertised for the past two weeks, and I'm the one who approved the newspaper ads!*

Her brown eyes danced with laughter at his awkwardness. "It starts at noon." Cocking her head to the right she sized the new administrator up. "If your executive responsibilities aren't too pressing," she teased, "the hired hands could use a little help."

Wes smiled. "I've been reading old board meeting minutes," he said. "Guess I could pull myself away. What do you want me to do?"

One hand on her cheek, she wrinkled her brow as though trying to solve a puzzle. "There's two dozen cakes in the **Pink Shop** with no one to load them. And in the employee parking lot there's a hospital van with nothing in it." A

Autoanalyzer. A laboratory instrument that performs many laboratory tests on the same specimen sample.

mischievous light sparkled in her eyes. "Think you could figure something out?"

"Manual labor?" Wes said in mock protest. "Not in my job description!"

"It's probably more productive than anything else you've done today," she replied with an impish smile.

He didn't mind the mirth, even if the humor was at his expense. "Sounds like you've been visiting with the board about my performance," he said.

She took a breath to speak, but he interrupted by holding his hands up. "Don't comment," he said. "Just show me the way." She pointed at the Pink Shop, and then at the exit. Wes complied.

"Niels," she said turning to the custodian. "We have two more posters to hang downstairs."

"Yeah. Ve better get to it," Niels said looking at his watch. Niels and Amy Castleton took the stairs to the basement.

As he drove the hospital van to the park, Wes admired the incandescence of the hillsides surrounding Park City. Almost overnight, the crisp Fall air had painted the electric green of the aspen trees shades of cinnabar, crimson, and gold.

Amy and Niels followed in the hospital pick-up. When they arrived, she gave orders, and Wes obeyed. He hauled cakes, refilled soft drinks, and emptied garbage cans. The affection of the employees for Amy was obvious. Most had known her since she was a young girl. To Amy, the employees were extended family, and she returned the affection with warmth and attention that charmed young and old alike.

The annual picnic was well publicized by the local newspaper and radio. In addition to employees and medical staff, over 600 people from the community turned out for the gala fund-raising event. There were pony rides for children and art displays for adults. Park City's country singers, the Benton Family, provided the entertainment. The bake sale raised enough money for a newborn ICU ventilator, and the five-dollar sack lunches raised enough money to pay off the **Autoanalyzer** in the lab.

For most, however, the highlight of the day was the *Dunk the Boss* event. The Pink Ladies brought a contraption that looked like it had been rented from the dungeon of a medieval castle. It had a gallows-like platform with a chair that dropped into a tub of ice water when a baseball hit the target. Employees were charged a buck a throw—members of the medical staff, three. Wes was the first to be offered the seat of honor, and everyone cheered when Dr. Flagg hit the target, and Wes dropped into the frigid water.

Someone was thoughtful enough to bring dry clothes—a cotton uniform from the laundry. It was four sizes too big, so Amy fashioned a belt from a rope. Wes looked ridiculous, but was happy with the response he received from the employees. Wes was still breaking down the barriers created when Wycoff fired Selman.

By late afternoon, the crowd had left and Amy was directing the cleanup. As the last car pulled out of the park, Wes loaded the sound equipment into the van. Sven had driven the hospital truck back to maintenance, so Amy climbed into the front seat, holding the only cake not sold.

Wes climbed in next to her, and turned the key. Silence—

He frowned. Once again, he tried. The engine didn't budge. Wes just sat there, his eyes wide with disbelief.

When he didn't move, Amy spoke. "Aren't you going to check under the hood?" she asked curiously.

"Wouldn't do any good—I don't know a carburetor from a crankshaft."

Amy studied the expression on his face, and then smiled with amusement. "I take it you're not one of those macho mechanics?"

"Hardly," he sighed. He blinked, and then focused his gaze on the empty parking lot. "Where are all the people?" he asked. "Doesn't anybody but the hospital use the park?"

"It's kinda remote," she replied. "Besides, in the evening it gets cold. We're at 7,000 feet you know."

Wes nodded dubiously.

"There's a phone at Country Corner," Amy volunteered. "It's about four miles down the canyon. It'll give you a chance to walk off dessert," she said, patting him on the tummy. She smiled, "I'll walk with you!" she said brightly.

Wes tried the engine one more time, nothing happened. Turning to Amy, he studied the cake she was holding—chocolate with green icing. Sliced bananas on the top spelled *"Buy Me!"* The heat had turned them a repulsive brown. "What are we going to do with that?" he asked glumly.

Amy examined the gastronomic monstrosity with mock seriousness. "Do you think there's a reason it didn't sell?"

Wes nodded. "I suggest we donate it to the dumpster," he replied.

Once they were on the road and had established a consistent pace, Wes started the conversation. Someone told him Amy had interrupted college to return for her father's funeral."

"So what's next?" he asked. "School? Work?"

"Mom still needs support; I'll stick around for a year."

"After that?"

"Probably return to the university."

"What do you want to be when you grow up?" He asked.

She gave him a sidewise glance and smiled. "English teacher. I'm majoring in comparative literature." The soft canyon breeze stroked her auburn hair. Now she turned and studied him carefully, her eyes dancing with curiosity.

"And you, Mr. Douglas? What do you want to be *when you grow up?*"

"Alive," he said.

"Things at the hospital can't be that bad," she sparred.

His face twisted into a contemplative frown. "My job lasts only until they find a permanent administrator. If my credibility is still intact, I'll probably return to my accounting practice. If I botch the job, then I'm not sure what I'll do, maybe pull up stakes, and return to Maine. There's a downside to the visibility this job has in the community."

"Is Maine your home?"

Wes nodded.

"Why did you leave?" she asked.

"Worked for a regional firm in Portland. Hated my supervisor, got tired of the city."

"That's all?" she asked.

There was another reason, and she sensed it.

"I lost a loved one," he said, "—automobile accident. Thought a change would help."

"Sweetheart?" she asked.

"We were engaged to be married," he said quietly.

"I'm sorry," she said. "How long were you engaged?"

"Three years."

"A long time."

"Too long," he said. "I was waiting until we were financially secure." He gazed at the mountains, silent and deep in thought. She didn't interrupt, and they walked.

"There's no such thing," he said presently.

"No such thing as what?"

"Security. You can plan your life to the smallest detail, but something always throws a wrench in the works."

She listened.

"When I was younger I believed there was some grand plan," he continued.

"Not now?" she asked.

His voice faded off. "It's just a game of dice . . ."

"You sound like my mother," Amy said.

"Not doing well?" he asked.

"Pretty shattered. Her faith is tottering."

"And you?" Wes stopped walking and they stood face-to-face. Her face softened as her eyes reflected a gentle optimism.

"I think there's a plan," she said. "It isn't ours," she continued, "and sometimes it's hard to see, but it's there. The key, I think, is patience." She continued walking and he followed.

"Do you like the hospital?" she asked, changing the subject.

Aspirate. To inhale fluid into the lungs.

Internal rate of return (IRR). A financial calculation of the profitability of an investment in plant or equipment. IRR is calculated by dividing the increased profit from purchasing a piece of capital equipment by the average investment in that equipment over a period of time such as a year.

Return on investment (ROI). A measure used to determine the financial attractiveness of an investment opportunity. It is calculated by dividing annual income from the investment by the amount of the average annual investment.

"It's interesting."

"Is that all?"

"Many of the issues are new to me."

"Have you ever worked in management before?"

"Yeah, but not in healthcare. Hospitals are a different breed of animal."

Amy raised her eyebrows in simple question, and Wes continued. "In most firms the goal is simple—maximize profit," he said. "In hospitals, issues get a lot more complicated."

"How?"

"You're dealing with people's lives. In manufacturing, we don't replace equipment that still works, unless it will cut costs or raise productivity. The Pink Ladies just paid off the new Autoanalyzer. It meets neither criterion."

"Then why did you buy it?"

"It's faster. That's important when the paramedics deliver someone to the hospital unconscious. The sooner the doctor gets an answer, the better chance he or she has of saving the patient. It won't happen often, and the revenues will never cover the costs, but occasionally it will save a life.

"Financial models," he continued, "like **return on investment** and **internal rate of return** are a great help in manufacturing." He shook his head soberly. "They don't work very well in healthcare."

"Sounds like something Dad would say," Amy said.

"Before I took this job, I blamed high healthcare costs on inefficiency. I'm starting to realize it's more complex. Thursday, I was visited by a delegation from obstetrics. We have a small nursery. Right now it's not staffed. The nurses have to monitor it from the nursing station across the hall. They watch the babies through a large window. The problem is, with the glass reflection, they can't always clearly see the baby's color."

"Our average occupancy is less than three babies a day," Wes continued. "Justifying a full-time nurse for that volume is difficult, especially when you remember we're talking three shifts a day—seven days a week. It takes four full-time employees to fill one slot."

"I did the math," he said. "Full coverage would cost $126,000 a year—that's $230 for a two-day stay. I told them I didn't think the nursery charge could absorb that.

"Thursday afternoon," he continued, "I was on the floor and happened to look in on the nursery. There were two newborns—twin boys, and one of them was blue. I called the nurse. The baby had thrown up and **aspirated**. She rushed in, got him breathing again."

"She looks at me like I'm Ebenezer Scrooge," he continued. "*'That's why we need full-time staffing coverage in the nursery!'* she snips as she returns to the nursing station. By that time, several nurses have gathered around the nursery window. They look at me like I'm an idiot, and nod their heads in agreement.

"They were right of course. All weekend I thought about what it means to have a twin brother. Playing together in preschool, venturing off arm in arm on their first day of kindergarten, double-dating in high school, serving as each other's best man at their weddings. Contrast that with the other scenario—*I had a twin brother, but he died several hours after we were born.*"

Wes shrugged. "Suddenly cost doesn't seem very important.

Amy looked up into his eyes, and vague electricity passed between them. With the back of his hand, he touched her cheek softly. Her mouth softened and her lips parted slightly. Without thinking, he kissed her, and then gathered her into his arms as she buried her face in his shirt.

Discussion One—Why Financial Ratios Don't Always Work in the Healthcare Industry

Investors organize most companies with the goal of earning a profit. Almost all decisions center on that goal. One tool managers of for-profit companies use to determine if they should buy a piece of equipment is a formula known as return on investment. They calculate return on investment by dividing the added income earned by buying the equipment, by the price of the equipment. For example, if a piece of equipment costs $100,000, and the yearly profit generated is $10,000, the return on investment is $10,000 divided by $100,000 or 10%.

Many financial tools employed by for-profit companies are not useful for hospitals. A hospital administrator may decide, for example, to buy a new piece of laboratory equipment even though the old equipment is not worn out, and even though there are more profitable ways to invest that money, simply because the new machine will save lives.

Hospitals operate on different decision models than typical businesses.

Discussion Questions

1. *Some people believe the decision not to operate a community hospital strictly like a business is a sign of inefficiency. Is there another explanation?*
2. *Wes Douglas tells a story about a request to raise nurse staffing in his newborn nursery. After witnessing a situation where a baby nearly died, he concluded: When you're faced with that situation, costs suddenly don't seem that important. Is he right, or is he just getting carried away with his emotions?*
3. *Several years ago, an administrator in a metropolitan hospital was proposing the purchase of fetal heart monitors for the Department of Obstetrics to his Board of Trustees. The equipment, maintenance, and training of the personnel would amount to many hundreds of thousands of*

dollars. One astute businessperson, who was serving as a trustee, asked how many babies the monitors would save. The administrator replied "maybe two or three a year." The board member then pulled a calculator from his shirt pocket and determined the cost was about $50,000 a baby. The board then discussed the question: "Is a baby worth $50,000?" The answer they settled on explains the difficulty facing most healthcare workers. "Probably not," they said, "unless it's my baby." Why are the daily operating questions facing allied health workers different from those facing employees in many other industries? Can you run a hospital like you would a bicycle manufacturing plant?

19

The Model

Edward Wycoff smiled as Tony Devecchi studied the architect's model. Wycoff commissioned it to raise capital, and it was doing its job! Jaxon White, the youngest architect of Denver's most prestigious architectural firm, waited at his side, his mouth twisted tight with expectation. Two of Devecchi's business associates watched from the sidelines.

Devecchi, wearing a black shirt, white tie, and alligator shoes, circled the model like a shark eyeing its prey. Placing his hands on his knees, he bent over for a closer look, his small rat-like eyes greedily drinking in every detail. He swore softly, and then nodded in approval.

"It looks different in three dimensions than it did on paper," he said, grinning broadly. "I like it! I think our young architect has done a commendable job."

Wycoff agreed. "Tell him about the project, Jaxon."

Jaxon took a deep breath and released it slowly. "We will call the project Wycoff Square," he said, pointing to the model. "It will consist of a hotel, condominiums, a retirement home with three levels of care, a hospital, doctor offices and a shopping center."

Devecchi nodded approvingly. "Ambitious project."

"You don't earn money by thinking small," an investor said.

Wycoff nodded. "It's a self-contained community. Except for the hotel, the project is similar to the retirement communities you've done in Arizona."

"Noticed that," Devecchi said, fishing a cigar from his shirt pocket. "Your design is better." He bit off the end of his cigar and spat it into the wastebasket. "After seeing this, I think my other projects need a new architect." Devecchi nodded at White who beamed proudly.

"You're lucky to have a good location," an investor commented. "Since the announcement of the Olympics, property in Park City is hard to come by."

"The project will be built on 100 acres south of Park City," Devecchi replied, turning to his associates. He pointed at the model with his cigar. "Wycoff's got the lien and assures us he'll have clear title to the property within 90 days."

Surrogate. Substitute.

Title. A legal document verifying ownership of property.

"The hotel will be leased to a major chain and will open before the games in 2002," Wycoff said. "Consolidated Healthcare will run the medical center. It will be a major publicity coup for your company to be the healthcare provider for the Olympics. The advertising alone will be worth millions of dollars." Wycoff turned to the investors. "And you gentlemen have the opportunity to provide the funding for the shopping center, provided, of course, you want in."

"We're in," an investor said. The others nodded. "Just see there are no complications in getting **title** to the land."

A sanguine smile cracked the cold lines of Wycoff's aging face. "Gentlemen," he said with characteristic self-assurance, "it's in the bag."

Wycoff was alone in the first-class section of Delta Flight 766 from Denver to Salt Lake City. He checked his watch—4:30 PM. The Boeing 737 sat isolated at the end of runway 32, awaiting final clearance for takeoff.

As Wycoff peered out his window, he noted the day, so full of promise that morning, was fading fast. At the airport, the temperature was dropping. To the north, a pack of gray clouds hobbled across the sky, driven by an impatient westerly wind. Wycoff could feel the cold in the joints of his hands.

"Ladies and gentlemen, this is the captain speaking. We apologize for the delay. We are twelfth in line for takeoff."

Wycoff shrugged. *What's the hurry?* he thought. His entire life he'd been impatient—anxious to arrive at some glorious future destination. He looked out the window at the threatening sky. *Is this all there is? The cheerless gray of old age?*

In rare moments of introspection, Wycoff reflected on the decisions of his early life. He decided then that he would avoid close personal relationships. It was a decision based on practicality—wealth and power were jealous mistresses; they wouldn't allow time for anything else. As a young man, he equated wealth and power with love and security—things he knew little of as a child. The word ***surrogate*** came to him. He mulled it over in his mind. Wealth was a surrogate for security and love—except it wasn't. *Counterfeit* is a better word, he reflected bitterly.

Edward Wycoff had a wife and family, but the warmth of those relationships died years ago, strangled by ambition that starved the affection from their marriage, and choked the love from his children. He had three sons—two attorneys and a doctor. A fourth child, a daughter, took her life at age 16.

The boys were polite, more out of respect to their mother than affection for their father. Their children never called him grandfather—something he took pride in during their younger years.

I don't need people, Wycoff shrugged. *Friends come and go—only enemies are forever.* He was silent for a moment, and then smiled sadly at his own self-deception. It was a good try. Denial worked well sometimes—today it didn't. At age 79, Edward Wycoff had concluded there were only two tragedies in life: *Those who don't get what they truly want . . . and those who do.*

Fifteen minutes later Edward Wycoff gazed quietly out the window as the flight was cleared for takeoff. As the Delta 737 lifted off the runway, he continued reflecting on how far he had come from the difficulties of his childhood.

Born the fifth son of a prosperous family, his father, Jeremiah Wycoff, was a successful merchant from Rexburg, Idaho. In 1918, Jeremiah met Peter Brannan who proposed he provide half the capital for a new bank. Although Jeremiah knew nothing about banking, the Brannans did, and he invested. The Brannans operated two banks, one in Park City, and a second in Price, Utah. Both were successful.

The new bank in Rexburg prospered for six years, investing heavily in the farming community. A series of crop failures from 1925 to 1928, coupled with the depression of 1929, severely dampened southern Idaho's economy, however, causing the bank to fail in 1931.

Although the family blamed stress caused by the bank failure on the subsequent death of Jeremiah, they had nothing but praise for Peter Brannan. Brannan arranged for the purchase of the family's assets by a Nevada bank, including the bank stock, although at ten cents on the dollar.

Edward Wycoff's older sister Alice was even offered a job in the Brannan household, providing domestic help for Peter Brannan's wife, who was in failing health. Inspired by Brannan, Wycoff later went east to get his schooling. Working his way through college, he got a degree in finance at New York University and took a job on Wall Street.

In 1933, a second tragedy struck the Wycoff family. Alice died giving birth to an illegitimate child. Edward Wycoff was told the father, a man named Ramer, left town shortly after learning Alice was with child. Once again, the Brannans came to the Wycoffs' rescue by arranging for the child to be raised in a home operated by the Order of Elks in Claremont, California.

Twelve years later, the fairy tale unraveled. In 1945, while researching a possible bank purchase, Wycoff discovered Peter Brannan owned the Nevada bank that bought the Bank of Rexburg. The person the family thought was their greatest benefactor profited from the family's financial difficulties.

Ten years later, at the deathbed of his mother, he was shocked to learn his nephew, Ryan Ramer, was none other than the son of Peter Brannan. The Ramer story was invented to spare the Wycoffs and Brannans the scandal the pregnancy would have caused both families.

Market Value. The price for which an asset can be sold now on the open market. Differentiate from book value which is the original purchase price.

A rancorous palsy shook Wycoff's frame as he thought of Peter Brannan. Since that day in 1955, he dreamed of nothing else but avenging his family. A caustic smile broke Wycoff's lips.

The chance came in 1996 while he was still on Wall Street. Word came that a small family-owned bank in Park City was for sale. The owner, he was told, a man named Brannan, had invested heavily in a software company that failed, consuming the family's fortune and placing them on the edge of bankruptcy. Further investigation showed that other family assets, including a local newspaper could also be bought for a small fraction of **market value**.

Wycoff organized a group of investors who bought the bank, the newspaper, and the mortgage. Wycoff was a silent partner—not even his wife was aware of his ownership interests in Park City.

Although the first motivation was revenge, the announcement Park City had won the bid for the 2002 Winter Olympics promised to make the transaction unbelievably profitable.

The bank originally held a note on 100 acres donated by the Brannans to build a new hospital. The land was an ideal location for a multimillion-dollar hotel resort he and Tony Devecchi hoped to build. Although the note was paid off by the funds from the sale of the bank and newspaper, Wycoff knew how to get it back.

Wycoff knew a little about Devecchi. He was an interesting character. Originally a Philadelphia slumlord, he made most of his money through hostile takeovers. At the height of his career, he had an ownership interest in more than 50 companies. Usually, he put himself on the payroll as CEO. This provided him with annual paychecks making him one of the highest-paid executives in the country. He then systematically looted each company.

Wycoff knew he would have to watch his back. He couldn't trust Devecchi. Devecchi, however, had the money, contacts, and resources necessary to build the complex.

Wycoff's hate for the Brannan family returned, choking off any thoughts of loneliness or remorse for the way he lived his life. For over 50 years, two goals had dominated his life. The first was a desire to earn money—a lot of money. Money could buy security; it could buy respectability; it could buy power. The second was revenge—retribution for the family responsible for the death of his father and the disgrace of his family. With one transaction—the purchase of the Brannan estate—he was close to achieving both.

Discussion Questions

1. *We live in a society that equates wealth with success. Given this value system, an outside observer might assume Edward Wycoff was a successful man. What has Mr. Wycoff sacrificed to achieve wealth and social prominence? Do you think it was worth it? Is it possible to be financially successful and still have a rewarding family and social life? What might Wycoff have done differently?*

20

Rachel

Rachel Brannan hummed softly as she polished the teapot from the sterling silver tea set her mother-in-law gave her the day she married James Brannan. She paused, holding the teacup up to a light. It was as beautiful and lustrous as the day Mrs. Brannan gave it to her.

Studying her reflection, she smiled. Unlike the silver tea set, she had aged. The chestnut brown hair Jim ran his fingers through the night he proposed was white, and the dark Welsh eyes he gazed into so lovingly now reflected the toils and trials of a life of hard work and service.

The older she got, the more she reminded herself of her grandmother, Amelia Price. Elizabeth immigrated with her husband in 1880. They came from the coal mines of Wales to the silver mines of Park City. Grandmother raised her after the death of her own mother. From Amelia, she learned the art of hard work, and hard work she did, even in her 68th year.

Rachel studied the tea set. For 30 years, it served as the centerpiece at the annual governing board and medical staff reception, always held at the Brannan mansion. Hosting the event would be different this year, Jim was dead.

Rachel turned and gazed lovingly at her husband's photograph on the desk. Jim had always provided direction in areas where she felt uncertain. Some members of the family felt he provided too much direction. Her oldest son David resented the domination. For Rachel, however, the granddaughter of a coal miner who had never felt comfortable in the presence of the rich or famous, Jim's self-confidence provided comfort and security.

A knock at the door interrupted her thoughts and her domestic helper, Hanna Brunswick, bustled into the room. Hanna carried a large linen tablecloth folded over her left arm. In her right hand, she held a large envelope, which she handed to Rachel. "David dropped this off this morning," she said. "You were resting. It's a list of those who confirmed they'll be at the reception."

While Rachel opened the envelope, Hanna laid the tablecloth on the desk. "I inventoried the linen closet this morning," she said. "This is the only linen large enough to cover the serving table."

Rachel gently caressed the linen tablecloth. Like her small hand, it was frail and delicate. "The tablecloth belonged to Jim's mother," she said. It's a shame it's getting old, but aren't we all?" She looked up at Hanna with brown eyes that still sparkled and nodded. "It will be fine," she said softly. Hanna reclaimed the linen and marched out of the room.

Rachel turned her attention to the guest list. Sixty-five people including spouses would attend: forty-five from the medical staff, twelve from administration, and eight from the board. *How the hospital has grown*, she thought as she contemplated the size of the medical staff.

As a child, she attended the groundbreaking for the building replacing the original Miner's Hospital. Jim's father presided at the ceremony. The Brannan family had given the funds for its construction. Through the years, whenever the hospital needed a new wing or major piece of medical equipment, the family foundation provided the funding.

Rachel turned her attention back to the guest list, scanning the names of those who would be attending. David would be there with his wife, as would her son Matthew. Matthew—now *Doctor* Matthew Brannan—had recently finished his internship and was a member of the medical staff.

Matthew was 28-years-old, 15 years younger than her first child, a daughter who died at childbirth. Rachel was proud of Matthew's accomplishments. Dyslexic, he struggled with reading, so much that many of their friends scoffed when Jim announced his son was going to become a doctor. Tutors and a generous donation to a medical school in Texas helped Matthew gain admission to medical school. With his education complete, now all he needed was a wife.

Rachel smiled thoughtfully. Matthew would be bringing Amy Castleton to the reception. Matthew had been a member of Hap Castleton's scout troop. He won the rank of Eagle his junior year of high school. As a college student, he served as Hap's assistant scout leader. Not, Rachel suspected, because he loved scouting, but because he loved Amy.

Outside, Matt Brannan had begun the annual ritual of winterizing the 30-room mansion. The job had fallen to him as David was too impatient for the job, and the hired help too old. Matt began by replacing the weather-stripping on all outside doors. Now he was ready to install the storm windows.

He decided to tackle the most difficult part first, an oval window on the Venetian tower. Matt studied the tower and he shook his head. The window was on the third floor. *Would have been nice if the carpenters had given some thought to energy conservation.* The original structure had no insulation, and single-pane windows. In 1880, coal was cheap. What's more, the man who built it—Great-grandfather Mike Brannan—owned the coal mines. Mike, and the era in which he lived, had energy to burn.

Mike's son Peter replaced the coal furnace. Thirty years later the heating bills were again too high, so Matt's father blew a foot of insulation into the attic and went shopping for storm windows. Modern aluminum windows wouldn't do, they would distract from the architectural integrity of the building. He hired a cabinetmaker and glazier to build wooden frames, consistent in style with the arched Italianate windows. They were pretty—but a bear to install.

Screwdriver in one hand and pliers in the other, Matt gazed in awe at the garish old house. He tried to imagine the shock on the faces of the conservative neighbors, when Mike Brannan unveiled the classical Victorian color scheme. Maroon walls, green trim, orange window sashes, and olive blinds. Three stories high, the Victorian mansion dwarfed the modest homes of the early miners. Atypical of 19th century Utah—very typical of its builder.

Mike Brannan was bigger than life—so was his house. Matt inherited his great-grandfather's features, but none of his genius, and little of his energy. Standing in the shadow of the old mansion, Matt felt small and inconsequential.

21

The Plan Takes Shape

Saturday evening, Rachel Brannan hosted the yearly medical staff reception. Wes Douglas used the opportunity to learn more about the medical staff's opinions of Brannan Community Hospital. Many were concerned about the vacuum created by Hap's death. Some doctors feared Wycoff would use the void to push for deeper cost cuts.

Dr. Emil Flagg bent Wes's ear on the dangers of corporate medicine. For 30 minutes, he praised the virtues of hospital administrators who were unwilling to subject the medical staff to the "dual degradation of budgeting and managed care." Flagg was especially critical of health maintenance organizations that dictated which doctors the patients were allowed to use.

"Some of our doctors spent 20 years building their medical practices," he said. "They aren't worth a nickel now. The HMOs own the patients.

"The older docs feel betrayed," he continued, "disconnected from the healthcare system they helped build. The people who run HMOs are nothing more than bookies. They hire statisticians to study the likelihood of somebody getting sick, then figure ways to earn a profit by shifting the risk to the doctors and hospitals."

Dr. Ashton Amos, president of the medical staff took a more moderate view. "I agree with what Krimmel says about the need for market forces. The old system wasn't good at involving all the stakeholders, but managed care isn't solving the problem either. We're substituting cost efficiency for quality. It's a scary trade-off when you're dealing with human lives.

"Since insurance companies pay the bill," Dr. Amos continued, "they think they can dictate how doctors should practice medicine. Managed care has become a huge bureaucracy."

The evening brought other revelations. Amy Castleton accompanied Dr. Matt Brannan to the reception. Wes noticed how he worshipfully followed her as she visited with the doctors and their wives. Wes was developing a deep visceral dislike for Matt.

Compensation system. A set of schedules listing the starting wage of each class of employees and pay steps given for experience.

External validity. As the term relates to pay, external validity means that pay for individual jobs is the same as the pay of similar jobs outside the organization. If employees at a military hospital earn less than their counterparts in the civilian world, the military pay system lacks external validity.

Internal consistency. A compensation management term meaning that pay is fair, and that employees are paid consistent with the education, skill, responsibility, and contribution to the organization.

Performance evaluation. A periodic evaluation by a work supervisor of the quality of work of a subordinate. Performance evaluations are often conducted at the time merit pay increases are awarded.

Salary schedule. A schedule listing the entry wage levels of different employee classes.

Salary surveys. Surveys to determine what other firms are paying for specific jobs.

Monday afternoon, Wes met with Emma Chandler to develop a plan to put the hospital at breakeven in 90 days. "Hospitals lose money by producing too little revenue or incurring too much cost," Wes said. "Let's focus on costs first."

Emma brought cost and productivity information from the Utah Healthcare Association to the meeting. Of special interest were comparative data on average cost per-patient-day for labor and materials for hospitals the same size as Brannan Community Hospital. The reports clearly showed the hospital's costs were higher than any other hospital the same size in Utah.

Labor costs were the biggest problem. For some jobs, Brannan paid significantly more than competing hospitals. For other jobs significantly less. There seemed to be no consistent basis for setting salaries. "It's who you know, not what you know," one employee told him.

Wes called Karisa Holyoak, the CPA that had helped him find Krimmel. "I need a consultant in hospital compensation," he said. Someone who can help me set up fair and consistent **salary schedules**."

Karisa gave him the name of Dr. Paige Adams, a professor of compensation at Weber State University, in Ogden, Utah. A meeting with Chandler was scheduled. Wes invited Don Yanamura, the hospital's human resource director to attend.

"The problem is your **compensation system** was developed over many years as the hospital added new positions," Dr. Adams said as the meeting started. "There were no guidelines—no governing philosophies. As a result, your salary schedules lack internal consistency and external validity."

"What does that mean?" Yanamura asked.

"**Internal consistency** means the system is *fair—employees get equal pay for equal work*. **External validity** means that a firm's salaries are *consistent with the market*. Utah Healthcare Association data shows your salaries are neither."

Yanamura gave Wes a side-glance. "I suspected that was the situation," he said. "I inherited the present system. I've never had the resources to fix it."

Adams smiled sympathetically. "That's a common problem," she said. "Human resource directors are often so busy with daily operations they don't have time to design good compensation systems. As technology continues to change job content, problems are created for pay, recruitment, training, and **performance evaluation**."

"It seems most hospitals would be ripe for the service you offer," Yanamura said. "If we hire you, what will you do for us?"

"I'll interview your employees and their supervisors to identify what each of your employees do. I will prepare a job description for each job, listing the major tasks of that position. Using **salary surveys** and statistical tools too complicated to explain here, I will determine what salaries should be. From that I will prepare a salary schedule."

Wes was pleased that Yanamura was receptive. "If we hire your firm, how long will it take until we have your report?"

Adams retrieved a calculator from her briefcase and punched in several figures. "You have about 350 employees—about 125 different job descriptions," she said. "My firm completed a similar project for Memorial Hospital in Colorado Springs. I think we could complete your study in about four weeks."

Yanamura nodded at Wes, who turned to Adams. "Let's do it!"

Discussion One—Wes' Approach to Saving the Hospital

In developing a plan to save Brannan Community Hospital, Wes Douglas first focused his attention on the healthcare industry. His goal was to understand the factors driving healthcare costs. Having a good feel for the industry, he now turns to the internal operation of his hospital. To reach breakeven, he can raise revenues or cut costs. He decides to look at costs first. Since labor is one of the hospital's largest costs, that is his first priority. He hires a consultant to help him determine what labor costs should be.

Discussion Question

1. *One way that a person might judge the efficiency of a hospital is to compare the number of hours of registered nurse time per-patient-day with that of other hospitals. If Community Hospital uses four hours of registered nurse time per-patient-day, and the University Hospital uses six, it is possible the University Hospital is less efficient than Community Hospital? What other explanations might there be for the difference?*

22

Inadequately Trained

Anterior. "On the front." An anterior x-ray, for example, gives a front view.

Cyanotic. Blue.

Epiglottitis. Inflammation of the epiglottis, (an elastic cartilage found on the root of the tongue that folds over the glottis to prevent food from entering the windpipe during the act of swallowing).

Intubate. The insertion of a tube into the airway to allow the patient to breathe.

Lateral. "On the side." A lateral x-ray, for example, gives a side view.

Pneumonia. an acute disease characterized by inflammation of the lungs.

Posterior. "On the back side." A posterior x-ray gives a back view.

Respiratory arrest. A situation where a patient has stopped breathing.

Except for Dr. Matt Brannan, the medical library was empty. At a table in the far corner he quietly read the medical record of a former patient. His eyes were wide with disbelief as he studied the **lateral** x-ray. *How could I miss that?* Small beads of perspiration formed on his upper lip as he reread the notes of Dr. Frank Almond, an emergency room doctor who saw the toddler four hours after Dr. Brannan sent her home.

In Brannan's pocket was a letter from the Morbidity and Mortality Committee, a peer-review group with the assignment to identify substandard practice on the medical staff. The letter requested that he come to a breakfast meeting the following Monday, prepared to discuss the case of Brittany Anderson. The letter charged that he misdiagnosed her case, with almost fatal results.

A week ago a young mother, Jonel Anderson brought her three-year-old daughter Brittany to his office. The first examination showed a barking cough and a mildly elevated temperature of 101.1 degrees. The child was drooling, a sign Brannan should have paid more attention to, but didn't—*toddlers drool*, he reasoned. Brittany's breathing was labored, which he misattributed to congestion or a stuffed up nose.

The lab work was normal, except for a slightly elevated white blood count of 11. To rule out **pneumonia**, Brannan ordered a chest x-ray, AP (**anterior**, **posterior**) and lateral views. He should have checked for **epiglottitis** but didn't.

Since her lungs were clean, he concluded that she had a viral, upper respiratory tract infection (URI). He sent her home. "There's nothing we can do for her in the hospital that you can't do at home," he told the worried mother. "Give her plenty of fluids, monitor temperature, give her Tylenol if her temperature raises, and call me if it gets worse."

Three hours later, **cyanotic**, and in acute **respiratory arrest**, Brittany Anderson was brought to the emergency room by ambulance. Her epiglottis, now severely swollen, sealed off her airway. So severe was the swelling, that it was almost impossible to **intubate** her. Brittany Anderson almost died in the hospital's emergency room.

Endowment. A charitable gift.

Family practice residency. A training program following the internship that trains a medical school graduate to be a family practice doctor. Family practice residencies are usually three to four years in length.

Thumbprint sign. A radiological sign of thickened tissues that encroach on an airway.

In today's review of Brittany's records, he saw what he missed earlier, the characteristic **thumbprint sign** on the lateral x-ray—a sure indicator of acute epiglottitis. Dr. Brannan finished reading and closed the medical record. This would be the second time in a year that he would be called before the committee. He was fearful they would conclude what he himself now suspected, that he was inadequately trained to practice family medicine.

Dr. Brannan was tired of feelings of inadequacy, thoughts he experienced since his father first made the decision that Matt would go into medicine. The Brannan family had an image in the community that was larger than life. Only medicine would be an acceptable career for the youngest heir to the Brannan legacy.

Matt explained to his father that he was a slow reader and not a good student. No matter, James enrolled him in the university and hired the best tutors money could buy. Hard study, good tutoring, and a family **endowment** of one million dollars to a small medical college on the east coast assured Matt's acceptance to the class of 1994.

It wasn't easy, but Matt hung in there. Four years later, he graduated, 95th in a class of 103 students. He finished a one-year internship and was applying for a residency in family practice when the family's fortune started to disintegrate. His father suffered a stroke, and Matt was called home to help put the family back together. As always, the family's needs came first. The residency would have to wait.

The library was quiet except for the ticking of a large grandfather clock on the far wall. Matt's mother presented it to the medical staff in appreciation for the care Jim received after his stroke. Dr. Brannan's eyes narrowed, and deep lines of determination formed around his mouth. *I need more training.*

Reviewing his options, he stared at a bookshelf on the far wall. On the second shelf was a directory that listed **family practice residencies** in the United States. He would apply for a residency; if that wasn't good enough, he would follow it with a fellowship. The only complication was Amy Castleton. He had given his heart completely; she had yet to do the same. They discussed marriage. She had not accepted his many proposals and was now dating others, among them Wes Douglas. If Matt went back to school without her, he was sure that she wouldn't be here when he returned.

"Knock, knock," Helen Castleton said as she slowly opened the door to Amy's bedroom.

Amy, sitting at her vanity by the window looked up and blinked brightly. "What do you think of the makeup?" she asked. "It's a new color."

"Absolutely stunning." Carrying a black dress, Mrs. Castleton crossed the room to Amy's closet. "Picked this up from the cleaners. Thought you might like to wear it tonight. It's one of Matt's favorites, isn't it?"

"Yes, but I'm not going out with Matt tonight," she said, returning to the mirror. "The film festival's in town and Wes Douglas has asked me to go with him."

Helen's eyes registered her surprise. "Wes Douglas?" she said. "The new administrator?"

Amy nodded. Her mother was silent as she processed Amy's message. Finally she spoke, choosing her words carefully. "I don't think things are going well for him at the hospital," she said. "In some ways I wonder if it's a good idea for you to date him."

"Why?"

"He has a financial background; some think he's a miniature Edward Wycoff. There are those who think he wants to change operations from the way they were under your father—to run the hospital more like a business, not a charity."

Amy shrugged. "That might not be all bad, given their current situation with the bank."

Helen shot Amy a withering look. "Your father would turn over in his grave if he thought you were siding with the accountants. You remember the fights he had with Wycoff?"

"I'm not siding with Wycoff," Amy said wearily. "It just seems like times have changed and—"

"The doctors don't like what's going on," Helen continued. "They're unhappy the board didn't consult them before appointing Mr. Douglas as interim administrator. There's talk of a revolt."

Amy started brushing her hair. "Where'd you hear that, Mom?"

"Rachel Brannan," Helen replied. "She thinks they should appoint Matt as interim administrator."

Amy smiled. "I'm sure she's unbiased," She replaced the brush on the dresser. Finished, she shook her head until her hair fell softly on her shoulders. Amy stood and retrieved her dress from the closet.

"Rachel says Matt's got many good ideas on how to run the hospital. Maybe they'd put him in permanently."

"Anybody ask Matt what he thinks of the idea?" Amy asked.

"Rachel thinks he'd make a fine administrator, and so do I. He would carry on the tradition of the family."

"Whose family—ours or theirs?" Amy asked dryly.

"Well, maybe both," Helen replied. "I thought you and Matt were talking of marriage."

"Matt's talking; I'm listening."

"You do love him?" Helen asked, her eyes reflecting her curiosity.

"Yes, I do, Mom," Amy sighed. "At least I think I do. It's just that I've known him since I was six, and sometimes it seems—"

"I think Rachel has her heart set on a Christmas engagement," Helen said.

"Well, I'm not engaged yet," Amy said as she slipped into her dress. Cocking her head slightly, she smiled. "I think that's the doorbell, Mom."

Helen gave her a resigned smile. Amy had her father's stubbornness as well as his charm. "I can see I'm not going to change your mind tonight," she said. "I'll get the door."

Amy shot her a look of warning.

"Okay, I'll even be nice," Helen said.

Actor Robert Redford started the Sundance Film Festival in 1981, hoping to create an event that would support independent filmmaking. Through the years it grew, gaining international stature. In 1999, over 300 young filmmakers showcased their work before many of Hollywood's most talented producers, writers, and actors. Each year the public is invited.

On the evening of their first date, Wes Douglas and Amy Castleton saw two films and later dined at the Olive Barrel Food Company, a small restaurant on Main Street. "I met your mother at the medical staff reception at the Brannans," Wes began while they were waiting for their order.

"It was difficult for her to go without Dad."

"You were there with Matt Brannan," Wes said, watching the expression on her face. He was interested in knowing more about their relationship. "How long have you known each other?"

"Our families have been close for many years. Father, of course, worked closely with Matt's father on the board."

Wes nodded, and waited for her to continue.

"Rachel and I are close. Before we moved to Park City, she and Jim lost a baby girl. Maybe I helped fill a void. I spent a lot of time in the Brannan household when I was growing up. It was only natural that Matt and I would become friends. Dad liked Jim Brannan; they were both good fishermen. Jim Brannan had a cabin on the Salmon River."

"Hap had many friends," Wes said.

"He got energy from people," Amy acknowledged, "and he was good to everyone. It was interesting to see the diversity of people that turned out for his funeral. Everyone from the governor to the humblest housekeeper was there; he always treated them the same. I think everyone there considered themselves a close friend of Hap Castleton.

"One of his pallbearers spent some time with me after the service," Amy continued. "A fellow named Arthur Skyros. Dad met him when Art's mother Marie moved to Park City in 1985, three weeks after her husband was imprisoned for holding up a liquor store in Los Angeles. Marie got a job in the hospital laundry. I think the transition from Los Angeles to Park City was difficult for Art. He was poorer than most of the kids at the high school. He looked different and talked different—and eventually, of course, the word got out about his father."

"Dad became aware of the situation when Marie left work one day to bail Art out of jail for shoplifting. That evening, Dad showed up at the basement

Pediatrics. A branch of medicine specializing in the treatment of childhood illness.

room Marie rented to invite Art to join his scout troop. Marie hesitated. Dad suspected it was because they didn't have the money for a scout uniform. Dad retrieved one from a former scout, and took him to the next meeting."

"Some scouts looked down their noses at Art—his father wasn't a doctor or an attorney. Dad was tough and never allowed down-talk. Eventually the other boys accepted Art, and he became one of Hap's best scouts. When Art graduated from high school, Dad used Art's rank of Eagle Scout to convince a former hospital trustee to fund a scholarship for him.

"Art worked hard in college. Four years later, Dad was the second person he called when he got his letter of acceptance to medical school. Art is now in his third year and wants to specialize in **pediatrics**.

"Shortly after Art joined the scout troop, Dad got the family out of their basement apartment. The hospital owned several homes next to the doctor's parking lot. They were bought for future expansion. One of these he rented to Marie for $150 a month. When her arthritis became so bad she could no longer work, he lowered the rent to $50.

"One day while reviewing the books, Edward Wycoff found out about it. The small house could have been rented out for 20 times that amount during ski season. He hit the ceiling and wanted Dad reprimanded for misusing hospital assets. Dad offered to pay the difference. The board listened to him, and then ruled that wasn't needed. Marie was a faithful employee for many years, and she stayed in the home. Not everyone on the board was as bottom-line oriented as Edward Wycoff.

"Dad may not have been the best businessman in the world," Amy continued, "but his heart was in the right place. He was intensely loyal to his employees, and most of them loved him for it."

"That's a tribute to your father," Wes said. He was starting to understand the motive for many of the actions Hap Castleton took during his tenure as administrator of Brannan Community Hospital. It was interesting to contrast the value systems of Hap Castleton and Edward Wycoff. Wycoff made millions, Hap died with few material assets. *I'm not sure I'm willing to judge who was the most successful,* Wes thought.

From deep inside the down comforter, Amy Castleton arched her back lazily. Curling her toes, she rubbed her legs against the soft flannel sheets, warm in the cold morning air of her attic bedroom. Sighing comfortably, she rolled onto her back, stretching her arms high above her head. It was Saturday morning. As she stirred, she gently pulled the covers from her head.

Sitting up, she hugged her knees, blissfully happy, but not sure why. She suspected Wes Douglas had something to do with it. The morning sunlight flowed from the compass window above her bed, giving the room an unearthly glow. The bedroom smelled of potpourri and cedar. Situated on the second floor, the bedroom windows were level with the maple trees that bordered Grand Avenue.

As a little girl, her bedroom was her castle tower—a place to wait for her prince. This morning, the same magic hung in the air. Had he come? Tilting her head, she lazily turned the idea over in her mind. She settled back into the bed as her eyes traced the sculpture of the heavy ceiling beams. Hap Castleton carved them himself from Cedar he hauled from southern Utah. She smiled as she remembered how her father loved working with wood. To Hap, there was something sacred about that medium. "Wood shouldn't be forced out," he said, "but shaped and fitted together like an interlocking puzzle." Dad took the same approach with people.

Hap built the home their first year in Park City. Carpentry served as an emotional outlet as Hap struggled to retool himself from a building contractor into a healthcare executive. The job change wasn't easy. He wouldn't have attempted it, but for the encouragement of Jim Brannan, the first to see Hap's managerial potential.

Hap, a contractor in Southern California, built a summer home for the Brannans in the foothills above Glendale, California. Brannan recognized his honesty and work ethic—but, most of all, his ability to work well with subcontractors of different backgrounds, temperaments, and personalities. Brannan Community Hospital's former administrator had announced his retirement, and Jim Brannan had his eye out for a replacement.

Park City was still transitioning from a primitive mining town to a sophisticated ski resort. Its struggling hospital needed someone who could pull the ethnically and culturally diverse community together. Not long after Brannan's summer home was finished, interest rates went through the ceiling, and Castleton's construction business folded. Brannan hired Hap to manage the hospital.

The move from Glendale, California, to Park City was easy for Hap—but not for his wife. She wanted a home. It was not easy for a man who had filed bankruptcy to get a construction loan. With a little arm-twisting by Jim Brannan, however, the bank loaned the funds for the materials and Hap provided the labor.

Hap built the home of stone, brick, and redwood. It had the architectural elements of a California bungalow. With broad latticed eaves, open porches, and expressive uses of wood, an article in the *Park City Sentinel* called it "Japanesque." Whatever its style, the gabled, trellised, and shingled home showed Hap's personality—functional, friendly, masculine, but, most of all, unique.

Sitting up now, Amy basked in the ambience of the room. She had many happy memories in this place—tea parties in kindergarten, sleepovers in junior high, prepping for dates with Matt Brannan in high school.

Her eyes narrowed thoughtfully as she considered Matt. He had been a part of her life from their first day in Park City. At first he filled the role of an older brother. Later she learned that his feelings were deeper. Three years

Billing code. A number used on a bill to an insurance company that identifies the diagnosis, test, or procedure being billed.

Bundling. As it relates to hospital billing, bundling is the practice of combining the charges of many services into one bill, rather than billing individually for each service. Some insurance companies prefer bundling, others like items billed individually.

older than she, he followed her through high school with worshipful awe, careful to do nothing that would frighten her away while he waited for her to grow up. He was always kind, always there. The relationship grew, and so did her feelings for him.

It was an effortless relationship—secure but not exciting. Did she love him? Or was she merely comfortable? With dating, school and volunteer work, her life had settled into a dependable routine, shattered now by her father's accident.

Amy musingly cocked her head. *And now there's Mr. Wes Douglas—am I falling for him?* She wasn't sure. Wes was different from Matt Brannan. Amy dominated the relationship with Matt. She led and Matt followed. Stronger, more deliberate, Wes Douglas stirred her feelings. Her forehead furrowed into a deep scowl. It was all too unsettling.

The return address was The Department of Justice in Denver, Colorado. Sensing its importance, the Controller's secretary pulled the official looking envelope from the stack of department mail and placed it prominently on Emma Chandler's desk where she would be sure to see it on returning from lunch.

In a few minutes, the young controller returned. Her secretary was right, it was important! Picking it up, she crossed the office and shut the door. Returning to her desk she opened the envelope, fingers trembling. She hoped her fears would be put to rest. She had an inclination to worry, and most of the things she worried about never happened. *Only, why had the Department of Justice waited so long to issue its report?* Carefully unfolding the document, she scanned the introductory letter, her pupils narrowing as she searched for key words.

She gasped in sudden surprise. *No—it couldn't be right, she must be missing something. Maybe she read it too fast.* More slowly now, she read the letter from the beginning, then read it again.

Two years ago, the hospital got its first letter from the Department of Justice seeking information on the hospital's billing methods. Eight months later, after spending $30,000 on audit fees, Emma gave seven years' worth of information. Sixteen months passed, and the hospital heard nothing. Now a letter told them that they owed $749,532, not for fraud, but for an infringement of rules. The hospital followed a long-standing practice of billing for laboratory tests one at a time. Medicare wanted them **bundled**.

This was the second infringement in a three-month period. Earlier, the hospital received a demand for the return of $1,200,000 in Medicare payments for radiology services provided over a three-year period. The government claimed the hospital used the wrong **billing code**. Although the difference in revenue between the two codes was only $125,000, the Feds wanted *all* the

Byzantine. Characterized by intrigue or deception.

Compliance officer. A person hired to see that an organization abides by specific rules and regulations.

Litigation. Filing a complaint in court.

money back. They claimed the deadline for rebilling under the correct code had passed.

The federal government was in trouble with healthcare spending and was determined to cut costs—by hook or crook. The number of FBI agents assigned to Medicare fraud was dramatically raised. *"It's almost a manhunt,"* an article in *Forbes Magazine* that Emma read reported. *"With that many cops out there, they've got to justify their keep. More and more, simple mistakes and misunderstandings are being labeled as fraud."*

The article quoted J. D. Klenke, a prominent medical economist: *"The whole focus on infringement, as opposed to flagrant violation, means everybody's guilty. There are 45,000 pages of Medicare reimbursement regulations. If you violate something on page 44,391—you're guilty. Full compliance is not possible. The regulations are* ***Byzantine****."*

Some larger hospitals in the state hired in-house **compliance officers** whose sole job was to read rules and regulations. Given the tight budget, Emma resisted increasing her staff. *Obviously a mistake, given The Justice Department ruling and the legal cost the hospital would incur to fight it.*

Emma wasn't opposed to going after the bad guys. With national spending for healthcare exceeding a trillion dollars a year, there was bound to be fraud. What she objected to, however, was a federal agency whose goal was revenue, not law enforcement. She shook her head as she laid the letter on her desk. *Hospital accounting wasn't fun anymore.*

Discussion One—Reducing Mistakes

Doctors occasionally make mistakes. Most hospitals have peer review committees to identify doctors who make more than their share. At Brannan Community Hospital, this committee is called the Morbidity and Mortality Committee. The procedure this committee follows is to review medical records, picked at random, from the Medical Records Library. When the committee finds substandard doctor practice, it is their responsibility to identify the cause. Inadequate training, carelessness, or sometimes infirmities from old age are just three of many causes.

Experience has shown the best course of action for a healthcare worker who has made a mistake is to own up to it and try to correct the problem to the best of his or her ability. Some studies have shown the primary cause of malpractice ***litigation*** *is a lack of communication. A family that might have shown some understanding had a doctor or hospital been forthcoming in admitting a mistake, is often enraged and thus, inclined to sue when they discover there was a cover up. Individuals can forgive honest mistakes; they are rarely forgiving of deception.*

Discussion Two—Legal Responsibilities of Healthcare Workers

As Wes Douglas becomes entangled with charges of possible malpractice against Dr. Matthew Brannan, it will help if he learns a little about medical law. This section reviews concepts that all healthcare workers should understand. Let's begin with several basic definitions.

A ***law*** *is a rule of conduct enforceable by a government entity. Laws govern relationships between people and impose punishments for violating proper behavior.*

There are five sources of law in the United States:

- *The United States Constitution*
- *Individual state constitutions*
- *Common law*
- *Statutes and ordinances*
- *Administrative regulations*

The person who starts a complaint against another in a court of law is the ***plaintiff****. The person against whom the complaint is sworn is the* ***defendant****. Laws can be grouped into two categories: criminal, and civil law.*

Criminal law *governs crimes against society. Examples of crimes tried in a court of criminal law include murder, robbery, and arson. The purpose of criminal law is to punish people who commit a crime.*

Civil law *covers all but criminal relationships. The goal of civil law is to make the harmed party whole. Successful civil cases incur liability for the defendant. A liability is a legal obligation.*

Crimes can be classified as:

- ***Misdemeanors****—crimes that are less serious than a felony and not punishable by long prison terms.*
- ***Felonies****—crimes that are punishable by imprisonment for more than one year.*
- ***Torts****—breaches of duty (excluding breach of contract) for which the court will provide a remedy.*

Criminal Law. Law is divided into categories called civil law and criminal law. Criminal law deals with crimes which have been defined as conduct that is immoral and for which there is no justification or excuse. Murder and robbery are crimes handled by criminal law.

Defendant. The person against whom a complaint is filed in a court of law.

Felony. A crime that is punishable by imprisonment for more than one year.

Law. A minimal rule of conduct enforceable by a controlling authority, usually a governmental entity.

Misdemeanor. A crime that is less serious than a felony and not punishable by a long prison term.

Plaintiff. The person charged in a civil action.

Torts. Breaches of duty (excluding breaches of contract) for which the court will provide a remedy.

Appeal. To take a case or complaint that has been decided by a lower court or administrative body to a higher one.

Civil law. Law is divided into categories called civil law and criminal law. Civil law covers all areas not addressed by criminal law. Specifically, civil law is concerned with the rights of citizens. An individual suing another for the accidental destruction of personal property would be under the jurisdiction of civil law.

Litigation. Filing a complaint in court.

Negligence. Failure to act with reasonable care; or failure to do something a reasonable person would have done; or performing an action a reasonable person would not have done.

Torts are handled in civil rather than criminal courts. Taking a complaint to court is called ***litigation****. Once a case is litigated, the defendant can* ***appeal*** *his or her case to a higher court.*

Torts can be classified as unintentional torts and intentional torts.

Unintentional Torts

Unintentional torts include negligence and malpractice.

Negligence *is defined as:*

- *The failure to act with care, or the failure to do something a reasonable person would have done, or*
- *The commission of an act a reasonable person would not have done.*

To prove negligence in a court of law, one must show that:

- *There was a legal duty*
- *There was a breach of that duty*
- *The breach caused damages*
- *Those damages resulted in an injury to the plaintiff*

Malpractice is defined as professional negligence. Malpractice is a major issue in healthcare. In medical malpractice lawsuits, judges will often rely on the following standards in determining if malpractice has occurred.

- *Did the practitioner fulfill his or her duty to the patient?*
- *Did he or she give the standard of care established by the hospital's policy and procedures manual?*
- *Is the hospital's policy and procedures manual consistent with standards required by the Joint Commission on Accreditation of Healthcare Organizations (JCAHO)?*
- *Was the incident foreseeable, given the nature of the incident and the training of the practitioner?*
- *Did the incident cause the patient harm?*
- *Did this harm cause financial damage to the patient?*

Abuse. An action that results in physical harm to a patient. Abuse can be physical, such as striking a patient; verbal, such as shouting or swearing; or psychological, such as threatening, intimidating, or belittling.

Assault. A threat or attempt to harm another person, or the fear of harm by a person threatened.

Battery. The illegal use of force against another person.

Defamation. The act of attacking the good reputation of another person.

False imprisonment. The unjustified restraint or retention of person without that person's consent, or the legal right to do so.

Informed consent. A legal document where a patient or his or her representative gives consent for treatment.

Invasion of privacy. Revealing personal information about a patient without that person's consent.

Intentional Torts

Intentional torts include:

- ***Assault***
- ***Battery***
- ***False imprisonment***
- ***Abuse***
- ***Defamation***
- ***Invasion of privacy***

Assault is defined as a threat or attempt to harm another person.

Battery is defined as the unlawful use of force against a person. Assault and battery are often charged together. Courts use the following criteria when determining assault:

- *Evidence that someone made a threat*
- *Evidence the threat, if carried out, would have caused harm*

Examples of assault and battery include:

- *Rough treatment*
- *Improper treatment*
- *Performing a procedure that a person has refused*

In most situations, a patient must give consent to be treated. Sometimes the consent is given in writing, in other situations it can be given verbally.

Failure to get consent before treatment can result in a charge of assault and battery.

To avoid this charge, a healthcare worker should get an ***informed consent*** *before treatment. Hospitals usually have the patient sign an informed consent when the patient is admitted. This document is in writing and must be signed by the patient, or his or her guardian.*

For an informed consent to be legal:

- *The consent must be voluntary*
- *The person giving the consent must be mentally sound*

Libel. Written defamation.

Slander. Spoken defamation.

- *The procedure must be explained*
- *Risks of the procedure, and of not having the procedure, must be explained in a way the patient can understand*

It is a good idea to have the person giving the consent repeat what he or she has been told. Consent is not required in an emergency where:

- *The emergency is life or health threatening*
- *The patient is unable to give consent, and*
- *The person who is legally authorized to give consent cannot be reached*

***False imprisonment** is the unjustified restraint or retention of a person without that person's consent, or the legal right to do so. Examples that courts have held to be false imprisonment in suits against health professionals include:*

- *Using physical restraint against a person without that person's permission*
- *Keeping a person hospitalized without his or her permission*

As with almost all rules, there are exceptions. A mentally ill person can be committed to a mental institution for treatment without that person's consent, if it can be proven that the person is a danger to himself or herself or to others.

Abuse is an action that results in physical harm to a patient. Abuse can be physical, such as striking a patient; verbal, such as shouting or swearing; or psychological, such as threatening, intimidating, or belittling.

*Defamation is an attack on the good reputation of another person. When defamation is spoken, it is **slander**. When written, it is **libel.***

Invasion of privacy is revealing personal information about a patient without that patient's consent. Courts have held that the following constitute invasion of privacy:

- *Unnecessary exposure during treatment or transport*
- *Disclosing information about a patient to people who are not members of the patient's medical team*
- *Discussion of a patient's personal information in the presence of other people*

Credentialing. To practice at a hospital, a physician must be a member of the medical staff and must have been given permission to perform specific medical procedures. Determining what procedures a physician is qualified to perform is called credentialing.

Nurse Practice Act. A state act that defines and regulates the practice of nursing.

- *Presenting case studies in educational settings or using data from a patient for research without hiding the person's identity*

Legal Regulation of Healthcare Practice

Controls over the provision of healthcare are established to protect patients, encourage quality, and define professional roles and practice boundaries. Controls can be classified as voluntary or involuntary.

***Voluntary controls** include guidelines issued by professional organizations for standards of care, and the defining of qualifications for certification and licensure. Organizations that provide voluntary guidelines include the Joint Commission on Accreditation of Healthcare Organizations (JCAHO) and the American Nurses Association (ANA).*

Insuring Competence

Professional competence is insured through credentialing. ***Credentialing*** *is the validation of competence. Credentialing includes:*

- *Accreditation—an evaluation that assures that an organization meets minimum standards*
- *Certification—recognition by a nongovernmental regulatory body that a person meets standards*
- *Licensure—recognition by a governmental body that a person meets minimum educational requirements and has the knowledge and skill to practice a specific profession*

Other Legal Issues

Execution of Physician's Orders

Hospital nurses are legally required to follow a doctor's orders unless they have reasonable expectation to believe the order will harm the patient. Good guidelines for nurses who are filling a doctor's orders include:

- *Understand your state* ***nurse practice act.*** *Know who can write orders (doctors only, or doctors and doctor assistants)*
- *Understand the hospital's policies with regard to doctor orders*
- *Where possible, get all doctors' orders in writing*

Telephone orders are permitted in an emergency. When taking a telephone order:

1. *If possible, have two nurses listen to the telephone order*
2. *Have one of the nurses document the order in writing*
3. *Repeat the order back to the doctor*
4. *Question an order that is:*
    - *Ambiguous*
    - *Contraindicated by normal practice, or by the patient's medical condition.*
5. *Get a telephone order* ***countersigned*** *within 24 hours*

Incident reports

Incident reports are used to report an event that injured, or had the potential to injure a patient, employee, or visitor. Examples of incidents include patient falls, medication errors, or malfunctions of equipment.

Incident reports include the time and date of the incident, events that led to the incident, the response of the patient, and an assessment of the impact on the patient. Some forms provide spaces for notification of the doctor and new assessments and medical orders. Healthcare workers should not include personal judgments or opinions about the incident in their report.

Medical Records

Courts have ruled that medical records are the property of the hospital and are confidential. They should not be available to anyone that is not on the patient's healthcare team. A patient, however, has the right to see his or her own medical record.

A ***medical record*** *is a legal document that can be presented in court. Erasures, therefore, are not permitted. Errors should be crossed out with a single line so the deleted information can still be read. The correct information should be signed and dated. It is always a good idea to give a written explanation for the correction.*

Patient medical records include the ***admission record****, nursing care plan, Kardex, nursing progress notes,* ***flow sheets****,* ***medication record****, and* ***discharge instruction sheets****.*

The ***admission record*** *is generated when the patient is admitted. The admission record may include* ***functional health patterns.*** *Functional health patterns are a method of organizing nursing assessment data. Functional health patterns include*

Admission record. A record created at the time a patient is admitted that is used by the billing department to track the patient and his or her services while in the hospital.

Countersign. To require a doctor sign a document verifying a verbal order given earlier by telephone.

Discharge instruction sheet. A document started at the time the patient is admitted, and finished at discharge. The discharge instruction sheet lists the teaching and discharge planning that took place during the patient's hospital stay. The discharge documents summarizes the patient's condition at the time of discharge, and lists instructions for care after discharge.

Flow sheets. Reports designed to allow patient information to be presented in graphical format. Flow sheets are a part of the patient's medical record.

Functional health pattern. A medical assessment that provides the basis or framework for collecting data about a patient. This information is used to assess the patient's health.

Medication record. A record of medications given to the patient.

Medical record. A record created on admission that records the treatment provided during the patient's hospital stay.

Nursing care plan or **nursing management plan.** A plan created when the patient is admitted detailing the nursing plan for treating the patient.

Change of shift report. A report given by nurses on the status of each admitted patient..

Intravenous. Literally, "through the vein."

Intravenous flow sheet (or intravenous flow chart). A flow sheet is found in the medical record that documents intravenous fluids administered to the patient.

PRN. Latin acronym for pro re nata meaning 'as needed or desired.'

entries on 11 areas of assessment, including: nutrition, exercise, sleep, self-perception, coping, stress tolerance, patient values, and beliefs.

***Nursing care plans** (also called nursing management plans) are also generated at the time a patient is admitted and are revised as the patient's condition changes. They contain:*

- *Nursing diagnoses*
- *Goals*
- *Outcome criteria*
- *Nursing interventions*
- *Evaluations*

*The Kardex is a portable file containing flip cards. Its purpose is to provide continuity of care from one shift to another. It is often used for the **change of shift report**. Data includes:*

- *The patient's name, age, occupation, doctor, date of admission, diagnosis, surgery, and emergency contact*
- *Basic dietary, activity, and hygiene needs*
- *Allergies*
- *Diagnostic tests*
- *Respiratory therapy treatments*
- ***Intravenous** therapy*
- *Daily nursing procedures, including dressing changes, and vital signs*
- *Medications*

The Kardex is used only for planning. Nursing care and the progress of the patient must still be documented in the progress notes and proper flow sheets.

Flow sheets document routine nursing procedures. They are designed to free the nurse from writing procedures that are done repeatedly. For example, vital signs including pulse, respiration, blood pressure, and temperature are shown graphically on a flow sheet. Other data documented on flow sheets include fluid intake and outtake, dressing changes, meals taken, and breath sounds.

*The medication record and **intravenous flow sheets** record the administration of medications. Medications are classified as routine or **prn** (medications given as needed).*

Durable power of attorney. A document appointing a legal guardian to make decisions in the event the patient is mentally incapacitated and unable to make medical decisions for himself/herself.

Living will. A document that gives specific instructions on the types of treatments that may or may not be used to prolong the life of an individual who is brain dead, or has a terminal illness.

The discharge instruction sheet is started at the time the patient is admitted to the hospital, and is completed at discharge. It includes notes on patient instruction and discharge planning. The discharge instruction sheet documents the patient's condition at the time of discharge, and gives instructions for post-discharge care.

Terminal patients

Legal issues surrounding the care of terminal patients have been complicated by new technologies that make it difficult to define the point of death. In 1981, the Presidents Commission for the Study of Ethical Problems in Medicine and Biomedical and Behavioral Research defined death as follows:

> *Death is present when a person has sustained either: (1) irreversible cessation of circulatory and respiratory functions, or (2) irreversible cessation of all functions of the entire brain, including the brain stem.*

Advance directives can simplify frustrations in dealing with people who no longer have the mental capacity to direct their treatment. Individual states have passed legislation that allows patients to specify whether they will accept or refuse certain medical treatments. These directives include:

- *The **living will**, which gives specific directives on the types of extraordinary procedures and treatments that may or may not be used to sustain or prolong life.*
- *The **durable power of attorney**, which appoints a legal guardian to make decisions in the event the patient is mentally incapacitated and unable to make such decisions. The durable power of attorney provides flexibility the living will does not.*

Treatment of Patients with Acquired Immune Deficiency Syndrome

Healthcare workers should be aware of current legislation about patients with Acquired Immune Deficiency Syndrome (AIDS). Legislation addresses discrimination in treatment, in-hospital transmission of disease, breach of confidentiality, and testing for the disease without an informed consent.

Risk Management

To lessen the incidence of negligence and possible malpractice, most hospitals have risk management departments. The goal of these departments is to identify potential risks to patients, employees, and visitors, and to take proper action to lessen these risks.

Risk management departments focus on the environment, products, and people.

Ergonomics. The science of designing the workplace to minimize worker injury.

The Environment

Hospitals can be dangerous places. Federal and state laws specify construction standards. ***Ergonomics****, the science of designing the workplace to minimize injury, can help with this design process.*

Hospital infections are a major source of illness for patients and employees. Infection control procedures, discussed in more detail in the chapter on quality assurance and safety procedures, are an important part of a risk management program.

Products

Risk management is responsible for ensuring all products used in the hospital are safe. Electrical equipment must be periodically inspected and certified by electronic technicians. Measures must be set up to ensure the correct drugs are given to patients in the right dosage.

People

People are the key to an effective risk management program. Employees must be trained to identify risks and take the proper action to reduce them. Employees must be familiar with federal and state rules and regulations and with hospital policy and procedure. When incidents occur, they must be reported and proper authorities must be notified.

As mentioned earlier, one method for reporting incidents is the incident report. The types of incidents reported include: falls, medication errors, complications from treatments provided by doctors or hospital employees, patient refusals of treatment, and patient complaints. Historically, some employees have been reluctant to report incidents, fearing reprisal. It is the duty of the hospital to stress that these reports will be used to prevent future accidents, and that in no situation will they be used for disciplinary action.

Discussion Three–Cost versus Quality

Most hospital administrators are caught in the crossfire between interest groups that have different goals and perspectives. The hospital's board of trustees wants lower costs. Many trustees would like to see hospitals run like businesses. Some doctors want the hospital to provide as many services as possible, even if those services are not cost-efficient. Nurses want higher quality, which they often equate with higher staffing. Families want loved ones cured regardless of cost, but then complain to trustees about high healthcare costs when they receive the bill.

No one wants hospitals to sacrifice quality for cost control, especially when the life of a patient is at risk. In any organization, however, money is limited. Hospitals that go bankrupt can no longer provide care. Continuing dialogue between healthcare professionals and the administrators charged with running their organizations with limited funds is essential.

Discussion Four–Everyday Ethical Issues

Not every situation a healthcare worker encounters is black-and-white. Code Blue purposely presents situations where good people sometimes do bad things, and vice versa. It also presents situations where there may be no clear-cut answer. The goal is to create classroom discussion that will help the student clarify his or her values. Healthcare is a value-laden profession.

Discussion Questions

1. *Dr. Matt Brannan has made a mistake in the diagnosis of a young child. What duty does he have towards the child's family, the hospital, the medical staff, and himself?*
2. *Reviewing the work of other doctors is a difficult, often emotional, task for many doctors. For many years, many doctors were unwilling to "blow the whistle" on substandard medical practice of peer doctors. Doctors justifiably feel some loyalty towards their profession and towards the other professionals with whom they must work daily. Doctors, however, also have a duty towards their patients. To whom does a healthcare worker have primary responsibility?*
3. *Some healthcare workers feel torn between the principles of honesty and loyalty. Studies have shown that some organizations prefer loyalty to honesty in selecting employees. Under what circumstances should you be loyal to an employer or a coworker? In what situations is honesty more important than loyalty?*
4. *What is the difference between negligence and malpractice?*
5. *Who is responsible for risk management in the hospital?*
6. *Hap Castleton was obviously a compassionate employer. Taking the son of a convicted robber under his wing when serving as a scoutmaster is an example. Perhaps more controversial, at least with Edward Wycoff, however, was his decision to rent a piece of property owned by the hospital to a disadvantaged employee at less than fair market value. List arguments for and against Hap Castleton's actions. Do you think he was justified? Is there a way he might have accomplished the same goal without raising questions by the board? Remember, how you do something is often as important as what you do.*
7. *Helen Castleton obviously doesn't have a good opinion of accountants. She feels they value profits above compassion and quality. (a) What can administrators and accountants do to correct the negative image they often have with allied healthcare workers? (b) How much should allied healthcare workers try to understand the financial constraints under which their*

administrators operate? (c) Is there any place for financial control in a healthcare organization?

8. *Describe a situation where a good person might do a bad thing for a good cause. Do you think "the end justifies the means?"*
9. *What is the goal and focus of a risk management department?*
10. *List five sources of law in the United States.*
11. *The person who starts a complaint against another in a court of law is the _______________. The person against whom the complaint is sworn is the _________________.*
12. *Explain the difference between criminal cases and civil cases.*
13. *What standards will judges rely on in deciding if malpractice has occurred?*
14. *What criteria do courts use in deciding if battery has occurred?*
15. *What are the elements of informed consent?*
16. *Give two examples of abuse in a healthcare setting.*
17. *What is the difference between defamation, libel, and slander?*
18. *Professional competence is insured through credentialing. Credentialing is the process of validating competence. List three forms of credentialing and define each.*
19. *What are some good guidelines for a nurse taking a telephone order from a doctor?*
20. *What is the purpose of an incident report?*
21. *Explain the proper procedure for handling an error on a medical record.*
22. *What is a flow sheet, why is it used, and what are some examples of flow sheets?*
23. *Explain what a living will and durable power of attorney are, how they differ, and what their goals are.*

23

Ramer

Take two tablets twice a day—on an empty stomach," groused Ryan Ramer, chief pharmacist, as he handed a prescription to the last customer of the day. It was 6:30, and his feet ached. He'd have been out of this prison if it weren't for the babbling of 82 year-old Zola Wayment, a retired hospital employee who frequented the pharmacy with small complaints and stupid questions.

Zola held the bottle close to her face as she slowly read the label. Ramer drummed his fingers on the white Formica counter, his lips drawn tight with impatience. Satisfied the pharmacist filled the prescription correctly, Zola carefully placed the bottle in her purse, retrieved a $20 bill, and handed it to him.

Without a reply, he grabbed it, shoved the change across the counter, and slammed shut the metal security window that separated the pharmacy from the hall. Most evenings, the end of the shift would have been a time for rejoicing. He was never meant for the drudgery of shift work. Tonight, however, things were different. In nine hours, he would be meeting with Barry Zaugg, a two-bit drug runner for Sid Carnavali, the main distributor for the drug lab he set up two months ago. It wasn't Zaugg he worried about. He didn't have the IQ to lace his shoes. Zaugg's boss, however, was a different matter. Carnavali was a mad dog and was capable of murder.

A wave of apprehension swept over Ramer. He removed a handkerchief and wiped the beads of sweat from his brow. He had problems—big problems—and Carnavali could make them worse. As he started the nightly task of balancing the cash register, his stomach churned. He reflected on the course that brought him to this frightening juncture in his life.

Money was the problem—and always had been—since he'd married Betty. The daughter of a successful doctor, Betty was raised to expect a lifestyle that Ramer couldn't provide. She never let him forget it. At first, he made up the difference between his income and her spending by taking money from the till. It was a slick routine.

Mental dementia. Insanity or confusion.

Narcotics number. An identification number issued to doctors certified to write prescriptions for narcotics.

Over-the-counter medications. Medications that do not require a prescription for purchase by a patient.

Purchase order. A document prepared by a buyer authorizing a seller to deliver and bill the buyer for the goods listed.

Volume discount. A discount given by a seller to a buyer who purchases a large volume of goods.

Each evening after closing, he would destroy the master tape from the cash register, then ring again the day's transactions. The new total would always be $200 or so less than the day's actual revenue—money he would pocket before leaving for home. The hospital had sloppy financial controls, his need was great, and the opportunity was there.

Over a three-year period, Ramer embezzled about $180,000 from the hospital. He'd have gotten a lot more, but an accounting student from Weber State University serving an internship in the business office noticed that transaction numbers on the master tape didn't match those shown on customer receipts. Ramer fired the student, claiming he made a pass at a high school girl who worked part-time in the pharmacy.

Ramer quit re-ringing the register. When financial pressures reappeared, he started moonlighting evenings at a local nursing home, filling prescriptions for patients from the extended care center's in-house pharmacy. At Ramer's suggestion, the nursing home started buying its drugs through the hospital. Hap Castleton approved of the practice because it provided the volume needed for **volume discount**s for both organizations.

One evening, a fire destroyed the nursing home's kitchen and adjoining pharmacy. Ramer didn't know how it started, but he took advantage of it. Returning to the hospital that evening, he filled a predated nursing home order for $6,000 of narcotics, which he removed from the hospital and sold to a drug dealer named Carnavali. The drugs, which netted $18,000 on the street, he reported as having been delivered to the nursing home, before the fire.

It was a good trick, but it couldn't be reproduced. He couldn't go around burning down nursing homes. One of the residents of the nursing home, however, was a retired doctor in early stages of **mental dementia**. With funding from Carnavali, Ramer set up a bogus home health agency in Salt Lake City, using the doctor's **narcotics number** to write prescriptions, which he sold to Carnavali. The practice ended six months later when the doctor died of old age.

Financial pressure returned when Ramer's son, Ronnie, announced shortly after high school graduation that he wanted to attend the same private university that Betty attended. Ramer heard of a group of pharmacists in Sweden who were caught making street drugs from **over-the-counter medications**. With his knowledge as a pharmacist and with help from the *Pharmacopoeia*, Ramer was soon able to duplicate the Swedish process.

His brother-in-law, Hank Ulman, owned part interest in a small flight service that operated out of the Salt Lake Airport. Business was slow, so Ramer helped him get a job to supplement his income in hospital maintenance. The plan was to have Hank fly the drugs to Phoenix. Carnavali would handle the marketing.

One obstacle was the large quantities of over-the-counter medications that would have to be bought as raw materials for the process. Large **purchase orders** from local distributors tipped off the authorities in Sweden. Ramer solved the problem by buying the medications through the hospital and running them through the books of his home health agency. To avoid having to remove the bulky raw materials from the hospital for processing, Ramer set up a small lab in a room beneath the pharmacy storeroom. It was a sweet setup.

Ramer's business was threatened, however, when Roger Selman hired a new assistant named Del Cluff. Cluff, a former auditor, became suspicious. Curious why a home health agency would buy so many over-the-counter drugs, he requested copies of all purchase orders from the home health agency. Ramer could have handled the problem, but Carnavali panicked.

The evening before Cluff was scheduled to fly with Castleton to Idaho, Carnavali paid to silence Cluff by sabotaging the plane. Hap stored his plane in a hangar near Hank Ulman's flight service. Castleton was killed, but Cluff survived, though in a coma at University Hospital.

Shortly after the accident, Ulman broke into Cluff's office and stole his audit work papers. A permanent solution to the Cluff problem was yet to be reached.

The cash register balanced. Ramer removed the day's receipts, depositing them in a small safe in his office. Finished with the day's activities, he turned the lights off, locked the pharmacy, and headed for the employee parking lot. In nine hours he would be back—this time to meet with Zaugg.

"Get in here before somebody sees you," Ramer whispered as he pulled Barry Zaugg through the pharmacy door.

Zaugg swore. "It's three in the morning!" he protested, twisting free from Ramer's grip. "This place is abandoned." He rubbed his arm and then slugged Ramer in the same place. "And keep your wretched hands off me!"

Ramer winced. "Hospitals are never abandoned," he warned as he shut the door. "Follow me." Crossing the room, Ramer fished in his pocket for his keys and then unlocked a door to the adjacent storeroom. Zaugg followed him through the door. A naked light bulb on the ceiling lit the bile green walls. An abandoned desk, filthy with dust, stood next to a yellowed 1971 calendar. Empty cabinets covered a bordering wall.

"Used to be the administrator's office," Ramer said, kicking his way through the boxes that littered the black and red linoleum floor. "When the administrative wing was added in 1972, the pharmacy took it over as a storeroom. "Don't use it for much anymore," he continued, "but it makes a good cover for the lab. That's why I always keep it locked," he said, waving his key.

"I don't see no lab," Zaugg said.

Ramer stopped and rested his right hand on a wooden storage shelf. "Used to be a door here," he said. "When my brother-in-law started work here, I had him build this cabinet. "It swings out," he said, "but you have to unlock it of course."

Ramer scowled as he searched for the right key on his chain. "Here it is," he said, bending over and inserting the key into a lock on the underside of the bottom shelf. There was a metallic click. Ramer removed the key and the cabinet swung open, revealing a small stairwell.

"They kept the safe down here," he said, entering the stairwell. He flipped a light switch. "Don't think anybody knows about it anymore." Ramer continued down the stairs, Zaugg following close behind. "All the old employees have retired, and I don't let any of the new ones into the storeroom."

At the bottom of the stairs, Ramer turned on another light. "Hank Ulman works at the shop. Got hold of the original hospital blueprints, the ones the carpenters use for remodeling. He redrew the wall so the stairwell doesn't show. On the master blueprint, it looks like the pharmacy on the other side is three feet wider at this point than it actually is."

Zaugg followed him through the door, then stopped. Lighting a cigarette, he inhaled deeply, letting the acrid smoke trickle out of his nose as he surveyed the room. Roughly 15 feet square, its concrete walls were bare, damp, and sour. A single frayed electrical cord dangled from the ceiling like an executioner's noose, its mustard light giving Zaugg's face a cadaver-like appearance. In the center sat an old autopsy table from pathology, cluttered with beakers, bottles, and a Bunsen burner.

"This is it?" Zaugg asked, gesturing with his cigarette. "This is the meth lab?"

"It's all it takes," Ramer replied, his eyes glowing with pride. "Took me a couple of weeks to figure out how it's done, another month to figure out how to get the raw materials without arousing suspicion. I've run two test samples, and now I'm ready for production."

Zaugg nodded, his eyes darkening dangerously. "Good thing," he said. "It's been two months since Carnavali paid you. Thirty thousand bucks. The boys in Phoenix are getting anxious for their delivery."

"You've seen the lab." Ramer blinked defensively. "Tell them they'll get their first shipment a week from Friday. I leave Friday for Connecticut. I'll be gone three days—I'm visiting my boy in college." Ramer removed a picture of his son and proudly placed it on the table. "His name's Ronny. He wants to go to medical school."

Ramer wasn't sure why it was important to impress this thug. Maybe it was to let him know that he wasn't a common crook, like Carnavali. "When I return Monday night," he continued, "I go to work. Figure in four days I'll have the first shipment—it'll pay off Carnavali and then some."

A cold silence engulfed him as Zaugg nodded slowly. "Hope so," he said. Zaugg's cold gray eyes were the color of death as he crushed his cigarette out on the boy's picture. "Carnavali don't have no patience for deadbeats. No patience at all," he said.

Discussion One–Fraud

Fraud is a concern for most organizations. Studies on corporate fraud identify two common characteristics of people who have stolen from their companies: (a) a pressing financial need—often created by living beyond one's means, and (b) opportunity.

Corporations can do little about (a), they can, however, reduce the opportunity for employees to steal by imposing acceptable financial controls. The previous controller of Brannan Community Hospital failed to do this.

In many situations, employees rationalize theft from their employer, with arguments such as "my employer doesn't pay me enough" or "everyone else is doing it." Whatever the rationalization, employee theft is wrong. It raises healthcare costs and destroys the character of those who engage in it.

One form of employee theft, unique to healthcare institutions, is the theft of controlled substances (i.e. narcotics). Healthcare professionals work long hours under stressful conditions. Drug abuse often begins innocently in an attempt to stay awake or go to sleep after a stressful shift. Healthcare workers have one of the highest drug abuse rates of any industry.

Discussion Question

1. *Does Ryan Ramer have any of the characteristics of employees who steal from their employers listed in the discussion above? If you were the supervisor of Ryan Ramer, might any of his actions have alerted you to a possible problem?*

24

Waste and Fraud

Director of materials management. The person in the hospital, usually a department head, who has responsibility for the purchasing and distribution of materials in the hospital.

Open purchase order. An agreement with a vendor (a hardware store for example) that allows specific employees to purchase without a purchase order. A purchase order is a formalized document that authorizes the purchase of materials or services on credit. Open purchase orders are subject to abuse by employees who may buy items on the company account for their personal use.

Monday morning, Wes turned his attention to data from the Utah Healthcare Association that showed that Brannan Community Hospital had a higher-than-average cost of materials per-patient-day. For the next two days, he reviewed the materials function with Anne Leavitt, **director of materials management**. At their concluding meeting, he summarized the following problems:

- In an effort to get volume discounts, most of Utah's hospitals had come together to buy as a group. Brannan Community Hospital was not participating and was paying a higher price for supplies than other hospitals.
- The hospital had many **open purchase orders** that allowed anyone from the hospital to buy building materials on the hospital's account with nothing more than a signature. Wes heard rumors that employees were using these orders to buy building materials for their own homes.
- Some nursing stations were carrying excessive inventory, as the staff was fearful of running out of supplies on weekends when Central Supply was closed.

Having received little direction from Hap, Anne was receptive to the new administrator's suggestions. Together, they prepared a plan to address these problems. Wes presented the plan to Emma Chandler the following morning.

Emma agreed with Wes's ideas and suggested that while he was investigating the hospital's purchasing practices, that he look into the practices of the pharmacy as well.

She observed that Ryan Ramer's lifestyle exceeded his income, often a sign of embezzlement. The pharmacy did not have financial controls that would prevent this occurrence. One concern was that the chief pharmacist did not deposit receipts nightly. This led to a discussion of other questionable practices that Hap had never allowed Emma to address.

Gatekeeper physician. A doctor selected by an insurance company who must approve a request for a patient to see a specialist. The goal of gatekeeper doctors is to cut the use of expensive specialists. Gatekeeper physicians were used extensively in the early days of managed care but have lost favor among patients and insurance companies in recent years.

Pre-certification. A process where an insurance company certifies, before admission that they will pay for a specific treatment or procedure.

In May, for example, an audit showed the hospital's maintenance supervisor built a fence at his home with materials bought on a hospital purchase order. Reimbursement had never been made. Castleton was reluctant to fire the supervisor, as he had worked at the hospital for 25 years and was two weeks away from an honorable retirement.

Emma suspected the business office Manager had an ownership interest in the agency used by the hospital to collect bad debts. This was an obvious conflict of interest. The business office manager was the one responsible for deciding which accounts were given to the collection agency and was channeling new, easy to collect accounts to his own agency for which he was receiving a substantial collection fee.

At the conclusion of their meeting, Wes asked that Emma conduct internal audits on the pharmacy, on maintenance, and on the business office. Wes hoped that audit findings would be negative and firing dishonest employees would not be needed. If employee terminations were required, however, Wes planned to handle them as soon as possible. *Move quickly and take no hostages,* he decided.

Fridays were slow days for the Pink Shop. Since few surgeons liked doing rounds on weekends, fewer procedures were scheduled in the operating room which meant fewer visitors and fewer Pink Shop customers. Amy Castleton served as the secretary/treasurer of the women's volunteer organization. Fridays were a good time to work on the books. Today, Amy's goal was to reconcile the bank statements. For the third time in an hour, she picked up the August statement and then laid it back on the counter.

Her mind wouldn't focus. The problem was Matt Brannan. Somehow, Matt got word that Amy was still dating the new administrator, and he was livid.

"He's a CPA for heaven sake," Matt's tone was accusatory, as though Amy were somehow to blame for his vocation. "He is cut from the same mold as Edward Wycoff. Profits are all he worries about; patients are means to an end, they're nothing more than work-in-process."

From her own work in the Pink Shop, Amy understood how important it was to break even. Given the financial condition of the hospital, she appreciated the problems the hospital's losses were causing for Wes. How to solve these problems was a primary source of debate between the board and the medical staff.

Before his death, Hap told her the board favored a managed care approach. He explained, "Managed care seeks to control hospital costs through more efficient use of resources. Some of the ways it does this are peer-reviews**, pre-certification**, financial incentives to encourage doctors to use fewer services, and the use of **gatekeeper physician** to assure that patients use expensive specialists only when needed."

CAT scan. Abbreviation for computerized axial tomography. CAT scans perform the same function as x-rays, but with a different technology that results in a clearer image. CAT scans are expensive, and must often be pre-certified (pre-approved) by insurance companies.

Invasive procedures. A procedure that requires the insertion of an instrument or device into the body for diagnosis or treatment.

Physician panel. A group of doctors who contract with an insurance company to provide services at a reduced rate.

Managed care troubled Hap. Insurance company clerks, who did not have the medical background needed to question doctor decisions, performed utilization review. Daily, insurance companies challenged doctors with questions like *"Is this procedure essential?"* or *"Can you use a less expensive medication or procedure?"* or *"Is this an experimental procedure?"*

"Medicine has always been *experimental,"* Hap said. "That's why they call it the *practice of medicine.* To refuse to pay for a procedure that hasn't been tried in the past is to close the door on innovation and future research. There are diagnostic procedures that are less expensive than **CAT scans**, but these are **invasive**, more painful, and often more dangerous to the patient. Specialists *are* more expensive than general practitioners," Hap continued, "but that's because they know more. Since when do we want to *'dumb down'* medicine?"

As for incentive payment, Hap recognized the problems with traditional fee-for-service and cost reimbursement but was not convinced that forcing doctors to select treatment choices based on cost rather than quality was the right approach.

To illustrate the point, he showed Amy a note an internist received from an insurance company about a CAT scan he had ordered. *"Approve this, and it will be your last,"* a handwritten note on the letter said. In the same envelope, the doctor received a list of the insurance company's participating doctors, sorted by cost per patient per diagnosis. The doctor's name was on the top third of the list. *"We plan on reducing our physician panel. One of the criteria will be average cost per procedure. Expensive providers will be eliminated from participation in our* ***physician panels*** *unless they change practice patterns,"* a note attached to the list explained.

Amy's father was hesitant to embrace managed care—until insurance companies and doctors assured him that quality would not suffer. Wycoff believed that Hap's reticence brought the hospital to the brink of insolvency. The medical staff believed that Wycoff's approach would destroy the reason they built the hospital in the first place—to provide the highest quality of care to patients, *regardless of ability to pay.*

Matt was certain that Wes Douglas was changing into a young Edward Wycoff. He accused Wes of using Amy's father as the fall guy for the hospital's current financial condition. "He's slandering Hap Castleton," Matt said. "If not with words, then actions. His intent is clear; the worse Hap looks; the better Wes will appear when he *'saves' the hospital."* Matt drew the words out sarcastically.

"Wycoff and Wes have created a crisis in the minds of the board and the employees. It's nothing more than justification for a power grab."

Given Amy's feelings for Wes and her father, Matt's accusations were troubling.

That evening, Wes reflected on the events of the past seven weeks. His first priority was to get the hospital in the black. Otherwise, the bank would pull its line of credit, and the hospital would close. To end losses, he could lower cost or raise revenue. Since costs are easier to manipulate in the short run than revenue, he focused on reducing costs first.

Wes started by studying the reasons for the dramatic rise in costs the industry experienced. He visited with administrators and doctors at the University Hospital. He learned that a breakdown in market forces created disincentives for the proper use of healthcare resources. He also learned about *managed care*, an initiative to create incentives for doctors and administrators to control costs.

Having a better understanding of the industry, Wes then focused on specific cost irregularities at Brannan Community Hospital. He found that labor and material cost for each patient day were higher at Brannan Community Hospital than at most of its competitors.

Satisfied with the progress made, he decided the next logical step would be to explore the revenue side of his hospital's profit equation. Revenue is a function of volume and price. Wes decided to address the volume issue first. He heard that St. Matthews Hospital was successful in increasing its share of the market.

Wes called Pete Lister, the director of marketing at St. Matthews with the hope that he would be willing to share some insights on how he could raise revenue by increasing patient volume. He made an appointment for Friday.

Discussion Questions

1. *Briefly discuss the steps that Wes Douglas might take to cut direct materials costs in his hospital.*

2. *Wes Douglas' Acting Controller, Emma Chandler, has noticed that Ryan Ramer, Chief Pharmacist, has a lifestyle that exceeds his income. What red flag does this raise?*

3. *Emma Chandler is also concerned that the pharmacy is not making nightly deposits. What problem might this suggest?*

4. *Outside collection agencies usually are given accounts receivables the hospital has not been able to collect. If the collection agency is able to collect the receivable, they receive a large fee, sometimes as much as 50% of the amount collected. Why would it be a conflict of interest for the business manager (the person responsible for selecting what accounts are given to the collection agency) to have an ownership interest in that collection agency?*

5. *Wes has decided that if fraud is discovered and he has to fire employees, he will "move quickly and take no hostages." If there are unpleasant tasks a new administrator must handle, why might it be to his or her advantage to handle them quickly? What impact might dragging out firing employees have on the morale of other employees?*

6. *Why do some health insurance companies try to second-guess doctors by challenging the treatments and procedures they order? Why do many doctors balk at the practice?*

7. *What are the incentives for a doctor to remain on an insurance company's doctor panel? How do insurance companies use this as a leverage to control healthcare costs? Do you think this is ethical?*

25

The Revenue Equation

Tertiary care center. A healthcare center that provides the highest level of specialty care.

From deep inside the office, Wes listened to the gas turbine engines winding up on the Bell 230 helicopter. The pad was a short distance from the east entrance of St. Matthew's Hospital. As heat from the compression ignited a mixture of fuel and air in the twin combustion chambers, the sleeping engines angrily awoke, shaking the building until the floors vibrated and the windows rattled.

Across the room, close up against the window, Pete Lister watched the Life Flight helicopter take off. Facing east, it hovered six feet above the ground while the pilot visually scanned his instruments. Then, smooth as a Lazy Susan, the aircraft rotated 180 degrees west and lifted off into the icy morning sky.

"It's a marketing tool, you know," commented Pete Lister, director of marketing as he turned from the window. Lister retrieved a pipe from the windowsill and fished for a tobacco pouch in the side pocket of his tweed sport coat. "With two helicopters and three fixed-wing aircraft, one of which is a Cessna Jet, we drop from the sky capturing patients from all over the state. These are patients that might otherwise be transferred from rural areas to Timpanogos Regional Medical Center or to the Ensign Peak Regional Medical Center."

Lister opened the pouch, gently filled the pipe, and then tapped the tobacco down with his thumb. "We think our care's better, and the flights are medically needed. But they are marketing tools, still the same," he said, placing the pipe in the corner of his mouth.

A **tertiary care center**, St. Matthews's Hospital was not a competitor with Brannan Community Hospital. The marketing director was gracious enough to spend an hour to teach Wes the fundamentals of hospital marketing. Wes guessed Lister's age at 45. A closely cropped salt-and-pepper beard framed his square jaw. With his pipe and tweed coat, he looked more like a philosophy professor than the successful marketing director of a $250 million a year organization.

Bigger-is-better syndrome. The perception of some physicians and patients that larger hospitals provide better quality than smaller hospitals.

Inpatient revenue. Revenue generated by treating patients admitted to the hospital.

Occupational medicine. A branch of medicine concerned with the impact of work on health. It addresses workplace hazards, social forces impacting physical and mental health in the workplace, workplace injuries and so on. Synonym for industrial medicine.

Out-migration. The practice of patients in a rural area to bypass their rural hospital to get healthcare services at a larger city hospital.

Outpatient services. Services provided by hospital departments to patients not admitted to the hospital for an overnight stay.

Outpatient surgery. Surgery performed on patients who have not been admitted to the hospital for an overnight stay (or in some cases patients who stay overnight, but are in the hospital for less than twenty-four hours). Also called ambulatory surgery.

Skimming. The practice of providing only those healthcare services that generate a profit, leaving to others (usually community hospitals) the responsibility to provide services that generate a loss.

Lister lit his pipe. "It hasn't been long, you see, that hospitals have had to market their services. In the old days, under cost reimbursement, our doctors were able to create demand. Prospective payment stopped that.

Although I haven't studied your hospital's statistics, there are probably several reasons for the decline in patient days your hospital's having.

"In Utah, DRG reimbursement cut the average length of stay in hospitals from seven to three days. In addition, many rural and suburban hospitals experienced **out-migration** as patients sought hospital care in larger cities."

"Why?" Wes asked.

"Transportation systems made it easier for patients to travel greater distances to get hospital care. Also, there's the **'bigger-is-better' syndrome**."

Lister returned to his desk. "The third reason is that many large hospitals have become more aggressive in marketing to rural areas. Since prospective payment systems have capped prices and cut patient days, the only way to raise volume is by capturing patients from other hospitals."

Wes was puzzled. "How do Salt Lake hospitals market to patients in Park City?" he asked.

"One way is by selling managed care programs to employers in your community that mandates employees only use Salt Lake hospitals," Lister replied. "If your hospital lost the Mountainlands contract, a significant number of patients would have been channeled by employers to other hospitals."

Lister's comments were consistent with Wes's observations. On his drive that morning to Salt Lake City, he saw several highway signs advertising HMOs sponsored by metropolitan hospitals. Most were directed to employers. HMO contracts were being sold to employers based on their cost savings. Wes realized they were also an effective hospital marketing tool.

"Then what's the solution to our declining inpatient volume?" he asked.

"There are several possible solutions," Lister said. He retrieved a marketing report from his desk drawer. "The first is to recognize that hospital patient days represent a smaller and smaller part of healthcare cost in the current environment. Notice the decline in **inpatient revenue** as a percent of total revenue," he said, handing the report to Wes. "If Brannan Community Hospital is to survive, it must supplement its inpatient revenue with other services."

Wes took notes attentively. "What types of services?"

"**Outpatient services** like laboratory and **outpatient surgery**, **occupational medicine** products, and durable medical equipment. For years doctors have been **skimming**—building their own outpatient surgical centers to perform high profit, low-risk procedures, while leaving the high-cost, high-risk, low profit procedures to the hospital. Hospitals have to take some of that business back."

"Give me an example," Wes said.

Alternative medicine. Medical theories or practices that are not accepted as being effective by most medical doctors. Some alternative medicine techniques have medical value but are not generally accepted because they have not been subjected to scientific studies that have shown them to be effective.

Diagnostic services. Tests and procedures performed to diagnose an illness.

LASIK surgery. Surgery in which a laser is used in place of a scalpel to correct vision.

Overhead. Hospital costs can be grouped into two general categories. Direct costs and indirect costs. Direct costs are those that can be easily traced to the patient. The cost of an injection or the nursing hours spent giving a bed bath are examples of direct costs. Indirect costs are costs that are essential to the operation of the hospital, but cannot be easily traced to a specific patient (payroll, human resources, and equipment maintenance are examples of indirect costs). Indirect costs within a specific department (the copy machine in the laboratory or the laboratory supervisor) are often referred to as overhead costs or department overhead. Patient bills must cover direct and indirect costs.

Self-pay patient. A patient who pays the cost of his or her own healthcare without the aid of an insurance company.

"**LASIK surgery**," Lister replied. "Some hospitals are selling vitamins, or offering limited forms of **alternative medicine**," Lister continued. "That might be a new revenue source for your hospital."

"What types of alternative medicine?" Wes asked.

"Meditation, Yoga, acupuncture."

"Aren't there liabilities to offering alternative therapies?"

"Yes, but in some situations, no more than for traditional treatments. You have to be selective," Lister said. "I'm not proposing crystal therapy, but research has shown that some forms of alternative medicine have therapeutic value."

Lister continued. "As insurance companies place more controls on the procedures they're willing to pay for, many hospitals have begun to market services to **self-pay patients**. There are shops in malls where a person can get a laboratory work-up without a doctor's order. The stores don't diagnose, and they encourage the patient to review the results with his or her doctor. Some provide **diagnostic services** that insurance companies won't pay for—procedures that are more expensive, but less invasive than those offered by the hospital."

"Doesn't this alienate hospital medical staffs?" Wes asked.

"Yeah, but they're already alienated. Let's face it, many of your doctors are draining off your high revenue procedures." Lister looked directly at Wes. "How many of your doctors run their own labs, x-ray machines, or outpatient surgery units?"

"I don't know."

"Check it out," Lister said. "To show how innovative some providers are in marketing to the self-pay market, there are group practices that have cut out insurance companies altogether. For $4,000 a year, a patient can enroll in a plan that entitles him or her to immediate telephone access to a doctor, 24 hours a day. The clinic guarantees a patient can always see a doctor within 4 hours of his or her first phone call."

"What acceptance have these plans had with the public?" Wes asked.

"Within two weeks of offering the plans, many group practices have sold out. Clinics cut **overhead** by not having to maintain large insurance billing staffs. Paperwork is cut, and doctors work fewer hours and see more patients."

"Okay," Wes said, still taking notes. "What else can I do?"

"A second approach to raising patient volume might be to educate local employers who buy HMOs on the negative impact that sending patients to distant providers has on the local economy. As patients leave, so do their dollars. Studies show that for every dollar that leaves the community for hospital services, an added 60 cents is lost in retail revenue.

"A third approach might be to raise inpatient volume by capturing a larger share of the local market. To do that, you might consider starting your own hospital-sponsored HMO."

Discussion One—Cutting Losses

There are two ways that Wes Douglas can cut the losses that Brannan Community Hospital is experiencing. He can cut costs, or raise revenues. If he decides to raise revenues, he has two options: (a) raise prices, or (b) raise volume.

Before the introduction of prospective payment, most hospitals wishing to cut losses chose option (a). Under DRG reimbursement and capitation payment, hospitals are no longer free to raise prices at will, however. For that reason, most hospitals are paying more attention to activities that will raise patient volume.

If the number of patients in a service area is fixed, the only way that a hospital can raise patient volume is by capturing market share from other hospitals. This chapter explored some marketing tools that focus on that goal.

Discussion Questions

1. *How can a hospital-sponsored HMO raise market share?*

2. *A decrease in the average length of stay for hospital patients has resulted in fewer hospital days and less inpatient revenue for the hospital. How has this influenced the provision of outpatient services by community hospitals?*

3. *Why have some doctors decided to offer their services only to patients who are able and willing to pay for their own healthcare services (i.e. self-pay patients)?*

26

The FAA Report

Employee productivity bonus pool. Money that can be distributed to employees based on increased productivity.

Flexible budget. A budget that changes with changes in volume.

Standard cost. What a procedure or service 'should cost' versus what it actually cost. A similar but not identical concept to budgeted cost. In the context of compensations studies, what the labor cost for a specific service should be.

On Monday Dr. Paige Adams was back to present the results of the compensation study. Both Wes and Emma were pleased with a method that allowed them to calculate **standard cost** for procedures. They called a meeting for department supervisors. The goal was to use these standards to develop **flexible budgets**.

Supervisors at first worried the standards would be used punitively. Enthusiasm for the program rose when Wes announced that he would share 50% of the expected savings from tighter standards with employees through an **employee productivity bonus pool**.

It was early afternoon when Wes returned from his meeting with his department heads. Two men were waiting outside his office. The larger one spoke first.

"I'm Officer Kuxhausen," he said, producing FBI identification. "Mr. Smith is with the Federal Aviation Administration. We'd like to visit with you privately."

Wes nodded, and they followed him into his office where he shut the door. "You're investigating Hap's accident?" Wes asked when all were seated. "Any clue about the cause?"

Kuxhausen nodded at Smith, who produced a large manila envelope.

"We have evidence that someone tampered with the plane," Smith replied. Opening the envelope, he laid two photographs on the desk taken by the FAA of the wreckage. Wes studied them, surprised that Del Cluff could have survived the accident. The impact broke the back of the aircraft. The fire that followed reduced the fuselage to a charred skeleton.

Smith removed a pointer from his shirt pocket. "This is a picture of the right engine, taken the morning after the accident," he said, leaning over the photograph. "The cowling surrounding the engine has been removed to expose the fuel pump. The nozzle connects to the fuel hose. Note the small hole—the probable cause of the fire.

"Notice the sticky residue here," Smith continued, pointing to the fuel line. "Kuxhausen was the first to notice it—the lab tells us it's a petroleum-based electrical tape that originally covered the hole."

Wes looked up. "A fuel line repaired with electrical tape?" he asked skeptically.

"No—sabotaged. The boys at the FAA lab tell us the hole was sanded with a three-sided file. Fuel pressure in a Cessna 340 comes through the line at 35 pounds per square inch," Kuxhausen injected. "Whoever made the hole covered it, knowing the aviation fuel would soften the tape, breaking the seal and allowing the fuel to escape. From the burn marks, you can see the fuel ran back along the hose until it contacted the hot magneto." He outlined the path with a ballpoint pen.

A menacing smile cracked Kuxhausen's face. "Clever way to bring a plane down, don't you think?"

"Not with you guys around," said Wes. "Any idea who did it?"

"Nope. That's why we're here. Are you aware of anyone who had it in for Hap Castleton?"

Wes frowned. "Everyone in the public eye makes enemies. It's no secret the hospital's got problems—big problems. Vendors haven't been paid, employees may lose their jobs, but no particular suspect comes to mind. You're welcome to interview the employees and staff."

"We will," Kuxhausen said. Removing a business card from his wallet, he slapped it on Wes's desk. "Meanwhile, if you think of anything else, give us a call."

Outside the hospital, Smith and Kuxhausen visited briefly in the parking lot before going their separate ways. "Do you think he's a suspect?" Smith asked.

Kuxhausen picked at the remnants of a steak sandwich between his teeth with a plastic toothpick. "He seemed stressed," he said. "But, what would he have to gain? Anyone who'd aspire to Hap Castleton's job isn't smart enough to sabotage an airplane."

Following Kuxhausen's visit, stories about Hap's death swept through the hospital like wildfire. Motives rumored behind the murder ranged from a crime syndicate interested in the hospital's undeveloped property to efforts of the hospital board to cover up illegal contracts they had taken to provide services at inflated prices to the hospital. One story even postulated an affair between Del Cluff and the wife of a jealous doctor. Wes had trouble seeing Del Cluff in the role of paramour, but as with all rumors, logic was irrelevant.

Wes had no idea why anyone would harm either Hap or Cluff. He was aware of a growing hostility in the community in general—and the hospital in particular—toward the financial problems plaguing the hospital. The hospital had $90,000 in payables to local vendors who would not be paid in the event of a bankruptcy.

Loss of work by several hundred employees was a similar concern. Tempers flared as employees, doctors, and board members deflected blame for what all feared was an impending financial disaster.

Though Wes didn't fear for his personal safety, he had concluded that a hospital failure would have a severe negative effect on his career. He wasn't responsible for the bad decisions that brought the hospital to the brink of ruin, but in the community's eyes, he would share the blame—as the hospital's last hospital administrator.

The advisability of circulating his resume with former associates from Portland, Maine crossed his mind. Late that afternoon, he drove to the Castleton home to visit with Amy and Helen Castleton, where he discussed with Helen Castleton the possibility of Hap's murder. Helen had no idea who would want to harm her husband.

Discussion Questions

1. *Assume that Brannan Community Hospital has 100 beds and, during the year, operates at a 70% occupancy. If there are 365 days in a year, how many patient days will Brannan Community Hospital generate in a year?*

2. *If the hospital uses, on the average, 4.0 hours of registered nurse time per-patient-day, how many hours of registered nurse time will it pay for in a year?*

3. *Assume that registered nurses earn $25 an hour. What will the annual cost of registered nurses be?*

4. *Now assume that Wes Douglas is able to negotiate a new standard of 3.8 registered nurse hours per-patient-day. What will the annual savings to the hospital be?*

5. *Assume that Wes Douglas agrees to share half the savings with the registered nurses as a year-end bonus. If the hospital has 100 registered nurses, what will be the year-end bonus for each nurse?*

27

An Audit of the Pharmacy

Methamphetamine. A psycho stimulant (drug with mood elevating properties) that exerts greater stimulating effects on the central nervous system than does amphetamine. Methamphetamines are widely used by drug abusers.

Percodan. A narcotic pain killer.

Pharmaceutical. Relating to the pharmacy.

Sudafed. An over-the-counter medication commonly used for patients with symptoms of hay fever.

With the exception of the running shoes and trophy rainbow trout, the administrator's office looked much the way it did when Hap died. Wes didn't care for the décor. It was overdone and out of date. If the hospital survived and the board offered Wes the permanent position of administrator, the velvet drapes and French Provincial furniture would go. For the present, however, there was little reason to change the décor.

Still, it would be nice to have a desk that worked, Wes thought as he struggled once more to open the top drawer, jammed for the second time in as many days. Grasping the handle, he jiggled it firmly to no avail and then hit it forcefully with the palm of his hand. Still, it didn't budge. Something was caught in the runner.

Pushing back the heavy executive chair, he retrieved a screwdriver from the bottom drawer, then climbed under the desk. From his position lying on his back, it took a moment for his eyes to adjust to the dark. The runners were covered by a 2' x 3' baseboard, securely attached to the side panels by four screws. Interestingly, an amateur carpenter had sawed an opening about the size of a legal envelope in the center. It was covered with a small door with two hinges and a small latch. *A hiding place?* Curious, Wes released the latch. A yellow envelope fell out, hitting him on the chin. Retrieving it, he crawled out from under the desk.

Sitting on the couch next to the door, he looked at the penciled label on the envelope. *"Ramer Investigation."* It looked like Hap's handwriting. Inside were several slips of paper. The first was a three-by-five card with the name of Randall Wynn Simmons penned on it. Beneath, also in Hap's handwriting, was the inscription, "Twelve **Percodan** prescriptions, January through March 1994."

There was a 1997 bill from the hospital to the Lycaon Home Health Agency for **pharmaceuticals**—16 cases of **Sudafed**. The order included four other items, which Wes recognized as over-the-counter drugs containing **methamphetamines**. A note showed that Ramer paid for these items personally.

Department of Business Regulation. A state agency, given the responsibility to license and regulate businesses within a specific state.

Invoice. A bill itemizing products or services provided.

Topical antibiotic. An antibiotic designed for application to an external wound.

Ziac. A medication commonly prescribed for high blood pressure.

The last items in the envelope were two receipts from the hospital, both dated February 27, 1993. The first was for a **topical antibiotic** for $7. The second receipt was for a prescription for a drug called **Ziac** for $12.52. A canceled check to the pharmacy from the account of Hap Castleton for $19.52 was stapled to the back of the second receipt. Wes studied the documents for a few minutes and then picked up his phone and called medical records.

"Hi, Shannon, Wes here. Have we ever had a doctor on the staff named Randall Simmons? … Never heard of him, huh? How about a patient? The full name is Randall Wynn Simmons . . . Yeah . . . check the files and give me a call. Thanks." Wes hung up and returned his attention to the documents. In a few minutes the phone rang.

"Hi, Shannon. No one by that name ever admitted here? At least as far as the records go back, huh? And how long is that? Okay, thanks anyway."

There was a knock at the door and Emma Chandler entered. "Come in," Wes said, "I was just going to call you." Emma crossed the room and sat down. "Ever heard of the Lycaon Home Health Agency?" Wes asked.

Emma shrugged. "I've sent them **invoices**," she replied. "We serve as the pharmacy for five nursing homes and three home health agencies—they're one of them. They have a post office box in Salt Lake City."

"Why do we sell them pharmaceuticals?"

"Hap approved it four years ago. It raises our purchasing volume—we share the volume discounts."

"Who owns Lycaon?" Wes asked.

"Don't know," Emma replied. "We just invoice them for the drugs they order, they pay their bills. We have an open purchase order from them in the file someplace."

"Why don't you pull it," Wes suggested. "I would like to see who signed it. I'd also like you to do some research on this home health agency to find out who owns them. Call the **Department of Business Regulation**," Wes said as an afterthought. "And while you're playing the role of detective, see if you can find out anything about a fellow named Randall Wynn Simmons. He may have filled an outpatient prescription at the hospital sometime in 1994. Check these prescription numbers." Wes handed Emma the card.

Emma's blue eyes reflected her curiosity. "What's this all about?"

"I'm not sure, but it may have some bearing on Hap's death. See what you can find out, but keep it low key, okay?" Wes cautioned.

That afternoon, Emma pulled the open purchase order from Lycaon Home Care. A Nancy Baum signed it. She listed herself as the purchasing agent. The name didn't ring a bell, and she couldn't find her in the Park City or Salt Lake City phone books. She called the administrative offices of the Social Security Administration and found Lycaon wasn't Medicare certified. *Strange,* she

Alzheimer's. A disease that causes the progressive loss of perception, judgment, and awareness.

Articles of incorporation. A legal document filed with the state when an organization is formed.

Blue Cross. The first health insurance company in the United States.

Business license. A license issued by a city or state allowing a business to operate.

ID. Acronym for identification.

Social Security Death Index. A database available over the internet listing persons with social security benefits who have died. The database lists the person's name, social security number, date of death, and the place the benefit check was mailed.

thought, *Medicare is the largest payer of home healthcare costs in the state of Utah. How do they stay in business?*

With a visit the following day to the Department of Business Regulation, she got a copy of Lycaon's **business license** and **articles of incorporation**. To her surprise, the owners were listed as Ryan Ramer and Hank Ulman, both employees of the hospital. Late that afternoon, she reported back to Wes.

"As far as I can discover from talking to the offices of Medicare, Medicaid, **Blue Cross**, and several other large insurance carriers," Emma said, "Lycaon has never billed a third-party payer for a visit. Yet they've run a good volume of drugs through the pharmacy over the past two years."

"Were we paid?"

"To the penny."

"Why would Ramer and Ulman own a home health agency?" Wes asked. "It's outside their expertise."

"Beats me! Neither has said anything to me about it." Emma said.

"What about Randall Simmons?" Wes asked.

"Almost forgot," Emma replied. "That's an interesting story in itself. I couldn't find his name in the phone book. I started to wonder if he was still alive, so I checked out the **Social Security Death Index** on the Internet. He died in Fillmore, Utah, in 1997. I called Millard County and got a copy of his death certificate. He passed away in a nursing home."

"I checked the phone book for the nursing home, no listing. I called the Utah Nursing Home Association and found the place burned down in '97. I was able to place a call to the former administrator. He retired and lives in Greeley, Colorado, with his daughter. He recalled Randall Simmons; said he was a patient there for four years before his death. He told me Simmons was a retired doctor from Panguitch, Utah. Practiced from 1949 to about 1989.

"Decided to call the Bureau of Narcotics," Emma continued. "The numbers you gave me were for prescriptions signed by Dr. Simmons in 1996—class three narcotics for a patient named Darin Erickson. No one knows who Erickson is, but they were filled at a pharmacy in Salt Lake City. Simmons' license was lifted two months later because of these prescriptions."

"Why?" Wes asked.

Emma smiled cynically. "Dr. Simmons had **Alzheimer's**—he didn't have his mental faculties after 1994. I wondered if Erickson was still alive, so I ran his name through the Social Security Death Index. I found a fellow with that name who died in 1966. I checked with the Drivers' License Division and found that someone using his name and social security number obtained a driver's license in 1989. Apparently, this person got a copy of his birth certificate from the data on his tombstone and used it for identification."

Wes was silent while he digested the information. "A doctor with Alzheimer's, who writes narcotics prescriptions, for a dead man with a renewed driver's license. What do you make of it?"

"I think someone's forging prescriptions and filling them using fake **ID**," Emma replied.

Wes nodded. "Good work, Emma, keep snooping. Let me know what you find."

Discussion Question

1. *Why do you think the healthcare industry has such a high rate of substance abuse? What might a healthcare organization do to prevent employee drug theft and abuse?*

28

Facility Problems

State Fire Code. Rules and regulations, many of which deal with construction standards designed to cut death and injury in the event of a fire. Hospitals are bound by law to abide by the state fire code.

Wes Douglas laid his glasses on the blueprint, then rubbed his tired eyes. He was perplexed. For the past two hours, he and his chief engineer, John Conforti, met with Brett Patterson, Park City's Fire Chief, to determine if there was a way to bring the building in conformance with the State Fire Code.

Wednesday, Wes got a six-page letter from Patterson's boss, the state fire marshal, detailing the building's violations. The letter threatened to close the hospital unless a remedy was agreed upon. Wes immediately called Patterson to set up a meeting.

Patterson, who had done his best to cooperate, shook his head apologetically. "My own kids were born here; we come here for healthcare. We don't want to see the hospital shut down, but it's got to meet code, Wes."

Many violations were resolved, but two remained. Wes replaced his glasses and studied the blueprint. "This main section of the building dates to 1935," he said, tapping the document with his knuckles. "What I don't understand is why the issue's coming to a head right now."

"The **State Fire Code** was amended in 1995," Patterson replied. "Back then, we put the board on notice they would either have to update the hospital or we would close it. The board promised they'd build a new hospital. With that understanding, we gave them a variance. All that changed in September when the board announced it was canceling the project." Patterson arched his eyebrows and shrugged. "No replacement—no variance."

Wes took a deep breath, then released it slowly. He understood Patterson's argument; he just didn't have much money. "Okay," he said with a tone of finality. "I'll agree to replacing the sprinkler system. Hate to do it, as we plan to tear the whole structure down in a couple of years anyway, but you leave me no choice." Wes turned to Conforti. "How much will that cost us?"

"Fifty thousand bucks."

Wes swore softly. "What's left?" he said, returning his attention to the blueprint.

"The newborn nursery."

"I can't close the newborn nursery," Wes said. "We can't survive if we get out of the baby business. Besides, Castleton just spent $30,000 recruiting and outfitting a new obstetrician."

"If you keep it, you have to get a code-approved exit," said Conforti. "The current hallway's too narrow. It's three feet wide; the code calls for ten. It met code when the wing was built but doesn't now."

"I have an idea," said Patterson. He pointed to an area near the nursery. "You could create a new hall by removing the west and south walls of the pharmacy storeroom. That would give you a 12 foot hallway emptying direct into the lobby—just 13 feet from the main entrance."

Wes nodded as he studied the blueprint. "Might work," he said. He turned to Conforti. "Why didn't you think of that?"

First Floor Brannan Hospital

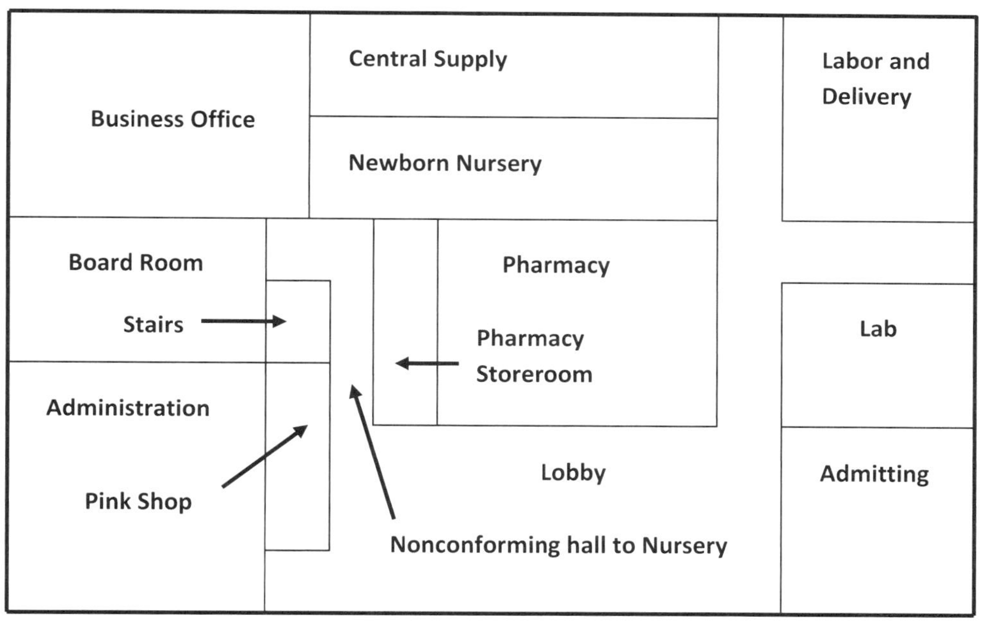

Conforti shrugged. "I don't know, but I like it. I'd rather lose a storeroom than a Nursery."

"There's one problem," Conforti continued. "Ryan Ramer's pretty possessive of the area. Two months ago, the director of volunteers tried to get it for the Pink Shop. Ramer lost his cool. Never seen anyone react that way; you'd have thought we were asking for the keys to the narcotics vault. Ask him again, and you'll probably get the same reaction."

“Then we won’t ask him,” Wes countered. “He’s gone for the weekend, and the fire marshal will be here Monday. Let’s get a crew in this afternoon. I’ll deal with Ramer later.”

Friday afternoon, Emma reported to Wes on the continuing investigation of Ryan Ramer. “He becomes more interesting by the day,” said Emma. “By policy, the pharmacy must deposit all funds received nightly. Ramer has always resisted—complaining he was too busy. I’m on the board of the hospital credit union; Ramer’s a member. In the past five years, he’s financed some expensive toys: a boat, a cabin, and a Lexus automobile. Usually, he pays the loans off early, making sometimes two or three extra payments a week. The dates always correlate with the dates on which he makes the pharmacy’s deposit.”

“What do you make of that?” asked Wes.

“I was puzzled by the pharmacy receipts you gave me from Hap’s envelope. I wondered why they were with the other documents. The prescriptions were for medications Hap was known to be taking. There was nothing unusual about them.”

“So?”

“So we pulled the cash register tape Ramer delivers with the pharmacy deposits. In theory, it is a copy of the receipts from the pharmacy sales for the day.”

“Why do you say ‘in theory?’” asked Wes.

“Because the dollar amounts for the transaction numbers found on Hap’s receipt for that same date are different. My theory is that after the pharmacy closed and the other employees went home, Ramer would re-ring the tape with fictitious transactions, under ringing the transactions by as much as $200 per day. He would then use that money to pay down his credit union loans. The cashier there said he always pays in cash.”

“You think Ramer was embezzling from the hospital?”

“Sure do, and there’s more. I got his Social Security number from his personnel file and used it to get a copy of his birth certificate. What was unusual was his mother’s maiden name—*Wycoff*. That’s not a common name, so I checked his pedigree with the Family History Library in Salt Lake City. His mom was the sister of your Finance Committee chair, Edward F. Wycoff.”

Wes raised his eyebrows. “Ramer is Wycoff’s nephew?” he asked. “I didn’t know that.”

“Neither does anyone else. It’s a well-kept secret. The question is why.”

“It would be interesting to find out,” replied Wes.

Saturday afternoon, the carpenters removed the pharmacy storeroom walls without incident, creating a hallway between the nursery and Pink Shop. The only surprise was a heavy bookshelf with a built-in cabinet attached to the east wall.

"Funny, it's not shown on the blueprints; must've been added later," said the carpenter. "Shall we tear it out?"

The supervisor studied it carefully, then shook his head. "It's not a bad-looking piece of furniture," he said. "Leave it. That new night security guard Wes hired after the burglary has been griping that he doesn't have a place for his stuff. We'll move a small desk there and it can serve as his workstation. Be sure to drill it, screw it to the wall securely. There'll be considerable traffic through this area. We don't want someone with a service cart knocking the darn thing over."

"What's up with him?" Paula Grable, pharmaceutical technician, asked as she opened the cash register. It was Monday morning, and as the pharmacy was about to open, Ryan Ramer blew through the door, screaming something about the remodeling project.

"Guess they hadn't told him. He takes a personal interest in any changes to the pharmacy," she said as she opened the retail window. "Frankly, I like the change. We never used the storeroom anyway. Now the nursery has a legitimate exit if there's a fire."

"Where'd he go?" asked the other pharmacist.

"He left as quickly as he came. Started off for administration," she said with a funny look in her eye. "Swearing a blue streak, he was. Then, strange . . . he stopped, about halfway down the hall . . . stood there a moment . . . white as a ghost. Looked frightened to death. Then he turned and, without saying a word, headed for the parking lot."

Discussion One—Safety in the Hospital

As the administrator of an aging hospital, Wes Douglas is responsible to take the steps needed to assure that patients, visitors, and employees are safe while in his hospital. He will be helped by a number of government agencies.

Occupational Safety and Health Administration (OSHA)

The Occupational Safety and Health Administration (OSHA) was created in 1970. Its mission is to prevent work-related injuries, illnesses, and deaths. It does this by issuing safety and health standards, conducting inspections and investigations, and issuing citations and imposing penalties. It has been credited with reducing occupational deaths since that time by 62%, and injuries by 42%.

Center for Disease Control and Prevention (CDC)

The Center for Disease Control and Prevention is a federal agency charged with protecting the health and safety of the American people. It serves as a source of credible information on disease prevention and control, environmental health, and health promotion and education.

The CDC plays an important role in identifying and controlling infectious diseases including HIV/AIDS and tuberculosis. In addition to identifying outbreaks, the agency uses "fingerprinting" technology to classify strains of the thousands of infectious diseases that impact populations around the world.

Clinical Laboratory Improvement Amendments (CLIA)

Congress passed the Clinical Laboratory Improvement Amendments in 1988 to set up quality standards for laboratory testing in the United States. The focus of the legislation was on accuracy, reliability, and timeliness of patient test results.

CLIA legislation defines a laboratory as a unit that performs laboratory testing on specimens taken from humans for diagnosis, prevention, or treatment of disease.

Discussion Two—The Hospital Fire Plan

Another important component of hospital safety is the fire plan. Usually, this is a written document that all employees must understand. Many hospital fire plans use the acronym RACE in training employees. RACE stands for: Rescue, Alarm, Contain, and Extinguish.

Discussion Three—The Hospital Disaster Plan

Hospitals are designed to handle patients who are admitted one at a time. What happens when a plane crashes or an earthquake occurs and the hospital is suddenly deluged with 150 patients? Who is treated first? How are the patients admitted? Who handles the flood of family members that may storm the hospital lobby demanding information about their loved ones? These are some of the issues that a hospital disaster plan addresses.

Communication is an important component of a disaster plan. Switchboards often use code language to communicate with employees. "Code Orange" when broadcast over the public address system may announce that the hospital disaster plan is being activated. "Code Red" announces a hospital fire, and "Code Blue" solicits help for a cardiac arrest at a specified location.

A hospital disaster plan may specify:

- *Line of authority*
- *Communication*
- *Triage*
- *Supplies and equipment*
- *Temporary morgue facilities*

Line of Authority

Often the following persons, in the order listed, will be in charge:

1. *Administrator*
2. *Director of nursing*
3. *Nursing supervisor*
4. *Emergency room supervisor*

Communication

The plan will specify where each of the following communications centers will be established, and who will be in charge:

Public Communications Center: A communications center for receiving outside calls and giving information to the press, radio, and relatives of injured patients will be set up in medical records.

Internal Communications Center: A center to coordinate and handle internal communications.

Emergency Room Radio Communication Center: The center that receives and sends messages to ambulances, police and fire vehicles, and governmental agencies.

Triage

Triage is the process of sorting people to determine who receives treatment first. The goal is "to do the most for the most." Triage is usually performed by a triage officer, who sorts patients, but does not give care. Patients are sorted into casualty categories, using tags that are numbered or colored.

DOA. *Abbreviation for "dead on arrival."*

An example of these categories is shown below:

Category	*Definition*	*Color*	*Treatment*	*Example*
1	*Life threatening*	*Red*	*Immediate*	*Severed artery*
2	*Urgent*	*Yellow*	*Urgent*	*Broken femur*
3	*Minor*	*White*	*Delayed*	*Twisted ankle*
4	*Dead*	*Black*		

Given limited medical personnel, category one would be treated first, followed by category two, and so on.

Supplies and Equipment

How bulk emergency supplies will be obtained internally and externally.

Temporary Morgue Facilities

This is where ***DOA****s (dead on arrival patients) will be taken. Decisions must be made as to whether personal belongings will be removed and how the Command Center will be notified for casualty list purposes.*

Discussion Questions

1 *Discuss the origin and goals of OSHA, the CDC, and CLIA. Why is it important for health workers to be aware of the regulations and procedures of these organizations?*

2. *Assume you are the new assistant director of maintenance at Brannan Community Hospital. At the prodding of the State Fire Marshall, Wes Douglas has decided that the hospital needs a fire plan and has appointed you as chairperson of the committee to prepare it. Using a search engine on the Internet, research "Hospital Fire Plans."*

   Using the research material you get from the Internet, write a one page memo to your committee outlining the goal of the committee. Include with the memo a brief topic outline of what the fire plan will contain.

3. *Why must typical policies for the admission and treatment of patients change when there is a major disaster that creates a large influx of patients? What special problems do you think this creates for: (a) admitting, (b) the emergency center, (c) the operating room, (d) administration, (e) the switchboard, and (f) the morgue?*

4. *Assume that you have been named triage officer for an accident involving the crash of a bus. Classify the following injuries into the four triage categories listed above:*

Injury	***Triage Category***
Patient has obstruction in airway, not breathing, but still alive	
Abrasions on face and hands	
Broken nose	
Massive head injuries, no respiration or heartbeat	
Massive bleeding from severed leg	
Broken ribs	

29

Ramer's Reversal

Amphetamine. A drug that stimulates the nervous system. Some amphetamines are abused by people seeking an unusual psychological experience.

"Why didn't you warn me?" Ramer screamed, his rage choking him. Ramer had just burst into Hank Ulman's office. His brother-in-law had never seen him angrier.

"Warn you 'bout what?" Hank asked as he took his feet off his desk.

"Warn me they were going to knock the walls of the pharmacy storeroom out."

"Didn't know they did," replied, surprised as Ramer. "Why would they do that?"

"Made it into a hallway," Ramer replied. "Connects the newborn nursery to the lobby."

"I never saw a work order," Hank said defensively. "It wasn't on the schedule board when I left Friday." His eyes widened as he thought about the hidden staircase, "Did they find the door to the lab?"

"I don't know—no, don't think so. The bookshelf is still there . . . but they bolted it to the wall. Worse still, they've put a desk with a phone and our security guard in front of it—now it's his workstation!"

A tense silence enveloped the room. "What are you going to do 'bout the delivery?" Hank asked. "You promised to ship Thursday. You can't renege again. Carnavali's capable of murder."

A nauseating wave of fear washed over Ramer—for a moment he couldn't breathe. "I don't know," he gasped. As his eyes darted about the room, he wiped the beads of perspiration forming on his forehead. "We don't have many options. We've got $55,000 worth of Sudafed down there. We can't get it out without tipping everyone off, and even if we had the money to replace it, it would take me a couple of months to do it without raising the suspicions of my drug reps. You don't order $55,000 of **amphetamines** without someone asking questions."

"We've got other problems here at home," Hank volunteered as Ramer evaluated his options.

"Like what?"

"An investigation Wes has started on the home health agency."

“What are you talking about?” Ramer asked. The tension in his abdomen tightened.

“I was installing a new phone line for a computer. In the business office, you know, on Friday. Heard Emma Chandler talking with Kayla Elmore,” Hank continued.

“Who’s Kayla Elmore?”

“High school student, volunteers in the business office. Anyway, Chandler’s askin’ her to pull all the home health agency purchase orders. She’s calling the State Division of Business Regulation in to do an audit of the agency’s prescriptions.”

“Why would he do that?” asked Ramer.

“Maybe they found Cluff’s work papers. Maybe they were in Hap’s desk. They sure as the devil weren’t in Cluff’s. I searched the place for 30 minutes the night I broke into the business office.” Hank shook his head. “You’ve got a problem, buddy.”

Ramer’s face hardened. “No, we’ve got a problem. If I go down, you go down.”

30

Paradigm Software

Holding company. An investment company organized to own stock in other companies.

Tuesday, Wes scheduled a meeting with David Brannan to discuss the foundation's pledge for funds to build a new hospital. From reading minutes of the Board of Trustees, Wes learned the Mike and Sara Brannan Foundation committed a gift of one million dollars for the new building. Originally, they were to pay it in four installments. The first installment was made in April of 1999, according to schedule. In June, David Brannan reported the foundation was having financial problems, and put the board on notice that more payments might not be forthcoming. Wes wondered why.

David Brannan arrived dutifully at 2:00 PM. It was clear to Wes that David was embarrassed by the family's default. As David took a chair in Wes's office, Birdie popped her head in to remind the administrator that he was two hours behind on his afternoon appointments. The waiting room was filled with hospital creditors, doctors, patients, and unhappy employees, all demanding immediate solutions to their problems.

Wes didn't waste time on small talk. "I met with the fire marshal," he said soberly. "The building doesn't meet code. We are making some changes, but in the long term, remodeling will cost more than replacement. Unless we can show progress on a new hospital, they plan to shut us down."

"With the hospital's current financial situation," Wes continued, "and without the foundation's endowment, we stand little chance of getting more financing. What are the odds the foundation will be able to help us with the remaining $750,000 on the pledge?"

"I wouldn't hold my breath," David said. "No doubt you have been told of the family's financial difficulties."

Wes nodded.

"There's less than a 50% likelihood the foundation can meet its commitment," David continued. "The foundation's assets consist of 10,000 shares of Brannan Inc., a **holding company**," he continued. "At its peak, it owned two coal mines, a major interest in Russell's bank, Park City's only

Industrial Espionage. The act of one company spying on a competitor to obtain trade secrets.

ICU. Acronym for Intensive Care Unit.

Venture capitalist. A person who provides the funds to start or expand a business.

newspaper, and Paradigm Systems, a software development house. All that's left is Paradigm. It's not yet profitable."

"But it does have value?" Wes asked.

David nodded. "It could. I have a potential buyer. He won't commit, however, until the company shows that it can turn a profit."

As a C.P.A. with Lytle, Morehouse, and Butler, Wes consulted with several high-tech firms in Maine and was familiar with the industry. Many fortunes were being earned in software development. Folding his hands he leaned forward. "Tell me more," he said.

"The company was formed in 1994 by a group of engineers and software programmers in Seattle, Washington. On their first contract they teamed with Tandem Computer and an electrical engineering firm to develop and install a hardware and software system for the Boeing Corporation.

"Boeing was concerned about the security of its aircraft plant in Renton. There was a lot of union unrest—concern about **industrial espionage**. Boeing contracted with Paradigm for a computerized security and environmental control system. The system was to provide security, access control, monitoring, and fire protection for their entire plant.

"Employees would be allowed to access only those areas for which they were authorized. A Tandem computer would control access through the central station. One of the requirements was that it have the ability to read and process 15,000 employee access control cards during the ten-minute period employees report to work each morning.

"It was an expensive project," David continued. "The hardware included a central command post, employee identification card readers, television cameras, monitors, and smoke and fire detectors—all in addition to the software code.

"Halfway through the project, Paradigm ran out of money. They underbid the contract. Father bought the company, thinking he could save it with an infusion of one million dollars. He was wrong; the software had a major design flaw. By the time the contract was finished, the overrun exceeded four million dollars. Unwilling to lose his first investment, Father came up with more money. The funds came from other companies owned by Brannan Industries. In retrospect, he wouldn't have bought Paradigm if he knew how much money it would take to finish the contract. He bled his other companies to get the cash."

"What's the status of the contract now?" Wes asked

"The project is finished, and there are new potential customers. Paradigm is negotiating with a large hospital chain to design and install a similar security system for its hospitals. This system would also include the monitoring equipment in the **ICU**s and nursery."

"What else is needed?" Wes asked.

"About $800,000 for development work. I have a **venture capitalist** who will fund us, but he is unwilling to put the money in until we can show our

Job order costing. A sophisticated accounting system that traces the costs of products.

Telemetry. The science of measuring something, sending the measurement by radio signal to a distant station, and then recording or interpreting the results. In a hospital, telemetry, for example, may be used to transmit heart monitor information from a patient to a central nursing station.

ability to control cost. If I can get the $800,000, we can modify the software and get the contract."

"Okay, so you have a computerized environmental control and security system."

"Right."

"And the software works."

"More or less. There are bugs, but I think they're few. The system's running in Texas and Washington," David explained.

"And you have customers, with money, willing to buy and modify the system, and a venture capitalist who will fund it," Wes asked.

"Right, and an investor that will buy the company if it turns a profit."

"What else do you need?" Wes asked.

"More sophisticated control systems—specifically **job order costing**."

"If I could help you put an acceptable system in place, how long would it take for you to finish the contract?" Wes asked.

"About three months," David replied.

"Then, you think you could sell the company for enough money to cover the foundation's commitment to the hospital?"

"Yes," David affirmed.

"I've developed costing systems for defense contractors," Wes said. "I don't have much time, but we can't survive without the prospect of a new hospital. I'll give you 40 hours of free consulting time. Let's see if we can get Paradigm Medical Systems in the black."

David's eyes lit up as he considered the possibility of a sale. "That would be great. Wes, I need one more favor," he said.

"Shoot."

"We are working on linking our computer with a telemetry unit that can broadcast a video signal at least seven miles to a central station. We need a place to test the **telemetry** component of the system in a reinforced concrete building. We'd like a room in the hospital."

"How large of a room do you need?"

"My engineers tell me we need a room with about 400 square feet. There has to be at least one floor above the test room, and it needs to be within 200 feet of other telemetry units like fetal heart monitors. We need to test for interference."

"How long do you need the room?"

"About a week."

"I'll give you the boardroom," Wes said. "Coordinate with Mary Anne."

"Ryan? . . . Ryan Ramer, isn't it?" A large man wearing a convention name tag stuck out his hand. Ryan Ramer's hand remained by his side. With more important issues on his mind, he was in no mood for petty conversation, especially from someone he didn't know.

"Do I know you?" Ramer asked. His lips puckered with annoyance.

"Peter Applebee. Don't you remember? The Elk's Home? Claremont, California? My wife and I are in Park City for a convention."

Ramer's eyes hardened. "Remember the school," he snorted. "Don't remember you." With that, he broke off and continued down Main Street. He didn't look back.

"My!" the conventioneer's wife asked "Who was that?"

"He was raised with me in the Elk's home—a real loner," her husband replied. "No one knew much about him. He started showing bizarre behavior in the sixth grade. Became obsessed with poisons and explosives, as I recall—started experimenting. They finally sent him to a lockdown institution when the headmaster's car blew up. We never heard what happened to him after that. The conventioneer shook his head. "He was a strange kid."

"Well!" his wife exclaimed, "it doesn't seem like he's changed much!"

31

First Management Reports

Actual costs. Costs incurred and reported in the financial records distinguished from budgeted costs which are projected costs.

Budgeted costs. Costs projected at the time a budget is prepared.

Standard costs. What procedures should cost as determined by a study.

Monday morning, Emma met with Wes to review the first reports of the new cost information system. From the start, Wes's goal was to empower the department heads by giving them the information they needed to make decisions. He believed that Hap often made decisions that should have been made on a department level.

The meeting was held in the boardroom, where Emma spread the reports on the table, then stepped to the whiteboard. "When we first met with the department heads last September," she said, "they told us they needed information for . . ."

Emma wrote on the board:

Information is needed for:

Pricing
Cost control
Strategic planning
Measurement of the efficiency of our hospital compared with other hospitals

"I think the system we have designed will meet the criteria. For pricing we can find standard costs per procedure, and compare it to the revenues we are getting. For cost control we can compare **actual costs** to **standard costs** or **budgeted costs**. For strategic planning we can see what procedures we earn money on, and which procedures we lose on, and for efficiency we can compare our standard costs to those of other hospitals.

"We can tell how much we earn or lose by DRG, insurance company, doctor, and so on under each of those reimbursement systems." She continued. Her mouth pulled into a frown. "Unfortunately, we're finding that revenue isn't even close to cost in some cases."

"I suspected as much," Wes interjected.

"Let's look at the reports," Emma said, "and I'll show you how they work." The first report shows us profitability by DRG. This report is for DRGs one through 7."

Brannan Community Hospital
Profit or Loss by DRG

DRG	# Cases	Actual Revenue Per Case	Actual Cost Per Case	Profit (Loss)
1	12	$3,240.00	$4,200.00	$ (960.00)
2	45	$1,270.00	$1,200.00	$ 70.00
3	15	$5,680.00	$6,130.00	$ (450.00)
4	67	$3,240.00	$3,100.00	$ 140.00
5	32	$1,200.00	$ 900.00	$ 300.00
6	45	$ 980.00	$1,020.00	$ (40.00)

Definition of Column Headings:

Column 1: The diagnosis related group (DRG).
Column 2: The cases in each group seen by the hospital for the period.
Column 3: The average actual payment received by the hospital for all patients in this DRG category (regardless of their insurer, or the reimbursement system used by their insurer). This is calculated by taking actual reimbursement received and dividing by the number of patients seen.
Column 4: The average cost to the hospital per case.
Column 5: The average actual profit or loss on all patients seen in this DRG category (the difference between Column 3 and Column 4).

"We earn the most money—$300 per case—on DRG 6. We lose the most money—$960 per case—on DRG 2. Strategically we should raise our volume of DRG 6 patients, and either phase out the procedure, or cut the costs of DRG 2."

"The next report," Emma continued, "is an analysis by insurance company for DRG 6—Circulatory Disorders. We'll use this report as we negotiate with insurance companies. Notice that 52% of our contractual adjustments come from Medicare Part A, on which we lose $100 per case on DRG 6. Our total revenue (number of cases x average charge) for Medicare was $38,400, while our total costs were $43,200."

"They're not exactly what you would call a profitable customer, are they?" Wes said.

"Nope."

Brannan Community Hospital
Average Profit or Loss by Insurance Company
DRG 6—Circulatory Disorders

Insurance Company	# Cases	Actual Revenue Per Case	Standard Cost Per Case	Profit (Loss) Per Case
Blue Cross	13	$1,320	$900	$420
Medicare Part A	48	800	900	($100)
Medicaid	4	750	900	($150)
Aetna	15	1100	900	$200
Western Health	6	1000	900	$100
United	2	1050	900	$150
Security Insurance	5	870	900	($30)

Definition of Column Headings:

Column 1: Name of insurance company.
Column 2: The total cases for the month for this insurance company.
Column 3: The average amount paid per case by the insurance company.
Column 4: The hospital's average standard cost (budgeted cost) per case.
Column 5: The profit or loss per case for this insurance company (revenue minus standard cost).

"The next report compares the average cost of each doctor, compared to standard cost, for DRG 6."

"Remind me once again what standard costs are," said Wes.

"It is what the procedure should cost."

"It's the budget?"

"Right."

Brannan Community Hospital
Physician Based Analysis
DRG 6

Doctor	# Cases	Standard Cost Per Case	Actual Cost Per Case	Variance
Brannan	5	$900	$1,850	($950)
Hemingway	2	$900	$700	$200
McDonald	8	$900	$890	$10
O'Reilly	12	$900	$1,100	($200)
Lee	1	$900	$1000	($100)
Chandler	9	$900	$500	$400
Avery	5	$900	$850	$50

Wes studied the report. "Why does Dr. Brannan have such a higher average cost than other doctors?" he asked. "He is $950 over budget per case."

"He has a different practice pattern. He uses more medications, more lab tests, and his patients stay in the hospital longer."

"How come?" Wes asked.

"We're not sure, but we think he has more complications. Whatever he is doing, his patients don't get well as fast as those of other doctors."

"That's interesting," Wes said. "I never thought we could pick out substandard practice through accounting data." He was quiet for a moment as he studied the report. "Let's give this data to the Morbidity and Mortality Committee," he continued. "It looks like Dr. Brannan could benefit from a little peer-review."

Thursday afternoon, Emma took the data to the University Medical Center where it was reviewed and confirmed. Friday morning, Wes met with Dr. Emil Flagg, Chairperson of the Morbidity and Mortality Committee, to discuss his concerns.

"The quality of Dr. Brannan's care has been a concern since he joined the medical staff," Emil admitted soberly as he reviewed the reports. "I'm not surprised at the data. He has more than his share of complications."

"After reviewing his training, I'm no longer convinced that he's qualified for family practice. As I look at his file, he applied for and got privileges in obstetrics and surgery for which he is marginally qualified. Dr. Brannan finished an internship, but never a residency. He's not board certified in family practice, obstetrics or surgery."

"How did that happen?"

"A rural hospital with a poor history of peer-review, a father who has funded its shortfalls for the past 20 years. It was politics," replied Emil. "Hap should have been more aggressive when Brannan applied for membership on the medical staff, but I think he had his hands full with problems created by managed care, and didn't want to risk his relationship with the Brannans."

"Who grants medical staff privileges?" asked Wes. "The administrator, the medical staff, or the board?"

"The medical staff, through the Credentials Committee, recommends. The final power lies with the board, however."

"After he joined the staff, Brannan ran into complications with several patients. The nursing staff is on record of having complained about him on at least two occasions. Where was the medical staff when this was happening?" Wes asked.

"Brannan's partner visited with Hap off the record, but was unwilling to criticize him openly as he had to practice with him. The doctors in the clinic across town also expressed concern, but felt since Brannan was a new competitor, they might be accused of having ulterior motives. Historically, doctors have been reluctant to criticize their peers. It's a brotherhood; there is a tendency to stick together."

"Hap was burned several years ago," Emil continued, "when he took disciplinary action against a radiologist. Everyone on the medical staff complained privately about him. When the administrator took formal action, however, it became '*them against us*.' The staff rallied behind the radiologist."

Wes removed his glasses and stared out the window as he collected his thoughts. "Okay, so what do we do?" he asked.

"Dr. Brannan will meet before the Morbidity and Mortality Committee next week. It will be his second time before that group in less than a year." Flagg was silent as he counted his power chips. The Brannans were no longer funding the hospital. Several members of the medical staff owed him favors. It was time to call in the political IOUs he held.

"With a new administrator," Flagg said, almost as though he were talking to himself, "and a renewed resolve by the board to fix the hospital, this well may be the time for me to push for a resolution." He turned to Wes. "It's not that I've been a laggard, it's just the problem has political ramifications, and the environment wasn't favorable."

"If there's a fight among the medical staff, it won't be pretty," Emil continued. "And you'll be right in the middle, taking sword blows from all sides." He looked Wes straight in the eyes. "When there are problems, the hospital administrator makes a good fall guy. The community can't fire the board, and they don't want to fire the medical staff, and so . . ."

"I get your point," Wes said. "No need to finish the sentence."

"Let's be candid, Wes. When the board went after you they wanted a hired gun. Taking the actions needed to save this place will create enemies. The board would be crazy to stand behind someone as unpopular as you're going to be in certain circles. You're too new to have many allies. Once the dirty work's done, you're expendable."

Wes was quiet while he absorbed the message. "Wish I'd have known this when they offered me the job," Wes said. "I guess I could have figured it out if I'd thought it through."

"Welcome to Politics 101," Emil said. "So, what do you want to do?"

"Let's do what's right," Wes said.

Monday afternoon, Dr. Emil Flagg reported to Wes. "The committee restricted Dr. Brannan's obstetric and surgical privileges," he said, "but rejected the proposal to suspend him from the medical staff. Their recommendation is that he go back and get a residency."

"What was his response?" asked Wes.

"He'll live with the restricted privileges; he has no choice, although he's angry about it. At this point, he doesn't seem interested in returning to school."

Continuous Quality Improvement (CQI). An approach providing products that stresses that the organization should never be satisfied with its product—that ways should be found to constantly improve quality.

Total Quality Management (TQM). A management philosophy that focuses on the creation of continuous quality improvement to provide products that exceed the expectations of customers.

"The problems we are having with Dr. Brannan are raising the issue of quality," Wes said. "I'd like to meet with someone who is doing research in the area to see if there is anything we can do to improve the quality of our product. **Total Quality Management (TQM)** and **Continuous Quality Improvement (CQI)** are big issues in manufacturing, and I think they deserve evaluation in healthcare as well."

"There are continuous studies conducted on those topics at the University of Utah Medical School," Emil said. "If you want, I'll see if I can get someone down here to talk to us."

"Let's do it!" replied Wes.

Discussion Questions

1. *What is the difference between standard cost and actual cost? If actual costs are higher than standard costs, is that good or bad from the standpoint of the hospital administrator?*
2. *Refer to the report entitled "Brannan Community Hospital—Profit or Loss by DRG 6." Calculate the total profit or loss (profit or loss times the number of cases) for each DRG. What is the total profit or loss for the period for DRGs 1 through 7?*
3. *Brannan Community Hospital loses $30 per case for Blue Cross patients on DRG 6. What choices does Wes have to cut this loss?*
4. *Why must the Board of Trustees rely on the medical staff to evaluate the quality of healthcare provided by doctors in the hospital?*
5. *When doctors given the responsibility for reviewing the quality of care of their peers fail in their responsibilities, what impact does it have on the integrity of the healthcare delivery system?*
6. *Our society has much ambivalence towards "whistleblowers." Many people believe it is wrong to "rat on someone." To whom should healthcare worker feel more responsibility: the welfare of a coworker who is providing substandard practice, or the health and safety of the patient?*
7. *Why is it important for a healthcare worker to show loyalty to a person? When is this loyalty superseded by "loyalty to principle?"*

32

Improving Patient Care Decisions

Biostatistics. Statistics is a discipline that finds relationships between different events through the study of numbers. Statistics can be used, for example, to determine if there is a correlation between a behavior such as smoking and cancer. Biostatistics is the science of statistics as applied to biological or medical data.

Hill Burton. A federal program from the 1950s that provided funds for hospital construction.

Dr. Tom Woolsey's eyes sparkled with approval. "Your interest in quality is timely," he said. He and Dr. Crystal Hammond were in the office of Wes Douglas at the request of Dr. Emil Flagg. Woolsey and Hammond were professors. Woolsey taught **biostatistics** in the Department of Preventive Medicine at the University of Utah Medical School. Hammond was a professor of business administration at Weber State University. At Wes's invitation, Dr. Emil Flagg and Dr. Ashton Amos were also present.

"I met Hammond at a symposium on marketing sponsored by the Healthcare Marketing Association," Woolsey said. "Much of what she said related to my research on total quality management. Since them, we have coauthored several articles on that topic together." Woolsey turned to Hammond. "Why don't you begin by reviewing your research?"

Crystal Hammond, a stocky woman in her mid-thirties, cleared her throat. "There are four stages in the evolution of markets," she said. "The first stage can be summarized by the phrase *"If you build it, they will come."*[2] In this stage, demand exceeds supply. The power is in the hands of the provider with the greatest assets."

"In the healthcare industry, this occurred in the 1950s," Woolsey added. "The country was concerned about a shortage of hospital beds. The federal government intervened with funds through the **Hill Burton** program for building new hospitals."

"Our 1956 wing was built with Hill Burton money," Dr. Amos volunteered.

Hammond nodded, and then continued. "In the second stage, supply catches and then exceeds demand. Firms begin to compete in the marketplace. This is the stage of selling and competition. In healthcare, this occurred in the early 1970s. Hospital beds alone no longer guaranteed success. Hospitals

---

[2] Berkowitz, Eric N., Ph.D. and Robert T. Kauer, Ph.D., "The Strategic Life Cycle," *The Journal of Strategic Performance Measurement,* August/September 1998, Volume 2, Number 4.

Clinical pathways. A clinical pathway is a guide for physicians and nurses. It is designed to provide decision paths to be followed in diagnosing and treating patients. The goal is to standardize the practice of care so that physicians and nurses use only those diagnostic and treatment options scientifically shown to provide the best medical outcomes.

Database. A collection of data arranged for easy retrieval.

Outcomes management. A quality management program that evaluates quality through an evaluation of patient outcomes.

Treatment protocol. Procedures that should be followed under specific conditions.

started marketing their services, although cost reimbursement softened the impact of oversupply.

"The third evolutionary stage is restructuring. The focus is on ending excess capacity. We have seen this in retailing, banking, and manufacturing."

"And the healthcare industry," Woolsey interjected. "Look at what's happened over the past decade as hospital corporations have bought and downsized competing hospitals. The focus has been on the elimination of duplicate hospitals."

Hammond nodded. "The final stage is customer value," she said. "Finally, the seller focuses on quality. That's where the health industry is today."

"How does one raise quality in a hospital setting?" Wes asked.

"One area that has received great attention is **outcomes management.**"

"What's that?" Wes asked.

"Outcomes management focuses on measurable improvements of patient health because of specific procedures or treatments."

Wes shook his head. "That doesn't sound innovative to me."

"It's not; the idea has been around for a long time. It just hasn't always been applied. The approach was first proposed in 1913 by a Harvard surgeon named Emery Codman. He called it the *end results idea.* It consisted of tracking surgical patients for a year to see how their treatment turned out. The goal was to discover the most likely cause of success or failure. Codman planned to collect the information into a **database** to improve treatment profiles. Unfortunately, his proposal to the American Medical Association was essentially ignored—it got only $500 in funding. More important to Codman, other doctors stopped sending patients to him, his practice suffered, and he abandoned the idea.[3]

"In 1919, the concept was resurrected by the American College of Surgeons that performed a study of 692 hospitals with 100 beds or more. The study showed that only 89 met the minimum standards. The response of The Board of Regents to the report was swift and uncompromising. They collected all the copies, carried them to the basement of the hotel, and burned them."

"The regents were men of action," Flagg said with a sarcastic laugh.

"Despite its rocky start," Woolsey continued, "outcomes management is receiving attention again because of pressures of employers and consumers who would like to be able to judge the quality of the healthcare services they are receiving. One approach is to build **clinical pathways**, doctor guidelines, and **treatment protocols**. Though this approach has its critics, it also has its supporters.

"Research conducted by several medical schools has shown there is a large geographical variation in treatment patterns among doctors. Patients like to think their doctor's approach is based on research, but unfortunately that isn't true. Doctors don't always follow the best practices. The result is that

[3] Many of the concepts in this section are drawn from an excellent article by Joey Flower entitled "Measuring Health," which appeared in the *Journal of Strategic Performance Measurement*, August/September 1998, Volume 2, Number 4.

Double-blind peer-reviewed scientific study. A double-blind study is a study that uses a placebo (harmless substance) as well as the drug being tested on separate patients to compare outcomes. Neither the researcher nor the patients getting the drugs know which is being administered. The objective is to distinguish between the actual action of a drug and the psychological effect taking a drug might have on a patient. Peer-reviewed means that the methodology and results are reviewed by scientists with similar qualifications.

Retrospective statistical analysis. Statistical analysis that occurs after an event, such as the treatment of patients.

resources are wasted, and, in some situations, patients die. A 1992 Harvard study estimates that as many as 180,000 patients die each year from medical mistakes.[4] A 1997 Rand Corporation study of autopsies shows a 35 to 40% error rate in diagnoses."[5]

"Why don't doctors follow the best practices?" Wes asked.

"There are two schools of thought on that one," Woolsey said. He wrote the following on the chalkboard:

Doctors don't know what the best approaches are.

Doctors get bogged down in dealing with the huge volume of information needed to make decisions.

"Let's address the first possibility," Woolsey said as he retrieved a professional journal from his briefcase. "Part of the problem is that we don't know what the best practices are."

"That's hard to believe," said Wes.

"Let me read from an article in the August/September *Journal of Strategic Performance Measurement,*" replied Woolsey. "Most practices in clinical medicine have never been tested in **double-blind peer-reviewed scientific studies**, or even through **retrospective statistical analysis**. When practice techniques have been firmly established or debunked in such studies, the knowledge often does not affect clinical practice. Many doctors fail to hear of the new knowledge; others routinely ignore it, preferring to continue to practice the way they were taught in medical school.[6]

"The first problem can be solved through research and education," Woolsey continued. "The second problem is caused by limits in human memory."

Hammond spoke. "Studies on human information processing shows that we have two types of memory. Long-term memory is almost unlimited in its capacity, while short-term memory is limited to six or seven chunks of data. Unless a doctor follows a decision tree when making decisions that involve many variables, it is easy to get confused."

"But we have the technology to supplement short-term memory," said Wes. "Computers can store, organize, and retrieve an almost unlimited amount of information."

---

4 Allen, Jane E. "Doctors, Insurers Meet to Highlight Ways to Reduce Medical Errors," Associated Press, October 14, 1996.

5 "U.S. Healthcare Can Kill, Study Says," San Francisco Chronicle, October 21, 1997.

6 Flower, Joe. "Measuring Health," The Journal of Strategic Performance Measurement, August/September 1998, Volume 2, Number 4.

Acute myocardial infarction. A heart attack.

Boundary guidelines. Guidelines that define acceptable medical practice.

Decision tree. A graphical representation, sometimes a flow chart, of all alternatives in a decision-making process.

Outcome audit. A medical audit that seeks to identify poor medical care through poor patient outcomes.

Pediatrics. A branch of medicine specializing in the treatment of childhood illness.

Practice protocols. Rules developed to guide doctors in the way they treat specific illnesses.

"That's right," Hammond replied. "And some teaching hospitals have developed **decision-tree** software programs for use by doctors in diagnosing. Unfortunately, not all doctors have embraced that technology. Many still rely on memory."

"I think we have pretty well covered the theory," Flagg said. "Now let's be more specific. What can the medical director of a small hospital like ours do to improve the quality of its doctor decisions?"

"There are several actions you can take," replied Woolsey. "Your Quality Control Committee can start performing **outcome audits**.

"You can encourage members of the medical staff to adopt **practice protocol**s that have been shown to have the best outcomes. These are essentially pathway guidelines, as opposed to **boundary guidelines** that define medical practices beyond which doctors incur penalties. You can also encourage doctors to use computer technology to store, organize, and retrieve these protocols. The use of computers to retrieve and execute decision trees can cut errors resulting from omissions of memory."

"What can hospital administration do?" asked Wes.

"You have installed a cost accounting system that will identify the medical resources used to treat patients. You might consider including outcomes data in your database."

Wes nodded as he took notes.

"You can also adopt many recent innovations of manufacturers in the areas of continuous quality improvement (CQI) and total quality management (TQM)," offered Hammond.

"Your first focus," she continued, "should be on improving customer satisfaction, market share, and profitability. It should also focus on ending waste and rework and on improving productivity. The most important part of this program will be managing the core processes in the hospital—processes that clinical trials have shown improve outcomes."

"To work," Flagg said, "the system will have to be clinically meaningful. That means we will have to gather and report clinical data."

"That's correct," said Woolsey. "One community hospital I'm consulting with has begun by identifying four high-volume critical medical conditions for outcomes assessment." He walked to the board and wrote the following:

Pediatric *asthma*
Pregnancy
Cardiovascular disease
Acute myocardial infarction

"Could we hire you to help us do the same?" Flagg asked.

"Dr. Hammond and I would be happy to help you in any way we can," Woolsey replied.

"Where will we get the money?" Wes asked.

"That's your assignment," said Flagg.

Discussion Questions

1. *What are the four stages in the evolution of a market? In what stage is the healthcare industry now?*

2. *Define outcomes management and explain how it can be used to improve healthcare practices.*

33

The Competition

Nonprofit hospital. A hospital whose surpluses cannot be kept or given for the benefit of specific persons but are used for the mission of the organization.

Vertically integrated. A vertically integrated company owns companies at all stages of production and distribution. A vertically integrated hospital chain, for example, might own doctor practices, primary hospitals, specialty hospitals, health insurance companies, and nursing homes.

With the successful completion of the first module of the information system, Wes turned his attention to the competition. One of the obvious reasons for the decline in patient volume was Snowline Medical Center, ten miles to the south. From visiting with Madeline McMillan of the Utah Healthcare Association, he learned Consolidated Healthcare of Arizona, a for-profit hospital corporation formed in 1985, built the hospital.

Madeline told Wes the company was well capitalized and that most of its hospitals were new. The company boasted saving from centralizing the purchasing, housekeeping, financial, and dietary functions. Its charges were slightly higher than many **nonprofit hospitals** in the state—not including Brannan Memorial Hospital, which raised prices in its struggle to remain solvent.

Madeline reported the company was **vertically integrated**, owning hospitals, nursing homes, and a health insurance company that served as the nucleus for its managed-care program. The corporation recently started an aggressive program of doctor practice buyouts in an attempt to control doctor referrals.

Although some criticized the company for its aggressive marketing practices, Madeline was impressed by its efficiency and financial strength. She suggested that Wes meet Jon Einarson, the local hospital administrator. At Wes's request, she called Einarson and set up the appointment.

"Today's hospital employees are too expensive," Jon Einarson snarled. At age 35, he stood six foot three and tipped the scales at a muscular 220 pounds. His closely cropped beard accentuated the rawboned features he inherited from his Icelandic ancestors, and his sea green eyes could pierce an opponent like a Viking pikestaff.

For the past two hours Einarson had given Wes a tour of his building, highlighting efficiencies in design that allowed the hospital to cut staffing by

20%. Now both dined in the private dining room next to Einarson's office. Einarson reached for his steak knife. "A good administrator knows how to slash labor costs," he said cutting the rim of gristle and fat from his thick steak. "That's why we ax old hospitals. We design our buildings to save labor. In five years we can pay for a new building in payroll savings alone.

"Before entering the market," he continued, "I approached your board with a purchase offer. Your Finance Committee chair, Edward Wycoff, killed it." Einarson took his first bite and nodded approvingly as he savored the flavor. "It was a mistake," Einarson continued. "Park City would have been a better location for us, but your board resisted our for-profit ownership. In the long run, the decision will hurt us both."

"Why?" asked Wes.

"Because there isn't a big enough population to support two new hospitals. That's why I was pleased when I heard you wanted to meet with me. I hope you've come to the same conclusion," said Einarson.

"The board will never support a consolidation," said Wes. "The community tradition is too strong."

"The tradition is wrong," Einarson retorted angrily. "Hospitals are too expensive to plop in every community along the Wasatch Front. What your board is doing is a disservice to the community. If you want to do what's right for Park City and yourself, you'll work with us. We can make it worth your time."

"What do you have in mind?"

Einarson swallowed, then wiped his face with his napkin. He leaned forward conspiratorially, dropping his voice to a whisper. "You don't have to take direct steps to sabotage the operations. Your hospital's a sick patient, Wes. Remove the life-support systems, and it will die on its own."

"What specifically are you suggesting?" asked Wes.

"We've heard about your efforts with budgeting, cost accounting, and so on. Don't waste your efforts. Let nature take its course."

"And if I do as you suggest?" Wes asked.

"When the hospital closes, there will be a position for you with Consolidated Health Systems, at a generous salary. We'll give you a two-year contract at $150,000 a year. You won't have to do anything; use the time to rest, or find a new job."

"Three-hundred-thousand dollars to close the hospital," Wes mused. "What you're talking about sounds like a bribe."

"Don't get caught up in semantics, Wes. When the place falls apart, you'll need a new job. Wycoff's not going to take responsibility for the stupid decisions the board has made. When he gets done with you, you won't be able to get a job in Park City waiting tables."

Wes was surprised at the boldness of Einarson's offer. Jon Einarson hadn't risen to the top of his profession by being timid. Wes believed that what Einarson was proposing was a conflict of interest. Wes paused in mock seriousness as though considering the offer. "You don't mind if I discuss your generous offer with my board?" he asked.

Einarson saw through the sarcasm and was offended. "Don't be stupid, Wes. We must be discreet. I'm doing my best to save your hide, and you're insulting me."

Wes Douglas folded his napkin and placed it on the table. "Thanks," he said as he rose to leave, "but I'm not interested."

"You'll be sorry," Einarson said.

"Perhaps."

"Quote me, and I'll deny it," Einarson said as Wes left the room. Wes closed the door behind him.

Thayne Ford swore—not a soft, mealy mouth cuss like his grandmother used when she burned the rolls or dropped a stitch in her knitting, but a blaspheming profanity that fermented angrily in his guts and exploded with the violence of an Irish pipe bomb. Slightly ashamed, he glanced over his shoulder to see if anyone was listening. That wasn't probable since the newspaper office was empty. It was 4:00 a.m. He was about to miss the deadline for the Wednesday edition of the *Park City Sentinel*. The press was broken—*again.*

He grabbed a rag from the table and wiped his hands. It wouldn't be easy to fix this time. Made in 1952, parts were hard to get, and money was tight. Subscriptions were down. It wasn't enough that national papers like *USA Today* targeted rural markets. Even the statewide newspapers like the *Salt Lake Tribune* had online editions that stole readers from the smaller biweekly rural newspapers.

At 6:00 a.m., he'd call Edward Wycoff, his silent partner. Wycoff would write a check to fix the press—but not to replace it. Ford doubted he would ever get that commitment. There would be a price, of course—not just the verbal abuse. Ford could take that, but Wycoff would require more. Ford would agree. If it were a question of ethics or of feeding his family, he would choose the latter. There weren't other options at his age.

Discussion Questions

1. *We learned that duplication of hospital beds and equipment has the potential to raise the costs of healthcare within a community. With a new hospital just a few miles down the road, is it possible that Park City no longer needs a hospital? Assign class members into three groups. The first group should role play the members of the Board of Trustees of Snowline Medical Center. The second group should role play the members of the board of trustees of Brannan Community Hospital. The third group should represent members of the community called together to hear a debate on whether Brannan Community Hospital should be closed. At the end of the debate, have each community member write a three-paragraph statement on his or her conclusions on the topic.*

2. *What do you think about Jon Einarson's proposal that Wes Douglas cooperate with Snowline Regional Medical Center by allowing Brannan Community Hospital to die a natural death? Would it be ethical for Wes Douglas to accept the pay offered?*

34

Power of the Press

Wes was elated. All morning he'd worried about the interview, and with good cause. Since assuming the post of administrator, the local newspaper was unrelenting in its criticism of Brannan Community Hospital. In a small town, hospitals operate in a fishbowl. Whenever news was slow—which was often in rural Utah—someone at the *Park City Sentinel* started poking the hospital's closets for a skeleton.

As Wes watched the front steps of the hospital, Thayne Ford unlocked the door to his car. He turned and waved at Wes with a smile before entering and driving off. *Won that one!* Wes thought.

Thayne disarmed Wes from the start. Contacting Wes's former employer in Maine, Ford checked his consulting references. "Their enthusiasm was overwhelming," Ford reported sheepishly. "They liked your style. Said you were good at identifying operational problems, and better still at fixing 'em. 'A real smooth cookie,' one reported."

"Sorry I've been so tough on you in my editorials," Thayne continued. "It's in everyone's best interest for you to succeed—at least if we want to have a hospital."

"Volume is down," Wes volunteered, "and the negative press hasn't helped."

Thayne's eyes narrowed with regret as he stared at the floor. "In the news media, we get carried away sometimes, maybe to the detriment of our communities." His face brightened. "Tell you what we'll do," he said. "Whenever a new president is elected, the press usually gives him a 60 day honeymoon—a period during which they lay off the negative press. Maybe we ought to do the same for you."

"That'd be great. I'll tell you whatever you want to know—so you don't think I'm hiding anything from you. Give us 60 days to get our act together. If we haven't fixed the problems by then, you're free to go after us."

"You're a tough negotiator," Ford said. Both laughed.

"Okay. Now tell me what's going on," Thayne began. "Is it safe to be admitted to Brannan Community Hospital?"

"Certainly," replied Wes. "We have our problems, like everyone else, but the overall quality is as good as any rural hospital in the state."

"What kind of problems?" Thayne queried.

"We have a doctor we are disciplining. The board has temporarily suspended his privileges."

"Anyone I know?" Thayne pressed.

"Can't give the name," Wes replied, "but we're working on the problem."

"Any trouble getting the medical staff to support you?" Thayne asked while taking notes. "I've heard some doctors are reticent to criticize peers."

"You said this was off the record?" Wes verified, nodding at the notebook.

"It's just for the files," Thayne replied.

"There was resistance from some members of the medical staff," Wes said, "but Dr. Emil Flagg, Chairperson of the Credentials Committee, handled the situation."

"I hear there's quite a bit of conflict on the board."

"I don't think we want to address that publicly," Wes said warily.

"Remember the deal," Thayne said. "It's just between us."

Wes nodded, and for the next 30 minutes he answered Ford's questions about the operation of the hospital as truthfully as he could. Topics discussed included board politics, and the problem small hospitals have competing with the resources and specialized staff of larger hospitals. *He probably didn't learn anything he didn't already know,* Wes thought as he concluded the interview. *Most of these problems will be fixed in 60 days; they'll be of little interest to the newspaper then.*

"I've enjoyed the interview," Thayne said as he closed his notebook. "It's given me new hope for the future of the hospital. Let's keep in touch; I need to know what's going on, but I'll support you—at least through the honeymoon period."

Standing on the steps of the hospital, Wes was elated to have found a friend and supporter.

He was about to receive the shock of his life.

In the security of his office, Thayne Ford reviewed his notes. The most interesting part of the interview was the malpractice scoop—the issue that caused the medical staff to suspend *"Dr. X."* The young administrator wouldn't tell him who that was. At that point Wes had been called out to talk to a fire inspector.

Thayne took the opportunity to look at the notes of the Credentials Committee meeting that Wes referred to. As Thayne suspected, the name of the doctor was scratched out. The patient's admission number was not erased, however, and Ford wrote it in his notebook.

HIPAA. Acronym for The Health Insurance Portability and Accountability Act. HIPAA was enacted by the U.S. Congress in 1996. One objective is protect confidentiality of health information.

He picked up his phone and punched in the phone number of Patricia Fielding—'Trish.' Trish was a medical records librarian in the hospital and one of Thayne's sources. He met her in a bar on her first night in town from Brooklyn. Crazy hair, but good figure.

"Heyyy, Trish! Guess who?"

The voice at the other end of the line bubbled with excitement.

"Thayne? . . . How ya doin'?"

"Doin' good. Got a favor though. Got a hospital admission number . . . wanna know who the patient is. . . . What's **HIPAA**?" he asked. "No one needs to know," he continued after her response. "Yeah, I can wait." He doodled on the notepad while she checked the files.

"Brittany Anderson? Seen in the emergency room, huh? What was the problem? Hmm . . . the doctor missed the diagnosis? Almost resulted in her death? Yeah, that's bad. Family plan to sue? Well, maybe they'll change their mind," he said, scribbling in a pad. "Who's the Doc? *Ah,* Dr. Brannan . . . the *Little Prince . . . "*

Thayne Ford held his notepad at arm's length as though admiring a beautiful work of art. A big Cheshire grin spread across his face. "I owe you one, baby."

Discussion One–Confidentiality

Confidentiality of sensitive information is an important issue in healthcare. Breaches of confidentiality can occur through idle gossip by employees in cafeterias and elevators, or through the inappropriate use of hospital records. Both can create significant legal liability for the hospital and its employees.

Health Insurance Portability and Accountability Act (HIPAA)

The first federal legislation to protect patient medical information took effect on April 14, 2002. This legislation limits the way that doctors, hospitals, insurance companies, and so on can use private medical information.

Key provisions of these new standards include:[7]

Access To Medical Records. *Patients should be able to see and obtain copies of their medical records and request corrections if they identify errors and mistakes. Health plans, doctors, hospitals, clinics, nursing homes, and other covered entities*

[7] Fact Sheet, Department of Health and Human Services, http://www.hhs.gov/news

should provide access to these records within 30 days and may charge patients for the cost of copying and sending the records.

Notice of Privacy Practices*. Covered health plans, doctors, and other healthcare providers must provide a notice to their patients on how they may use personal medical information and their rights under the new privacy regulation. Doctors, hospitals, and other direct-care providers must provide the notice on the patient's first visit as of April 14, 2003 compliance date and on request. Patients will be asked to sign, initial, or otherwise acknowledge that they got this notice. Health plans must mail the notice to their enrollees by April 14 of each year and again if the notice changes significantly. Patients also may ask covered entities to restrict the use or disclosure of their information beyond the practices included in the notice, but the covered entities would not have to agree to the changes.*

Limits on the use of Personal Medical Information*. The privacy rule sets limits on how health plans and covered providers may use individually identifiable health information. To promote the best quality care for patients, the rule does not restrict the ability of doctors, nurses, and other providers to share information needed to treat their patients. In other situations, however, personal health information may not be used for purposes not related to healthcare, and covered entities may use or share only the minimum protected information needed for a particular purpose. In addition, patients would have to sign a specific authorization before a covered entity could release their medical information to a life insurer, a bank, a marketing firm, or another outside business for purposes not related to their healthcare.*

Prohibition on Marketing*. The final privacy rule sets new restrictions and limits on the use of patient information for marketing purposes. Pharmacies, health plans, and other covered entities must first get a person's specific authorization before disclosing their patient information for marketing. At the same time, the rule permits doctors and other covered entities to communicate freely with patients about treatment options and other health-related information, including disease-management programs.*

Stronger State Laws*. The new federal privacy standards do not affect state laws that provide added privacy protections for patients. The confidentiality protections are cumulative; the privacy rule will set a national "floor" of privacy standards that protect all Americans, and any state law providing added protections would continue to apply. When a state law requires a certain disclosure—such as reporting an infectious disease outbreak to the public health authorities—the federal privacy regulations would not preempt the state law.*

Confidential communications*. Under the privacy rule, patients can request that their doctors, health plans, and other covered entities take reasonable steps to ensure that their communications with the patient are confidential. For example, a patient could ask a doctor to call his or her office, rather than home, and the* *doctor's office should comply with that request if it can be reasonably accommodated.*

***Complaints**. Consumers may file a formal complaint about the privacy practices of a covered health plan or provider. Such complaints can be made directly to the covered provider or health plan or to HHS' Office for Civil Rights (OCR), which is charged with investigating complaints and enforcing the privacy regulation. Information about filing complaints should be included in each covered entity's notice of privacy practices. Consumers can find out more information about filing a complaint at http://www.hhs.gov/ocr/hipaa or by calling (866) 627-7748.*

Discussion Questions

1. *Did Thayne Ford do anything illegal by violating his agreement to keep the information learned in his interview with Wes Douglas confidential for 60 days? Did he do anything unethical? Is there a difference?*
2. *Did Trish do anything illegal in giving out patient information? What legislation did she violate? How can you, as a healthcare provider, protect your patients and yourself? List ways a professional might prevent a breach of confidentiality.*

35

Anniversary Dinner

Dr. Emil Flagg smiled with satisfaction as he gazed at his wife and the children that gathered around the table. It was not often the whole family was together. Tonight they were celebrating his sixtieth birthday, and all were here for dinner at the Yarrow Inn. It was to be a surprise party, and Emil played the part well. Having been married to Edith for 35 years, however, there were few surprises. Edith never forgot an important occasion, and he knew she wouldn't forget this one. As he gazed at her, she radiated back the love that kept the family together through the good times and the bad.

Emil was not the easiest man to live with. His impatient and explosive personality often put him in conflict with his sons, who inherited their mother's dislike for conflict. Edith was the magnet that kept them together; and tonight the boys were here for her, as much as for him.

Robert, the oldest son, was an electrical engineer from Seattle and had flown in that evening with his wife and three sons. *A handsome family*, Emil thought. Seated across the table were Tom and his fiancée, Megan. At age 28, Tom had just been accepted to George Washington Medical School. It was high time that he take a bride, and Megan couldn't have been a better match if Emil picked her out himself.

Tom and Megan met last summer in Hawaii. Emil was presenting a paper at the annual meeting of the American College of Pathologists and took the family with him. Tom and Megan met at the hotel pool. Megan's father was the president-elect of the college. Already, he had approached Emil about the chairpersonship of an important committee. An honor Emil hadn't sought, it would mark an important milestone in his career. Technically proficient, Emil was never politically wired. Some of his colleagues said it was his abrasive personality. Emil believed it was his unflinching honesty.

A good pathologist doesn't use euphemisms. He wouldn't call a tumor a cyst to make someone feel better, yet that's what often happened in the world of hospital politics—incompetence was couched in softer terms in the reports of Peer-review and Credentials Committee. Emil silently scowled. *Incompetence is incompetence—spare the euphemism!* Earlier that week, he had an explosive argument with the other members of the Credential Committee over the surgical privileges of Dr. Matt Brannan.

Brannan was not board certified, and twice in the past year his lack of training got him into trouble. True, he was the youngest member of a family that faithfully supported the hospital for two generations, often reimbursing year-end shortfalls from family coffers. Money, however, shouldn't be the driving force in decisions about the practice of medicine. If Dr. Brannan wasn't competent, he shouldn't have certain medical staff privileges—maybe he shouldn't even be a member of the medical staff! On this final point, other members of the staff differed. Emil prevailed. He smiled with satisfaction as he remembered the meeting.

Across the room, a tall gentleman with gray hair entered the restaurant with his wife. It was Paul Jameson, an attorney and a first cousin to Edith. *He's not here for the party,* Emil thought. Emil and Paul had not spoken for years. The distinguished couple was shown across the dining room by the maître d' and seated at an adjacent table.

"How are you this evening, Paul?" Emil said, startling the old buzzard. Emil even stood and shook his hand. "I'd like you to meet Tom's fiancée, Megan."

Paul hadn't seen Emil and his family when he entered the restaurant and was surprised at Emil's cordial response. "How do you do, Megan?" he sputtered.

"I've been wanting to come by and settle that easement problem," Emil continued, before Paul could catch his balance. Paul and Edith owned bordering cabin sites in the High Uinta mountains north of Kamas, Utah. They inherited the property from a common grandfather. Edith got the west section, near the highway—Paul got the east. Both pieces of property had water and timber. Paul's had a better view of the valley but lacked one important feature—access to the road.

If their grandfather had been an attorney like Paul, he would have divided the property north and south, or at least would have provided a legal access to the road. He wasn't, though; he was just a poor sheepherder who wanted to do something special for his grandchildren.

Shortly after the inheritance, Paul approached Emil about the problem. All he wanted was a ten-foot easement through Edith's property. Emil was still smarting, however, about a lawsuit Paul's client filed against the hospital. Emil wasn't affected personally, but the case was without merit, and Emil told him so.

When Paul refused to drop the case, Emil took offense. An argument resulted where Paul suggested the best way to cut malpractice suits was to remove incompetent doctors, and Emil countered the ethics of attorneys was one step above that of the Mafia. For ten years, they hadn't spoken, while the property sat vacant. Paul's forehead arched suspiciously. "How much money do you want?" He asked.

Emil smiled generously as he put his arm around Paul's shoulder. "I don't want anything except to put this bitter saga to rest. Bring the papers by my office Monday. I'll sign them." Paul weighed the comment with a critical squint as he took his seat.

Emil's wife raised her eyebrows in pleased surprise. "That was nice of you, Dear," she said, when Emil was reseated. "I know his children have dreamed about building a cabin on the land for many years. I'm proud of you for putting an old feud behind you."

Emil shrugged good-naturedly. "If it makes you happy, it makes me happy," he said, placing his hand on hers.

"It's been a good year," he continued as he scanned the table. "Tom's been accepted to medical school and has a lovely fiancée. Robert is doing well with Boeing, and his children are growing up to be fine boys. In addition, in November we had the largest volume in pathology ever. It's time to share our good fortune with others."

Indeed, things were getting better at the hospital. Emil was suspicious of Wes Douglas from the start. *What did a CPA know about running a hospital?* Still—his analytical approach and never-give-up attitude were having a positive effect.

Patient volume was up and cost was down—thanks in part to a new cost information system Wes installed. Best of all for Emil, the board and medical staff were—at least for the moment—not at each other's throats. There was even talk of resurrecting the building program that was canceled shortly before Hap's death. Emil smiled with satisfaction.

A young man in a white shirt and black bow tie arrived at the table and nodded at Emil. "I'll be your waiter tonight," he said. "The house special tonight is chicken Jerusalem with artichoke hearts. It comes with a green salad with a light vinaigrette dressing."

Emil looked at his wife. "It sounds good to me, dear," she said.

"I'll take the same," he replied, without even looking at the menu.

"Maybe we should build a cabin too," Edith said, as the waiter moved down the table to take Robert's order. "We'll be having more grandchildren in coming years; it would be nice to have a family retreat."

"Even if the kids don't use it, it might make a romantic getaway for us," Emil said with a wink. Edith's brown eyes registered pleased surprise—romance was not Emil's strong suit. "As a matter of fact—" Emil's sentence was cut off by a pat on the shoulder. Looking up, he saw Thayne Ford from the newspaper.

"What a fortunate coincidence catching you together!" Thayne said, nodding at Paul Jameson.

Emil's eyes mirrored confusion as he studied Paul, then bounced a quizzical look off Thayne.

"You two are going to be spending quite a bit of time together the next few weeks, what with depositions and all," Thayne continued.

"What are you talking about?" Emil asked.

"Haven't you heard?" Thayne chortled. "Matt Brannan is suing the hospital for public defamation of character. Paul is his attorney. As Chairperson of the Credentials Committee, you are listed as a defendant. It's here in tonight's paper." Ford held up the nightly edition of the *Park City Sentinel*. The headlines read, *Wes Douglas Spills All—Dr. Brannan's a Quack, Board's Incompetent.*

Flagg gasped. He grabbed the paper, spilling the ice water on his wife. She stood up, knocking her chair over, which tripped a waiter, who spilled a large Caesar salad on Paul. Flagg glared at the headlines, read the first three paragraphs of the article, and then swung angrily to face Ford.

"When did Wes say this?" he snorted.

"Copyrighted article from an interview at the hospital yesterday," Thayne replied brightly. He pulled a stenographer's pad from his pocket. "Do you have a statement to make?"

"Be careful," Paul said from the bordering table. He was wiping salad dressing from his coat with a linen napkin. "Anything you say can be used against you in the courtroom."

Emil's face flushed red. Jumping up, he grabbed Paul by the coat lapels. "I'll give you a statement—you two-faced SOB!" he shouted.

"Careful," Edith said. Emil looked at her, and then shoved the frightened attorney into the buffet table, which collapsed onto the floor, taking Paul and Emil with it.

Thayne Ford snapped a picture.

"Tomorrow's lead story," he said to himself brightly.

36

Last Official Act

Wes Douglas reached for the last pile of vendor checks Birdie Bankhead gave him before leaving for the evening. Unless a miracle occurred—which was unlikely—approving them for payment would be his last official act as administrator of Brannan Community Hospital.

Downstairs in the cafeteria, the joint meeting of the medical staff and board had begun—he was specifically asked 'not to attend.' In a few minutes, Dr. Emil Flagg would present a resolution from the medical staff to the board asking that they release the hospital administrator. Edward Wycoff would read it, and then move the board accept the resolution. Another member of the board, probably David Brannan, would second the motion, and Wes would be history.

Wes removed his phone from the hook. A story like this hadn't hit the community since the silver mine explosion of 1910. He wasn't in the mood to talk to reporters. Picking up the pen, he started signing the vouchers and then leaned back in the large leather chair that once supported Hap Castleton. He stared at the evening edition of the *Park City Sentinel* on his desk. *Why did Thayne Ford do that?* Not only had he broken his word by immediately publishing everything, but he badly distorted what Wes had told him. Wes would never call Dr. Brannan a *quack* or the board *incompetent*. The motivation had to be more than a good story.

Wes shook his head as he retrieved the pen and started signing again. He was embarrassed—embarrassed for the board that trusted him with their hospital and embarrassed for the medical staff who, despite their faults, were doing their best to provide a high quality of healthcare to the residents of Park City. But most of all, he was embarrassed for the employees who deserved more than the ridicule the *Park City Sentinel* was heaping on them and their organization.

He smiled sadly. One person he would not have to be embarrassed for was Amy Castleton—she could hold her own. The afternoon the paper hit the streets, she cornered him in his office. Choked with anger, she read aloud Wes's derogatory *"quotes"* about her father. Wes tried to tell her that Thayne Ford invented them, but she wasn't listening.

"Father may not have been a polished CPA," she said, her eyes glistening with tears, "but he was honest . . . and he treated people with dignity." She slammed the door behind her as she left.

From the window, Wes watched her leave the hospital with Matt Brannan in his Mercedes. Wes was in love with her, but there was no way the relationship was going to work. Wes signed the last check and placed it on top of the pile. Birdie would retrieve and process the checks in the morning. There was nothing left but to pack a few personal belongings.

He removed a pen set he received when he left Lytle, Morehouse and Butler and a book of poetry Kathryn had given him. From the locked bottom drawer of his desk, he retrieved the file he collected on Ryan Ramer. He would mail it to the district attorney later that evening.

Downstairs the meeting was heating up. He could hear the shouting all the way up the stairwell. *It's all over but the screaming,* he thought. There was no reason to stick around; if they needed him, they could reach him at his apartment before he left town.

Heavy with fatigue, he stood and snapped shut the briefcase that held the few belongings he would take with him. Picking it up, he crossed the room, and then paused at the door. Several days earlier, he found a picture of Amy. Hap apparently misfiled it with an old financial report. It was taken when she was eleven-years-old, on a fishing trip with her father. He returned to the desk, opened the top drawer, and placed it in his side pocket without looking at it. Shutting the drawer, he crossed the office, locking the door on the way out. He would leave the keys at the switchboard.

37

Carnavali

Ryan Ramer's hands were still shaking as he unlocked the door to his Lexus at the Salt Lake Airport. He and Hank Ulman finished a meeting with Barry Zaugg, Sid "Sugar" Carnavali's drug runner and sometimes hit man. Carnavali was ticked, and Ramer was frightened. Carnavali paid $30,000 for drugs Ramer had still to deliver. Thanks to Wes Douglas, the lab and the raw materials were sealed away.

Zaugg was unsympathetic to Ramer's story. As he left, he slammed a wrench through the cockpit window of the small private plane Hank Ulman was servicing. "Worse things than this will happen if Carnavali doesn't get his shipment," he said.

Ramer slipped into his car and settled into the heavy leather seats, deep in thought. Problems were multiplying faster than he could find solutions. As he pulled out of the parking lot and onto the freeway, he realized that his life, and perhaps those of his family, were riding on his ability to solve the problem.

By morning, Ramer had a plan. He and Hank discussed it as they ate their lunch privately in his office. "We've got three goals," he began. "Satisfy Carnavali, retrieve the materials from the lab if possible, and get rid of the evidence uncovered by Cluff. I still think there are work papers out there, someplace. If Chandler hasn't found them, she will."

"Emma is onto something," Hank affirmed. "The past couple of days she's been hanging around maintenance, asking lots of questions. I think she knows about the home health agency."

Ramer nodded. "I've got a plan that will solve all three problems. Carnavali wants drugs; he doesn't care what kind. I've got 50 ten-cc bottles of morphine, another 70 bottles of Demerol in the narcotics safe that I could give him. It's two weeks' worth of hospital inventory."

"But you get audited on that stuff, don't you?" Hank asked.

"That's where you come in," replied Ramer. "Several years ago, I moonlighted at a nursing home in Salt Lake. One night the place burned; I don't know how the fire started, but it provided the cover for me to process an order for drugs that I was able to sell on the streets.

"You want to burn the hospital down?" Hank asked incredulously.

"Just the administrative wing. It would destroy the pharmacy, evidence of the lab, and Cluff's work papers," Ramer said.

"What about Emma?"

Ramer shrugged. "Maybe she perishes in the fire."

Hank was silent as he mulled the thought in his head. "No good," he said. But maybe I got a better idea. How 'bout an explosion? I've been tellin' administration for two years the boiler's got troubles, that someone's gonna get hurt or worse if they don't fix it. It's right beneath, and close enough to the pharmacy. It probably would take out the whole wing if I rig it right."

"Is the boiler big enough to destroy all the evidence?"

"We've got 200 gallons of gasoline in maintenance for the backup generator. The fire marshal told us to get it away from the generator. I'll put it in the storeroom in the basement; if anyone asks, I'll tell 'em that Wes told me to do it."

Ramer reviewed the proposal in his head, then smiled and nodded in acceptance.

"When do we do it?" Hank asked.

"Saturday morning, a little after 7:00 a.m. It's the monthly meeting of the board. With Wes gone, Chandler will be representing administration."

"What about the stuff in the lab? You gonna let it blow?"

"Friday night we get it out. We either tunnel through the wall in the basement or go down through the floor of the Pink Shop."

"The Pink Shop would be easier, it will be closed; the wall in the basement is too close to the cafeteria."

"I'll meet you tomorrow night at the Pink Shop—provided that gives you enough time to rig the boiler."

"I can do it in an hour," Hank said. "One more question—what about your uncle, Edward Wycoff? Won't he be at the meeting?"

"He's in Denver, completing the details on the closure of the hospital. We're going to simplify it for him," Ramer said with a smile.

The mood was sober at the Castleton household. In the past four months Hap died, a murder investigation had followed, the hospital's financial problems were revealed, Matt Brannan's hospital privileges were suspended, and now Hap's replacement had been fired.

It was Friday evening, and Helen Castleton and Amy were finishing a quiet supper. "Your father would never have allowed the situation to deteriorate at the hospital like it did under Wes Douglas," Helen said, as she cleared the dishes from the table.

"Mom, to be honest, Dad *did* allow the situation to deteriorate," responded Amy, surprised that she was willing to criticize her own father. "He did a great job for many years, but he didn't adjust his style to accommodate the demands of managed care. The hospital's financial problems aren't all Dad's fault, but he played a role."

"At least he was never vindictive," her mother replied. "After all the Brannans have done for the hospital, to single out Matt like he did . . ."

"Whatever Wes's mistakes, he's gone," Amy said sadly. "He's closed his CPA practice and has probably left town."

"Do you think the hospital will close?" Helen asked.

"I don't know. If it does, a large piece of Park City's history dies with it."

"Our family has a lot invested in that hospital," Helen added.

"I know. Some of my happiest childhood memories were the Saturday mornings I spent with Dad at the hospital when he would check the mail and catch up on paperwork."

"I remember those days," Helen said. "I always thought you'd be bored to death. What was there to do while he worked?"

"Dad had one of the carpenters build a playhouse in the old safe room, below his office. They furnished it with a small table and chairs that they built in the carpenter shop."

"I didn't know there was anything in the basement but the cafeteria and boiler room," Helen replied.

"You couldn't access it from anywhere but the administrator's office. There was a small stairway behind a bookshelf in the closet. Originally, that's where they kept the payroll."

"Is it still there?"

"I don't know; I'm not even sure where to look for it. Dad's old office became a pharmacy storeroom when they remodeled the administrative wing. It would be interesting to know what happened to the small furniture, though."

"Is the storeroom still there?"

"No, that area is part of the new hall to the newborn nursery." Amy's eyes flickered with curiosity.

"That's strange," she mumbled. *"Where are the stairs?"* Amy was silent for a moment as something Wes said about Ramer started to make sense.

"What did you say, dear?" Helen Castleton asked as she finished the dishes.

"Nothing," Amy replied.

Standing in the remodeled hall outside the nursery, Amy tried to reconstruct in her mind the original administrator's office and the placement of the stairs leading to the old safe room. *Assuming the pharmacy wall is the same, Dad's desk must have been about here,* she thought, standing in the middle of the hall. *The room was about twelve feet wide . . . that would place the closet and the stairway about where the display shelf is. The shelf isn't new; it looks like it's a remnant from the storeroom days, and it must have been used to seal the entrance.*

Moving closer she examined it. *Certainly the pharmacists must have known about the safe room. On the other hand, not many people were allowed in there; Ramer was always so possessive of the area . . .*

Her thoughts were interrupted by the muffled sound of hammering from the direction of the Pink Shop. From the space under the door, she noticed a light. Retrieving her keys, she unlocked the door to investigate.

Except for the toolbox on the counter, the room looked the same as when she closed the Pink Shop earlier that evening. Crossing the room, she looked at the tools, then noticed the hole in the floor, six inches or so behind the cash register. The cash drawer was empty. Quietly, she walked behind the counter and looked through the hole into the room below—*my old playhouse!*

Careful not to be seen, she looked closer. Someone was down there, assembling a cardboard box. The room was the same as she remembered but was cluttered with tables and bottles connected with tubing that resembled a chemistry set. *Who is down there and what is he doing?*

There was a noise behind her and she turned, startled. In the doorway to the Pink Shop stood Hank Ulman, in filthy coveralls. His hair was covered with chalk dust, and he was holding a crowbar. He smiled, exposing his chestnut colored teeth.

"Well, it's little Amy Castleton," he chortled. "And she's come to play house."

38

The Boardroom

The fear tightened in Emma's stomach as she studied the faces of the other members of the board. Directly across the table, David Brannan peered anxiously through a pair of broken glasses perched precariously on his nose. Ryan Ramer was kind enough to replace them—after punching him squarely in the face. To the left was Edward Wycoff, hands securely tied behind his back. Wycoff's eyes reflected terror, stark and naked. Emma didn't understand. *Wycoff is Ramer's uncle. . . Isn't he in on this?*

Emma had never studied Ramer carefully before. With his coarse cranial features and darting black eyes, Ramer reminded her of a trapped animal. *So Ramer was responsible for Hap's death. I should have suspected him earlier. What does he plan to do with us?*

Emma's stares irritated Ramer. He swore under his breath and checked his watch. "*Twelve minutes . . .*" he whispered to himself, "*then the fireworks start. Hank should have been back by now; hope he knows what he's doing.*" Hank made one last trip to the boiler room. "*Back or not, in another eight minutes I'm out of here.*"

Cocking his gun, he laid it on the highly polished boardroom table. He retrieved a small bundle from his coat pocket and unfolded it, placing its contents next to his revolver—one syringe and three small vials. *Too bad Wycoff showed up. Meetings must have finished early.*

Breathing heavily, he removed a handkerchief from his shirt pocket and wiped the sweat from his face. *Strange twist of fate. Uncle Ed . . . the final victim of his own hatred.* Picking up one of the vials, he held it to the light. *None of this would have happened if Cluff hadn't stuck his nose where it shouldn't have been.* He snapped the head off the vial, nostrils flaring as the pungent odor wafted in the air. *Cluff is gone . . . in a few minutes, they'll all be gone.*

Hands trembling with anger, Ramer rotated the vial between his thumb and forefinger to dissolve any remaining crystals, and then picked up the syringe. *Coroner'll never pick this up,* he thought, *if there's anything left to autopsy.*

Sergeant Pete O'Malley's frown dug deep furrows into his sunburned forehead. "Darndest thing I've ever seen," he said. He stared into the video monitor, scratching the scruff of his beard. "It don't look like no joke to me."

For the past four minutes, Sgt. O'Malley, Frank Davis, chief engineer of Paradigm Systems, and Wes Douglas watched Ryan Ramer take over a meeting in the boardroom of Brannan Community Hospital. Frank spent the previous day installing a video security system at the hospital and arranged a demonstration Saturday morning with O'Malley in the basement of the City Hall.

Wes was there at the request of David Brannan as Paradigm's consultant—his last assignment before leaving Park City. O'Malley picked up the dispatch radio in his office. "Unit Seven."

The scratchy response was immediate. It was officer Charlie Thurgood. "Unit Seven here."

"Charlie, I think we have a hostage situation at the hospital. I'm in the middle of a demonstration of a video security system here, and on the screen we see this guy burst into the boardroom with a gun. Sgt. Mason is off today, but Fuller's directing traffic on Main. Pick him up and then head over to investigate. I'll call the sheriff for backup. I'll see ya there."

"I'm rollin," Charlie said.

O'Malley spoke into the dispatch radio again. "A large fellow in a blue maintenance uniform may be implicated. He was in the room with the hostages but just left on an errand. See if you can intercept him before he returns."

Five minutes later, the phone in the boardroom rang, just as Ramer started to fill the first syringe. Since Emma Chandler was the only hostage who didn't have her hands tied, Ramer motioned with his gun for her to pick it up. She complied.

"Boardroom." Face expressionless, Emma listened for what seemed like an eternity, and then held out the phone.

"It's for you," she said.

Ramer's jaw dropped. "For me? Who is it?" he whispered.

Emma said nothing, and Ramer took the phone.

"Hullo," Ramer said, his eyes wide with curiosity.

"Ryan, this is Sergeant O'Malley." O'Malley chose his words carefully. Suspecting that Ryan Ramer was emotionally unstable, he purposefully kept his voice calm. "There are officers at each exit from the hospital, including the one leading from the boardroom to the hall. Throw your gun out and release the hostages. When the room is empty, come out slowly with your hands high above your head. We will give you further instructions then."

Ramer squinted at the floor with disbelief. *How did they know? Was it Hank? That doesn't make sense. He's in as deep as I am. It must be Amy*

Castleton. Maybe she escaped and the police were waiting for Hank when he went to arm the boiler room.

"Stay on the line," Ramer said. He needed time to think. *If the police nabbed Hank before he armed the boiler, then the clock isn't ticking. There's time to negotiate. If not, I've gotta get out of here.* He lifted the receiver to his ear.

"Lemme talk to Hank ."

"Hank's busy."

"Then unbusy him," Ramer said, "or I start shooting people." He fired the gun through the door. Immediately they put Hank on the phone.

"It's me."

"Did they get you before or after the errand?" Ramer asked.

"After."

Ramer swore under his breath. "How did they know we were here?"

"Dunno."

"Have you told them anything?"

"Won't talk to no one but a lawyer."

"Good." Ramer paused, concerned the conversation was being recorded. "Do you think they know . . . about the surprise?"

"I can't tell, but I want outta here!"

"That's enough," O'Malley said, taking the phone back. "The building is surrounded, Ryan. Throw your weapon out and release the hostages."

"I'm not goin' to prison," Ramer whispered to himself. "I grew up in a boy's home; I know what institutions are like."

"I have three nurses in here and four of the babies from the nursery."

"We know better," O'Malley said. "You have four hostages, all members of the board."

Ramer searched the room for a camera, but couldn't see anything. "Okay," he said. "I'll trade three of the hostages for a car. The fourth is going with me."

"Is there a bomb?" O'Malley asked.

"No."

"We know there's a bomb, Ramer. You told the hostages there would be an explosion. Where is it, and does it have a timer?"

Ramer's eyes searched the room. *How do they know? Is the place bugged?*

"I'll tell you about the bomb when I have the car," he said. "I have a cell phone."

O'Malley persisted. "When is the bomb set to go off?"

"It isn't. It's armed or disarmed by radio." Ramer lied. "There's an electronic safety device," he continued. "I have to be at least three miles from the hospital to arm it. Give me three miles and if no one is following me, I'll disarm the bomb."

The phone was silent while O'Malley conferred by radio with a SWAT team that was coming in from Salt Lake by helicopter. The estimated time of arrival was three minutes.

"You want a car, and you plan on taking a hostage with you." O'Malley affirmed when he returned to the phone.

"Right."

"We'll get the car. Stay on the line."

Several minutes earlier, O'Malley and Wes Douglas met Officer Thurgood in the cafeteria, where Thurgood first detained Hank Ulman. On the way over, Wes told Thurgood he received a phone call from Helen Castleton earlier that morning. Amy had not returned home last night. Wes suspected that Ramer had something to do with her disappearance and worried about foul play.

There was a speakerphone in the dietitian's office; O'Malley used it so they could listen when he called Ramer. "You heard the conversation," O'Malley said to Hank. "Ramer says there's a bomb, but no timer. Nothin's ticking; no reason to worry, right?" Hank said nothing. O'Malley noticed that Hank was perspiring profusely.

Hank looked at the clock and then at the sheetrock wall that separated the cafeteria from the boiler. "I'm hot; let's go outside," he said.

"The temperature's 68," O'Malley said, pointing to the thermostat on the wall. He turned to Officer Thurgood. "I'm not hot. How about you Charlie?"

"Actually I'm kinda cold," Thurgood said with a nervous shiver.

"I've got a medical condition. It's too hot in here for me. Take me out," Hank pleaded.

"The hospital's a good place to be if you aren't feeling well," O'Malley said. "Would you like me to call a nurse?"

"Tell us what's going on," Thurgood said, tiring of the small talk.

Hank's voice was tight. "I'm not talkin' to anyone without a lawyer. I have a right to be taken downtown."

O'Malley raised his eyebrows. "The only lawyer in town is Phillip Thornton. He's the Little League coach. It's Saturday morning, and he doesn't like to be disturbed during practice. We'll wait here and call him at noon." O'Malley put his feet on the table and looked at his watch. "We got plenty o' time."

Wes heard the loud *whoop whoop* of the helicopters as the SWAT team landed in the parking lot. Hank looked at the clock again, the fright clearly reflected in his eyes. "Okay, okay . . ." he said. "There's no time for the attorney. The boiler on the other side of that wall is going to blow in another five minutes. It shouldn't hurt the nursing units, but it will take the whole administrative wing! You can't stop it. The room's booby-trapped from the inside. Now get me outta here!"

"O'Malley was immediately on his feet talking to the SWAT team by radio. "Get the hostages out—*NOW!*" he shouted.

Wes Douglas, pumped full of adrenaline, grabbed Hank by the throat and threw him against the wall. "Helen Castleton called this morning; Amy went to the hospital last night and never came home. Where is she?" He screamed.

"In a room," gasped Hank , "below the floor of Pink Shop. We dug a hole and—"

"Take him!" Wes shouted as he shoved at Thurgood. "I'll be back . . . " he started to say, but his voice was blotted out by the sound of an explosion in the boardroom.

39

SWAT Team

Code Red. A distress call broadcast over the hospital intercom announcing to employees that there is a fire.

Sergeant Chapman was recruited out of high school to pitch for the Pirates. He was good—no, he was fantastic! Within seven seconds of the call from O'Malley, he threw the concussion bomb right where he wanted it—through the heavy glass of the boardroom window and onto the center of the large maple conference table. *You're out!* he thought as he dove for cover.

The detonation blinded and deafened everyone in the boardroom. It was temporary, but before the sound died, four members of the SWAT team burst through the heavy maple doors, disarming Ramer and pinning him to the floor.

Downstairs, Wes Douglas, who was knocked to the ground, was on his feet and up the staircase to the Pink Shop. Kicking the door in, he found the hole Hank described, covered by a 3' x 3' square of plywood. In an instant, he climbed through it, handing Amy up to a SWAT team member that followed him from the hall. "Hit the fire alarm!" he shouted as he emerged from the hole, hoping it would evacuate the building before the explosion.

With four minutes to go, Wes, O'Malley, and three members of the SWAT team searched both floors of the administrative wing for Saturday employees, while other officers checked to see the ICU Nursery was empty. In the distance, Wes heard *"**Code Red**, Code Red, Code Red"* over the intercom as the switchboard activated the fire and disaster plan.

Amy and the board members were being taken a safe distance from the hospital. Ramer and Hank were under the watch of the deputies. Running down the hall Wes thought of the nursing units housed in a separate wing to the south. Unless Hank's bomb was a blockbuster, only the administrative wing would blow. He said a prayer for the nurses and patients.

With less than a minute to go, Wes and the three remaining officers broke through the French doors of the administrator's office, crossed the lawn, and dove into an empty irrigation canal. The explosion from the boiler room was heard all the way to Heber.

40

The Dedication

Two years later—

Assistant administrator. A member of the hospital management team who reports to the hospital administrator. The assistant administrator is often responsible for a group of hospital departments.

Harbinger. A person or event that predicts the future.

MBA. Acronym for Masters of Business Administration.

The local population couldn't remember a more beautiful Fall. An early chill turned the soft Kelly green of the aspen to shades of crimson, gold, and orange. As 32 year-old Parker Richards stepped from his car onto the sidewalk of the new Brannan Community Hospital, it occurred to him the festive colors were a **harbinger** of a new era for Park City. Only recently completed, the new hospital would be dedicated in less than two hours.

Richards was well prepared for the position for which he was hired. After completing a degree in accounting and an **MBA** in healthcare administration, he served as an administrative resident at the Mountainview Hospital in Las Vegas, Nevada. His preceptor was an able administrator and an effective teacher. Parker Richards's arrival in Park City was timed to coincide with the dedication of the new hospital.

The building is certainly modern, he thought. *As different from the old hospital as the 20th century would be from the 21st. Fewer hospital beds, more outpatient services, a helicopter pad, and telemetry that linked the ICU to the University of Utah Medical Center.* Richards had only seen pictures of the old hospital. An explosion and fire destroyed its administrative wing in 1999. No one died, and fortunately the injuries were minor.

Crossing the lawn, he entered the modern lobby and took an elevator to administration on the third floor, where Birdie Bankhead, who had just been promoted to administrative assistant, met him. "Welcome," she said. "We're happy you could make the dedication. It's appropriate—a new hospital and our first **assistant administrator**. Wes is still meeting with the board. I'm sure he will be out in a few minutes."

She handed Parker a program for the dedication. "While you're waiting, you can look at this. Beautiful drawing, isn't it?" she said, pointing to the architect's drawing on the cover.

"I'm on my way downstairs to check on seating for the dedication," she continued. "If you need anything, Mary Anne will be happy to help you. You might congratulate her, she's just been promoted to administrative secretary."

Mary Anne looked up from her new desk and blushed.

"Congratulations to both of you," Parker said.

Birdie picked up a bouquet of flowers delivered for the speaker's podium, and hustled off to the elevator. Parker took a seat and studied the program. An introduction and welcome was to be offered by Wes Douglas, administrator. A musical number by the high school band was next on the program, followed by remarks by David Brannan, representing the Brannan family. The hospital had been made possible by a generous contribution from the Brannan Family Foundation, funded by the family's prospering software company.

As Parker finished reading the program, David's brother, Dr. Matt Brannan, entered the room accompanied by a lovely young woman. She was carrying a three-month-old baby. Parker had seen Matt on the picture of the Brannan family that hung in the new boardroom. He was told that Dr. Brannan was finishing a residency at Johns Hopkins Hospital in Maryland and would be joining the staff in another year. Parker hadn't met the woman, however.

Mary Anne stood and greeted them at the door, hugging both of them.

"Parker, I don't think you have met Amy," she said taking the baby. "She is the daughter of our former administrator, Hap Castleton." Parker reached out and shook Amy's hand.

"And this is Hap Douglas," Mary Anne continued, holding the baby up.

Richards looked puzzled.

"Oh yes, Amy is Wes's wife."

"Amy and I were childhood friends," Dr. Brannan explained. "With family and staff tied up with preparations for the dedication, she was nice enough to pick us up at the airport. My wife, Kayla, and I flew in for the dedication. Kayla is coming over with her mother."

The administrator's door opened, and David Brannan and Wes Douglas emerged. Wes and Amy embraced as Mary Anne continued to hold the baby.

"How's the residency?" Wes asked shaking hands with Matt.

"Be done in a year," he said.

Birdie returned with a cameraman from the *Deseret News*. "We need a picture for the paper," she said. While Wes Douglas, David Brannan, and Parker Richards lined up by the architect's model, Mary Anne made small talk.

"I understand you've taken up flying," Mary Anne said, addressing Matt.

"I have!" Matt replied. "It provides a good diversion from studying. As a matter of fact, I'm picking up a new plane tomorrow in Salt Lake City. Before flying back to Baltimore, I hope to take Wes in it on a fishing trip."

"Hold still," the cameraman said as he snapped the picture. He took two more.

"Where to?" Parker Richards asked when the cameraman left.

"McCall, Idaho."

Matt took the baby from Mary Anne and held him high above his head. "It was a favorite spot of this little fellow's grandpa. Who knows," Matt continued, making a funny face at little Hap. "Maybe I can turn your workaholic dad into a first-rate angler."

Wes smiled graciously. “It would be nice to take a break,” he said, “and someday I would like to learn to fish.” He shook his head as he put his arm around Amy. “But as for flying to McCall tomorrow, I think I’ll just stay here and keep my feet on the ground.”

With that, the group was off to the dedication.

Epilogue

Genetic engineering. A technique of changing DNA by adding genes to a molecule to change the type of protein an organism can produce.

It was 7:30 a.m. as the small Cessna Skyhawk 172P pulled onto the taxiway leading to Runway 16-left. The pilot, Dr. Matt Brannan, turned COM one to 118.3 to check in with the tower.

"Citation jet five miles inbound. Hold for arriving aircraft," the tower directed. Matt applied the brakes and stopped the aircraft short of the runway. To the north, the Citation jet, now at 7,000 feet, turned on its landing lights.

Matt throttled the aircraft to 1700 rpm. to check the magnetos. The rpm. drop didn't exceed 125 rpm—everything was in order. The Citation jet was now three miles out, its landing gear down and engines on idle. Once more, Matt reviewed his checklist: *brakes, flaps, carburetor heat.*

Matt was happy that, after considerable arm-twisting, Wes Douglas consented to join him on the fishing trip. It would give them the opportunity to mend some fences. If Matt was going to return to the hospital after his residency, he would want a better relationship with the administrator.

Wes, through the medical staff, started the action that forced him to apply for a residency. Now, two years into the process, Matt saw that it was the best thing he ever did. He ran into Kayla Elmore at church, the skinny HOSA volunteer from the business office. Except Kayla was no longer in braces, and her mature figure would no longer be called skinny.

Matt never paid her much attention at Brannan Community Hospital, but she had blossomed into the prettiest young woman he had ever seen. Kayla was working at Baltimore Community Hospital. They dated for a year before getting married.

The Citation jet landed and turned left onto the taxiway.

"Cessna five-seven Zulu cleared for takeoff. Fly heading 320, climb to one three niner, contact departure on 124.3," said the tower.

"Ready?"

Wes smiled nervously and gave Matt a "thumbs-up."

"Cessna five-seven Zulu, rolling." Matt released the brakes, pushed forward on the throttle and started his take-off roll. As the plane left the runway, both Matt and Wes thought of Hap Castleton. Three years ago, he took this same flight, and the tragedy that followed set into motion a series of events that changed both of their lives.

History would not repeat itself. Matt and Wes would complete the trip for Hap, and the experience would be the start of a better relationship between two professionals who would contribute significantly to the quality of healthcare in their communities.

Wes Douglas would eventually tire of the hassles of managed care, refocusing the direction of his hospital from primary to specialty care. Capitalizing on the **genetic engineering** breakthroughs of the first decade of

Cultured pancreatic beta cells. Pancreatic cells grown in a culture disk for transplant to patients with insulin dependent diabetes.

Genetic endocrinology. Use of DNA technology to produce tissues and drugs that secrete hormones.

Insulin dependent diabetes. A disease in which there is elevated glucose in the blood resulting from defects in insulin secretion, insulin action, or both.

Specialty care center. A health center that specializes in one area of care.

the 21st century, the Brannan **Genetic Endocrinology** Medical Center would become regionally known for the implantation of **cultured pancreatic beta cells** in the treatment of **insulin dependent diabetes**. In later years, Wes would serve as the president of the American **Specialty Care Center** Association and would contribute to the quality of healthcare and reduction of costs through the development of similar high-volume specialty centers throughout the country.

Shaken by his close call with death, Edward Wycoff would retire from the board. Reevaluating his value system, he would spend his remaining years trying, with some success, to build a relationship with his wife and children.

Del Cluff would recover from his injuries and return to work at the hospital. Unable to get along with the other hospital employees, he would eventually return to school to get a Ph.D. On graduation, he would teach Human Relations at a major University.

Dr. Matt Brannan would return from his residency. As the focus of the hospital changed, he would leave Park City for a general practice in Montrose, California. Unlike Wes Douglas, he would never gain regional attention; but would be remembered in the hearts of his patients for the quality of his care and the sincerity of his compassion.

Abbreviations Used in Text

AHA	American Healthcare Association
AHS	American Hospital Supply
AIDS	Autoimmune deficiency syndrome
APG	Medicare's ambulatory classification or grouping system
CAT	Computerized axial tomography
CCU	Coronary care unit
CEO	Chief executive officer
CFO	Chief financial officer
CNO	Chief nursing officer
CQI	Continuous quality improvement
CVP	Cost-volume-profit
DME	Durable medical equipment
DOA	Dead on arrival
DRG	Diagnosis related group
EC	Emergency Center
FAA	Federal Aviation Administration
FTE	Full time equivalent
GIGO	Garbage-in-garbage-out
HCFA	Healthcare Financing Administration
HFMA	Healthcare Financial Management Association
HIPAA	The Health Insurance Portability and Accountability Act
HMO	Health maintenance organization
HOSA	Health Occupation Student Association
ICDA-8	International Classification of Diseases Amended Version Eight
ICDA-9	International Classification of Diseases Amended Version Nine
ICU	Intensive care unit
ID	Identification
IRR	Internal rate of return
IV	Intravenous
JCAHO	Joint Commission on Accreditation of Healthcare Organizations
JIT	Just-in-time
MEC	Medical executive committee
MRI	Magnetic resonance imaging
OB	Obstetrics
OR	Operating room
PRN	As needed
PT	Physical Therapy
RBC	Red blood count
ROI	Return on investment
TPA	Third-party administrator
TQM	Total quality management

UAH	Utah Healthcare Association
VOR	Very High Frequency Omni Directional Range
WBC	White blood cell count

Glossary of Medical and Administrative Terms

Abuse. An action that results in physical harm to a patient. Abuse can be physical, such as striking a patient; verbal, such as shouting or swearing; or psychological, such as threatening, intimidating, or belittling.

Accounts Receivable. An organization's record of bills for goods or services provided that have yet to be paid.

Accreditation. An evaluation by an official organization to assure that another organization meets minimum standards of quality. In healthcare, accreditation is an activity conducted by an group named the Joint Commission on Accreditation of Healthcare Organizations. Since patients are usually unable to judge the quality provided by a hospital, accreditation is designed to guarantee that the hospital provides a high level of care.

Actual costs. Costs incurred and recorded in the financial records, distinguished from budgeted costs, which are projected costs.

Actuary. An individual who calculates insurance premiums.

Acute myocardial infarction. A heart attack.

Administration. The department responsible for the management of the hospital. The hospital administrator heads this department.

Administrative council. Department heads that meet regularly to coordinate activities of the hospital.

Administrator. The manager of the hospital.

Admission record. A record created at the time a patient is admitted that is used by the billing department and other departments to track the patient and the services he or she receives while in the hospital.

Adverse drug event. An unfavorable reaction to a drug. This can be caused by giving a patient the wrong drug, or a by a drug that causes an allergic reaction.

AIDS. Acronym for autoimmune deficiency syndrome. A deficiency in immunity caused by an infection.

Alcohol rehab. Short for alcohol rehabilitation. A unit or process of helping people with alcohol addiction.

Alternative medicine. Medical theories or practices that are not accepted as being effective by most medical doctors. Some alternative medicine techniques have medical value, but are not generally accepted because they have not been subjected to scientific studies that have shown them to be effective.

Altimeter. An instrument in the cockpit of an aircraft that reports the aircraft's altitude.

Alzheimer's. A disease that causes the progressive loss of perception, judgment, and awareness.

Amphetamine. A drug that stimulates the nervous system. Some amphetamines are abused by people seeking an unusual psychological experience.

Anesthesiologist. A physician who specializes in putting patients to sleep during surgery.

Anterior. "On the front." An anterior x-ray, for example, gives a front view.

Appeal. To take a case or complaint that has been decided by a lower court or administrative body to a higher one.

Aptitude. Natural ability.

Arms-length purchase price. A negotiated price between two unrelated individuals.

Articles of incorporation. A legal document filed with the state when an organization is formed.

Aspirate. To inhale fluid into the lungs.

Assault. A threat or attempt to harm another person, or the fear of harm by a person threatened.

Assistant administrator. A member of the hospital management team who reports to the hospital administrator. The assistant administrator is often responsible for a group of hospital departments.

Attending physician. The doctor who admits and supervises the care of a specific hospital patient.

Auditor. A person who reviews records to verify that transactions have been accurately reported.

Autoanalyzer. A laboratory instrument that performs many laboratory tests on the same specimen sample.

Average length of stay. The average number of days spent by a patient in a specific hospital. It is calculated by dividing total patient days by the number of admissions.

Bacilli. Rod-shaped bacteria.

Backwards thinking. A system of analysis that starts with the final goal in mind, then works backwards, analyzing how each activity contributes to the goal.

Bacteria. A one-celled microorganism.

Bad debt. A bill that will not be paid.

Bank loan committee. A committee that reviews applications for loans and approves or denies those requests.

Bankruptcy. A situation where a person or organization is unable to pay its bills. Often in bankruptcy, the court seizes the bankrupt person's or organization's assets and sells them to pay creditors (the people to whom debts are owed).

Battery. The illegal use of force against another person.

Bias. A point of view that prevents unprejudiced consideration of an issue.

Bigger-is-better syndrome. The perception of some physicians and patients that larger hospitals provide better quality than smaller hospitals.

Billing code. A number used on a bill to an insurance company that identifies the diagnosis, test, or procedure billed for.

Biostatistics. Statistics is a discipline that finds relationships between different events through the study of numbers. Statistics can be used, for example, to determine if there is a correlation between a behavior, such as smoking, and a result such as cancer. Biostatistics is the science of statistics, as applied to biological or medical data.

Blood pressure. The pressure of blood on the walls of veins and arteries.

Blue Cross. A health insurance company.

Board certified. The process of having been examined and certified that one has at least the minimum level knowledge and experience needed to practice within a medical specialty such as surgery, internal medicine, or obstetrics.

Board of Trustees. A group of individuals who oversee the operation of the hospital. The Board of Trustees has the authority to hire and fire the hospital administrator, approve the strategic plan and budget, and approve applications of doctors for membership on the medical staff.

Bond. A type of borrowing instrument. Hospitals can issue bonds to borrow money to pay for buildings and equipment.

Book value. An accounting term—book value is the value an item was purchased for. It may be different from the current market value because of such things as inflation. A hospital built in 1970 may have been built for $12,000,000, which is its book value, even though its market value (the amount for which the hospital could be sold) may exceed $100,000,000.

Bottom-line. Synonym for profit (found on the bottom-line of the income statement).

Boundary guidelines. Guidelines that define acceptable medical practice.

Breakeven. A situation where an organization neither earns nor loses money; where revenues equal expenses.

Broad spectrum antibiotics. Antibiotics that treat a wide variety of infections.

Budget director. The person responsible for preparing and monitoring the hospital's budget.

Budgeted costs. Costs projected at the time of budget preparation.

Bundling. As it relates to hospital billing, bundling is the practice of combining the charges of many services into one bill, rather than billing individually for each service. Some insurance companies prefer bundling, others like items billed individually.

Business license. A license issued by a city or state allowing a business to operate.

Business office manager. The hospital manager responsible for the creation, management, and collection of patient accounts receivable.

Business plan. A written document explaining how a company will reach its goal of profitability.

Byzantine. Characterized by intrigue or deception.

Call a loan. To demand that a loan be immediately repaid.

Capitation payment. A payment system where a hospital or doctor gets a fixed monthly payment to provide medical services to a person covered under a health insurance program. Capitation payment is a form of prospective reimbursement. Prospective reimbursement means that the cost of the medical treatment is negotiated in advance.

Captive health plans. A health plan, often owned by a hospital corporation, that dictates to its enrollees what hospitals and doctors patients must use.

Cardiac arrest. A condition where the heart has stopped beating.

Carotid artery. The artery that supplies the brain with blood.

Case manager. A person who continually monitors the quality of care provided to patients in the hospital. This is usually done by reviewing medical records to see that proper procedures have been followed and the right treatment has been given.

CAT scan. Abbreviation for computerized axial tomography. CAT scans perform the same function as x-rays, but with a different technology that results in a clearer image. CAT scans are expensive, and must often be pre-certified (pre-approved) by insurance companies.

Central line infections. Catheter-associated blood stream infections.

Central supply. The department that orders and distributes medical supplies to hospital departments.

CEO. An acronym for chief executive officer. In a hospital, the CEO is the hospital administrator.

Certification. Recognition by a nongovernmental regulatory body that a person meets minimum standards to provide healthcare services.

Chairperson of the board. The person appointed to lead the board. The chairperson usually sets the board agenda, appoints committees, and represents the board to the administrator and medical staff.

Chairperson of the finance committee. A member of a hospital board who has responsibility for monitoring the financial health of the hospital. In Code Blue, Edward Wycoff has this responsibility.

Change of shift report. A report conducted between nursing shifts to update nurses coming on duty on the status of each patient.

Chief dietician. A dietician is an individual who has been trained in the use of nutrition to treat illness. Dieticians work in the dietary department where food is prepared for hospital patients. The chief dietician is the supervisor of the dietary department.

Chief nursing officer (CNO). The director of nurses.

Cholecystectomy. An operation to remove the gall bladder.

Circle electric bed. A bed for patients who cannot or should not move. A circle electric bed looks like a Ferris wheel. The patient is strapped in the position of one of the spokes, enabling him or her to be rotated from time to time to remove pressure from parts of the body that may develop sores called decubitus ulcers. Decubitus ulcers are painful and difficult to cure.

Civil law. Law is divided into categories called civil law and criminal law. Civil law covers all areas not addressed by criminal law. Specifically, civil law is concerned with the rights of citizens. An individual suing another for the accidental destruction of personal property would be under the jurisdiction of civil law.

Clinical pathways. A clinical pathway is a guide for physicians and nurses. It is designed to provide decision paths to be followed in diagnosing and treating patients. The goal is to standardize the practice of care so that physicians and nurses use only those diagnostic and treatment options scientifically shown to provide the best medical outcomes.

Cocci. Spherical-shaped bacteria.

Code Blue. A distress call broadcast over the hospital intercom announcing to the code blue team that there is a cardiac arrest and that aid is needed.

Code Red. A distress call broadcast over the hospital intercom announcing to employees that there is a fire.

Collateral. An asset held as security for a loan.

Comorbidity. The existence of two or more unrelated diseases in one person.

Compensation system. A set of schedules listing the starting wage of each class of employees and pay steps given for experience.

Compliance officer. A person hired to see that an organization abides by specific rules and regulations.

Consultant. An expert who has knowledge that an organization lacks. Consultants are hired to provide this knowledge for a fee. Hospitals use many consultants, as the medical field is complex and most hospitals cannot afford to employ full-time employees in every area in which expertise is needed.

Continuous quality improvement (CQI). An approach to providing products that stresses that the organization should never be satisfied with its product—that ways should be found to constantly improve quality.

Controller. The individual responsible for managing the financial activities of a hospital. Responsibilities include accounting, working with banks to borrow money, and supervising the collection of accounts receivables.

Co-payment. An amount not covered by insurance that is paid by a patient at the time of treatment. Co-payments are designed to prevent unnecessary care.

Coronary Care Unit (CCU). The medical unit where patients with coronary (heart) diseases are treated and housed.

Cost reimbursement contract. A contract where the price of a product or service is not finalized until after the work is done. The customer pays full cost, even if there is a cost overrun from what the contractor originally estimated. Hospitals were originally paid under cost reimbursement contracts by insurance companies. Regardless of how efficiently or inefficiently care was provided, full costs were reimbursed by patients and insurance companies. Cost reimbursement contracts sometimes include an additional amount for inflation, new technology, and so on. This amount is sometimes called a fee to differentiate it from the profit earned by for-profit hospitals.

Cost reimbursement. A payment system where the provider (doctor or hospital) gets paid total billed costs as payment. Often an additional mark-up is added to pay for inflation. Since the doctor or hospital gets paid for all costs, regardless of inefficiency, there are few incentives for cost control. Cost reimbursement was the dominant payment system for many years for Medicare, Medicaid, and Blue Cross.

Cost. The cash or cash equivalent value sacrificed for goods and services that are expected to bring a current or future benefit to the organization.

Cost-per-patient-day. Total hospital costs divided by the number of hospital patient days.

Countersign. Making a doctor sign a document verifying a verbal order given earlier by telephone.

Cowling. The shield or covering of an aircraft engine.

CPA. Abbreviation for certified public accountant. A certified public accountant has passed an exam that shows a minimum level of knowledge in accounting and tax.

Crash cart. A cart containing instruments and medication used in a cardiac arrest or Code Blue.

Credentialing. To practice at a hospital, a physician must be a member of the medical staff and must have been given permission to perform specific medical procedures. Determining what procedures a physician is qualified to perform is called credentialing.

Credentials committee. The medical staff committee that reviews the application of physicians to perform specific procedures in the hospital and recommends to the hospital Board of Trustees that the physician be given or denied these privileges.

Credit limit. The maximum amount, as determined by the bank, an individual or firm can borrow.

Cresyl violet. A dye used in staining slide specimens to be examined under a microscope.

Criminal law. Law is divided into categories called civil law and criminal law. Criminal law deals with crimes which have been defined as conduct that is immoral and for which there is no justification or excuse. Murder and robbery are crimes handled by criminal law.

Critical condition. The most serious classification of patient illness.

Cultural blindness. A condition where persons assume that cultural differences do not exist.

Cultural sensitivity. An appreciation for the cultures and beliefs of others.

Culture. Social, artistic, and religious structures and manifestations that characterize a specific society; beliefs and traditions handed down from generation to generation.

Cultured pancreatic beta cells. Pancreatic cells grown in a culture disk for transplant to patients with insulin dependent diabetes.

Cyanotic. Blue.

Database. A collection of data arranged for easy retrieval.

Dean of the School of Medicine. The chief academic administrator in a school of medicine.

Decision tree. A graphical representation, sometimes a flow chart, of all alternatives in a decision-making process. Sometimes one component of a clinical pathway.

Defamation. The act of attacking the good reputation of another person.

Defendant. The person against whom a complaint is filed in a court of law.

Defibrillator. Equipment used to restore a patient's heart from fibrillation to a normal heart beat.

Demand. As used in economics, the amount of goods bought by customers at each level of pricing.

Deontological school. An ethical school of thought that studies moral obligations. Followers believe in the existence of good and evil, and that individuals have an obligation to do good for other people.

Department head. Hospitals are complex organizations. To make them easier to manage, administrators organize them into departments, usually by function. There are clinical departments such as nursing and laboratory that provide medical services; and support departments such as medical records, administration, accounting, and housekeeping that provide support services. The supervisor of a hospital department is usually referred to as a department head, or sometimes department supervisor. Department heads usually report directly to the hospital administrator or, in larger hospitals, to an assistant administrator.

Department of Business Regulation. A state agency, given the responsibility to license and regulate businesses within a specific state.

Department supervisor. Synonym for department head.

Deposition. Written testimony under oath.

Diagnosis Related Group (DRG) reimbursement. Historically, hospitals were reimbursed actual costs, regardless of how high those costs were due to inefficiency. This provided little incentive for cost control. In the early 1980s, the administrators of Medicare recognized the problem and decided to cap costs by paying one amount to the hospital for each diagnosis regardless of the services offered. They decided to change from cost reimbursement to fixed-price (prospective) reimbursement. The DRG system is a prospective payment system designed to provide an incentive for cost control. The agency responsible for administering Medicare has divided all illnesses into 400 or so diagnostic related groups. A numerical code is assigned to each DRG. A hospital that treats a person with DRG 14, for example, gets $8,658 for the treatment of that patient whether the actual costs to the hospital are above or below that amount. The DRG payment system has significantly affected the way medicine is practiced in the hospital and influences everyone from the controller to the floor nurse. For this reason, clinical personnel must understand at least something about prospective reimbursement.

Diagnosis Related Group. A disease grouping developed by the administrators of Medicare for payment to hospitals.

Diagnostic services. Tests and procedures performed to diagnose an illness.

Diagnostic tests. Tests performed to diagnose an illness.

Dietary department. The department responsible for preparing patient meals.

Dietician. A person trained in the practical application of diet in the treatment of illness.

Director of materials management. The person in the hospital, usually a department head, who has responsibility for the purchasing and distribution of materials in the hospital.

Director of nursing. The chief nursing officer (CNO). This person has line responsibility for all nursing activities in the hospital.

Director of purchasing. The person responsible for purchasing supplies, materials, and contract services for the hospital. Synonym for director of materials management.

Director of reimbursement. A hospital manager responsible for negotiating contracts with insurance companies, training hospital managers how to make money on these contracts, and managing the contracts.

Discharge instruction sheet. A document started at the time the patient is admitted, and finished at discharge. The discharge instruction sheet lists the teaching and discharge planning that took place during the patient's hospital stay. The discharge documents summarizes the patient's condition at the time of discharge and lists instructions for care after discharge.

DOA. Abbreviation for "dead on arrival."

Double bypass. An operation where two arteries are grafted to divert blood beyond an obstruction.

Double-blind peer-reviewed scientific study. A double-blind study is a study that uses a placebo (harmless substance) as well as the drug being tested on separate patients to compare outcomes. Neither the researcher nor the patients getting the drugs know which is being administered. The objective is to distinguish between the actual action of a drug and the psychological effect taking a drug might have on a patient. Peer-reviewed means that the methodology and results are reviewed by scientists with similar qualifications.

DRG reimbursement. See Diagnosis Related Group reimbursement.

Durable power of attorney. A document appointing a legal guardian to make decisions in the event the patient is mentally incapacitated and unable to make medical decisions for herself.

Economics. The study of scarce resources.

Elective surgery. Surgery that is not essential for the life or good health of the patient. A facelift is an example of an elective surgery.

Emergency call. Physicians at some hospitals are required to provide coverage of the emergency room. This is referred to as emergency call.

Employee council. A committee of hospital employees, often elected, whose purpose is to represent the viewpoints and concerns of the employees to management.

Employee productivity bonus pool. Money that can be distributed to employees based on increased productivity.

EMTALA. Acronym for Emergency Medical Treatment and Active Labor Act, also known as the Patient Anti-Dumping Law. This law is designed to keep hospitals from transferring patients who cannot pay for their care to other hospitals. Heavy fines are involved for those who do.

Endowment. A charitable gift.

Enrollee. A person covered by a health benefit plan.

Entry point. The place where a patient enters the healthcare delivery system. The American health care delivery system does not have a well-defined entry point, especially for minorities and the underprivileged.

Ependymoma. Cancer of the spinal cord.

Epiglottitis. Inflammation of the epiglottis, (an elastic cartilage found on the root of the tongue that folds over the glottis to prevent food from entering the windpipe during the act of swallowing).

Epinephrine. A stimulant used to increase heartbeat and the force of heart contractions.

Equality. Treating all people in the same manner.

Ergonomics. The study of work, more specifically the study of ways the workplace can be improved to lower employee injury and fatigue.

Ethics. The study of the principles of right and wrong.

Ethnicity. The unity that comes from a common religion, belief, language, or culture.

Ethyl alcohol. Synonymous with rubbing alcohol. It is often used as a disinfectant.

Evidence-based care. Treatment approaches to a disease that have been verified through scientific studies.

Expense. A cost recorded on the income statement.

External validity. As the term relates to pay, external validity means that pay for individual jobs is the same as the pay of similar jobs outside the organization. If employees at a military hospital earn less than their counterparts in the civilian world, the military pay system lacks external validity.

FAA. Acronym for Federal Aviation Administration.

False imprisonment. The unjustified restraint or retention of person without that person's consent or the legal right to do so.

Family practice residency. A training program following the internship that trains a medical school graduate to be a family practice doctor. Family practice residencies are usually three to four years in length.

Family practice. A medical specialty similar to general practice.

Federal Aviation Administration (FAA). A federal agency charged with regulating aviation.

Fee-for-service. A traditional doctor payment system. The doctor would bill for his or her services and the patient or insurance would pay the amount billed. Fee-for-service was a retrospective payment system, one where the price of a product or service was set after the care was delivered, and usually not subject to negotiation.

Felony. A crime that is punishable by imprisonment for more than one year.

Finance committee. A committee of the Board of Trustees responsible for supervising the financial operation of the hospital.

Finance department. The department responsible for accounting and finance within a hospital.

Finance mechanism. The system used to pay the cost of healthcare.

Financial analyst. A person who earns his or her living by studying the financial statements of companies and making recommendations, often about investments.

Financial reports. Reports that show the financial condition of a firm. The three most common financial reports are the income statement, the balance sheet, and the statement of cash flows. The income statement shows revenues minus expenses. The balance sheet lists assets (items that have economic value), liabilities (debts), and owner equity (the value of the owner's investment in the firm). The statement of cash flows shows cash that has been received and disbursed by the firm during the accounting period.

Financial resources. Funds used to pay for the salaries of healthcare personnel, the buildings, equipment, and supplies used to treat patients and the financial institutions that loan or disperse these funds.

Fixed price. A price fixed in advance that is not adjustable, regardless of the actual price of the product or service finally delivered.

Fixed-price contract. A contract where a price is set before the work to produce the product is carried out. Many homes are built under fixed-price contracts. If there are cost overruns, then the building contractor must absorb the loss. DRG and capitation payment systems for doctors and hospitals are examples of fixed-price contracts.

Flexible budget. A budget that changes with changes in volume.

Flow sheets. Reports designed to allow patient information to be presented in graphical format. Flow sheets are a part of the patient's medical record.

Formaldehyde. A pungent gas used as an antiseptic and disinfectant.

For-profit hospital. A hospital that is organized and incorporated to earn money for investors.

Foundation. A charitable organization that dispenses services or goods for the benefit of the community.

Free market. An economic system where people are allowed to decide what is produced, who produces it, and for whom it is produced. Prices in a free market are usually established by the interaction of supply and demand.

Fully-insured. In a fully-insured health insurance program, the insurance company assumes full risk for the difference between the health premiums paid by the employer and the actual cost paid to doctors and hospitals. Compare with self-insured in the Glossary of Medical and Health Administrative Terms in the appendix.

Functional health pattern. A medical assessment that provides the basis or framework for collecting data about a patient. This information is used to assess the patient's health.

Fungi. Plantlike pathogens (molds and yeasts).

Gatekeeper physician. A doctor selected by an insurance company who must approve a request for a patient to see a specialist. The goal of gatekeeper doctors is to cut the use of expensive specialists. Gatekeeper physicians were used extensively in the early days of managed care but have lost favor among patients and insurance companies in recent years.

Genetic endocrinology. Use of DNA technology to produce tissues and drugs that secrete hormones.

Genetic engineering. A technique of changing DNA by adding genes to a molecule to change the type of protein an organism can produce.

Gram stain. A process of staining bacteria that allows the classification of bacteria into two categories; those that take a gram stain from the application of Cresyl violet and those that do not.

Gram-negative bacteria. A bacteria that does not take the Cresyl violet stain

Gram-positive bacteria. Bacteria that takes a Cresyl violet stain.

Guarantee the line of credit. A line of credit is an agreement that allows a customer, at his or her discretion, to borrow funds from a bank for operations. Lines of credit are often secured by assets that may be sold if the loan is not repaid.

Harbinger. A person or event that predicts the future.

Health economics. Economics is the study of scarce resources—the study of how resources are produced and distributed. Health economics is an area of economics that focuses on the healthcare industry.

Health Maintenance Organization (HMO). An organization that delivers healthcare. Originally, HMOs tried to control health care costs by: (1) paying physicians and hospitals capitation instead of billed charge payments, (2) requiring patients to use specific doctors and hospitals, (3) providing financial incentives for patients to adopt healthy lifestyles, and (4) requiring second opinions or prior approval for expensive procedures that are often abused.

Health Occupation Student Association (HOSA). An organization for high school and college students interested in the healthcare field. HOSA provides information and activities designed to help students decide on a healthcare career.

Healthcare Financial Management Association (HFMA). A professional association for accountants and other finance professionals who earn their living in the healthcare finance industry.

Healthgrades.com. An organization that surveys hospitals and awards quality grades. Grades can be found on www.healthgrades.com

Hepatitis. Inflammation of the liver, often caused by infection.

Hill Burton. A federal program from the 1950s that provided funds for hospital construction.

HIPAA. Acronym for The Health Insurance Portability and Accountability Act. HIPAA was enacted by the U.S. Congress in 1996. One objective is to protect confidentiality of health information.

Hispanic. An American of Spanish or Portuguese descent. The term is sometimes used as a demographic classification of those who speak Spanish.

HMO. Abbreviation for Health Maintenance Organization.

Holding company. An investment company organized to own stock in other companies.

Home health agency. An organization that provides healthcare services to patients in their home.

Horizontal stabilizer. The short horizontal wing on the tail of an aircraft.

Hospital controller. The person responsible for all finance and accounting operations in the hospital.

Human Resources. The personnel department.

Humerus bone. A bone of the arm.

ICU. Acronym for intensive care unit, the unit where patients in critical condition are treated.

ID. Acronym for identification.

In the black. Financial slang for operating an organization with a profit.

In the red. Financial slang for operating an organization at a loss.

Incentive payment. A payment system designed to decrease cost by penalizing hospitals and doctors for poor efficiency, and rewarding them for high efficiency. A synonym for incentive reimbursement.

Incentive reimbursement. See incentive payment.

Incident report. A document used to report an incident that harmed or had the potential to harm a patient, employee, or visitor. Incident reports include medication errors, falls, patient refusal of treatment, safety violations, and patient complaints. Incident reports are an important part of a risk management program, a program designed to cut the risk of injury to those entering the hospital (patients, visitors, doctors, employees, and so on).

Indemnity insurance plan. A traditional insurance program design that provides few incentives for cost control. Indemnity policies usually: (1) pay billed charges, (2) allow patients to select their own doctor and hospital, and (3) provide little peer review.

Industrial espionage. The act of one company spying on a competitor to obtain trade secrets.

Infection rate. The number of infections per organization or similar case.

Infections committee. A hospital committee consisting of doctors, nurses, and other hospital employees responsible for monitoring hospital infections, finding their cause, and correcting these causes.

Inferior vena cava filters. Filters placed in the inferior vena cava to prevent deep venous thrombosis and embolisms.

Informed consent. A legal document in which a patient or his or her representative gives permission for treatment.

In-house collection agency. An agency owned by a firm (as opposed to an outside agency) that attempts to collect the firm's bad debts.

Inpatient revenue. Revenue generated by treating patients admitted to the hospital.

Inpatients. Patients admitted to the hospital for diagnosis or treatment. To be classified as an inpatient, many insurance companies require that a patient stay in the hospital twenty-four hours or more.

In-service director. A hospital employee responsible for the continuing education of the hospital's staff.

Insulin dependent diabetes. A disease in which there is elevated glucose in the blood, resulting from defects in insulin secretion, insulin action, or both.

Insurance premium. A payment paid by an employer or enrollee for health insurance.

Interdisciplinary team. A group of people with different educational backgrounds who come together for a specific project.

Interim administrator. A temporary hospital administrator who serves at the discretion of the board until a permanent replacement is found.

Intermediary. See third-party payer.

Internal audit. An audit conducted by hospital personnel (as opposed to an external audit conducted by outside auditors, such as certified public accountants).

Internal consistency. A compensation management term that means that pay is fair and that employees are paid consistent with the education, skill, responsibility, and contribution to the organization.

Internal rate of return (IRR). A financial calculation of the profitability of an investment in plant or equipment. IRR is calculated by dividing the increased profit from purchasing a piece of capital equipment by the average investment in that equipment over a period of time such as a year.

Internist. A specialist who focuses on diseases of adults.

Internship. A training program, usually one or two years in length, immediately following graduation from medical school, designed to give the medical school graduate real world experience in applying the theoretical concepts learned in class.

Intravenous flowchart. A flowchart found in the medical record that documents intravenous fluids administered to the patient.

Intravenous. Literally, "through the vein."

Intubate. The insertion of a tube into the airway to allow the patient to breathe.

Invasion of privacy. Revealing personal information about a patient without that person's consent.

Invasive procedures. A procedure that requires the insertion of an instrument or device into the body for diagnosis or treatment.

Invoice. A bill itemizing products and services provided.

JCAHO. Acronym for Joint Commission on Accreditation of Healthcare Organizations—an accreditation body.

Job description. A document detailing a position's: (1) job title, (2) salary range, (3) reporting line, and (4) duties.

Job order costing. A sophisticated accounting system that traces the costs of products.

Joint Commission on Accreditation of Healthcare Organizations (JCAHO). An organization that accredits hospitals and other healthcare organizations. Accreditation provides legitimacy in the eyes of the consumer, who is often unable to judge the quality of healthcare services.

LASIK surgery. Surgery in which a laser is used to correct vision.

Lateral. "On the side." A lateral x-ray, for example, gives a side view.

Law. A minimal rule of conduct enforceable by a controlling authority, usually a governmental entity.

Left renal vein. A vein running from a kidney.

Legality. Compliance with laws.

Length of stay. The number of consecutive days a patient stays overnight in the hospital.

Liability. A legal obligation. A mortgage, for example, is a legal obligation to repay a sum of money loaned to purchase a building.

Libel. Written defamation.

Licensure. Official recognition by a governmental body that a person meets minimal educational requirements and has the knowledge and skill to practice a specific profession.

Lien free. Without a lien.

Lien. The right to keep another organizations property until a debt is paid.

Life flight. A group that transports critically ill patients by aircraft to the hospital.

Line of credit. Many organizations need to borrow money to meet short-term obligations. Supplies must be purchased, and employees must be paid before payment for the services provided is received from the patient or insurance company. A line of credit from the bank is designed to temporarily provide these funds.

Liquidity. A measure of the ability of a company to pay its short-term debt (debt that must be repaid within a year).

Litigation. Filing a complaint in court.

Living trust. A legal document that holds title or ownership to a person's assets. In many ways it is like a will, in that it includes instructions on the disposition of that person's property on his or her death, often to charitable organizations.

Living will. A document that gives specific instructions on the types of treatments that may or may not be used to prolong the life of an individual who is brain dead or has a terminal illness.

Loan committee. A bank committee that reviews loan applications and approves or denies these applications.

Localizer. A transmitter used in an instrument landing system that provides the pilot with information regarding his alignment with the runway centerline during a landing approach.

Magnetic resonance imaging (MRI). A technology used by radiologists to create an image of internal body structures clearer than those shown by x-rays.

Maintenance department. The hospital department responsible for maintaining buildings and equipment.

Malpractice. An act of professional negligence that injures a patient.

Managed care. An approach to cost control that includes preauthorization for expensive procedures, incentive reimbursement, retrospective (after-the-fact) quality audits, and second opinions.

Managing partner (CPA firm). The senior partner in a public accounting firm.

Market value. The price for which an asset can be sold now on the open market. Different from book value, which is the original purchase price.

MBA. Acronym for Masters of Business Administration.

Medicaid. A governmental program funded with state and federal funds to provide healthcare to the poor.

Medical director. A doctor (often employed by the hospital) who has responsibility for representing the medical staff to the Board of Trustees and administration, and supervising the activities of the medical staff.

Medical executive committee (MEC). The primary governing committee of the medical staff. The goal of the MEC is to conduct business in the hospital for, and in behalf of, the medical staff.

Medical record. A record created on admission that records the treatment provided during the patient's hospital stay.

Medical staff membership. To practice medicine within a hospital, a doctor must apply for and be granted membership on the medical staff. Medical staff membership allows him or her to apply for privileges (the right to perform specific procedures), to attend medical staff meetings, and to participate on medical staff committees.

Medical staff privileges. The procedures a doctor is approved to perform in the hospital.

Medicare. A federally funded program that pays the costs of healthcare for individuals sixty-five years and older.

Medication error. The prescription or administration of the wrong drug.

Medication record. A record of medications given to the patient.

Mental dementia. Insanity or confusion.

Methamphetamine. A psycho stimulant (drug with mood elevating properties) that exerts greater stimulating effects on the central nervous system than does amphetamine. Methamphetamines are widely used by drug abusers.

Minority group. A member of a small group within a larger group.

Misdemeanor. A crime that is less serious than a felony and not punishable by a long prison term.

Misdiagnosis. An incorrect diagnosis.

Morals. Personal standards of right and wrong.

Morbidity and Mortality Committee. A committee in some hospitals responsible for monitoring the quality of care provided to patients.

Morbidity. The number of cases of a specific disease in relation to the general population.

Mortality. The hospital's death rate. The number of hospital deaths divided by the number of people in a specific population.

MRI. Acronym for magnetic resonance imaging. MRI images are clearer than those produced by x-rays and do not expose the patient to radiation.

Multiethnic. Being composed of members from more than one ethnic group.

Mutual insurance company. An insurance company owned by its enrollees.

Narcotic. A drug—natural or synthetic—with effects similar to those of opium.

Narcotics number. An identification number issued to doctors certified to write prescriptions for narcotics.

Needle stick. An accidental penetration of the skin of a healthcare professional by a contaminated needle used to administer medication or draw blood.

Negligence. Failure to act with reasonable care; or failure to do something a reasonable person would have done; or performing an action a reasonable person would not have done.

Net income. Revenue minus expense.

Neurologist. A specialist in the diagnosis and treatment of diseases of the neurological system.

Nonprofit hospital. A hospital whose surpluses cannot be kept or given for the benefit of specific individuals, but are used for the mission of the organization.

Nonprofit organization. An organization formed to provide services often not available through the private sector. Surpluses of nonprofit organizations cannot be kept or given for the benefit of specific persons but are used for the mission of the organization.

Nosocomial infection. An infection acquired in the hospital.

Note. A document showing the existence of a loan.

Nurse practice act. A state act that defines and regulates the practice of nursing.

Nursemaids elbow. A partial dislocation of the elbow, which occurs when the lower part of the forearm slips out of its normal position at the elbow joint. The injury is also called radial head dislocation.

Nursing care plan or **nursing management plan.** A plan created when the patient is admitted detailing the nursing plan for treating the patient.

Obligation to do good for others. An ethical responsibility. Health-care workers are obligated to take the action that will result in the best outcome for the patient.

Obligation to do no harm. An ethical responsibility. The first obligation of a healthcare practitioner is to avoid injury to his or her patient.

Obstetrician. A specialist concerned with the care of women during pregnancy.

Obstetrics. A medical specialty concerned with the care of women during pregnancy.

Occupancy rate. The percent of hospital beds occupied.

Occupational medicine. A branch of medicine concerned with the impact of work on health. It addresses workplace hazards, social forces impacting physical and mental health in the workplace, workplace injuries and so on. Synonym for industrial medicine.

On-call nurse. A nurse not assigned a specific time to work, but who agrees to be available to be called in on short notice.

Oncologist. A cancer specialist.

Open purchase order. An agreement with a vendor (a hardware store for example) that allows specific employees to purchase without a purchase order. A purchase order is a formalized document that authorizes the purchase of materials or services on credit. Open purchase orders are subject to abuse by employees who may buy items on the company account for their personal use.

Operational issues. Issues relating to the management or operation of a hospital.

Operations. Relating to the functioning or management of an organization.

Outcome audit. A medical audit that seeks to identify poor medical care through poor patient outcomes.

Outcomes management. A quality management program that evaluates quality through an evaluation of patient outcomes.

Out-migration. The practice of patients in a rural area to bypass their rural hospital to get healthcare services at a larger city hospital.

Outpatient services. Services provided by hospital departments to patients not admitted to the hospital for an overnight stay.

Outpatient surgery. Surgery performed on patients who have not been admitted to the hospital for an overnight stay (or in some cases patients who stay overnight, but are in the hospital for less than twenty-four hours). Also called ambulatory surgery.

Outpatient. A patient diagnosed or treated at the hospital without being admitted to the hospital (or in some cases a patient admitted to the hospital for less than a twenty-four hour period).

Overhead. Hospital costs can be grouped into two general categories: direct costs and indirect costs. Direct costs are those that can be easily traced to the patient. The cost of an injection or the nursing hours spent giving a bed bath are examples of direct costs. Indirect costs are costs that are essential to the operation of the hospital, but cannot be easily traced to a specific patient (payroll, human resources, and equipment maintenance are examples of indirect costs). Indirect costs within a specific department (the copy machine in the laboratory or the laboratory supervisor) are often referred to as overhead costs or department overhead. Patient bills must cover direct and indirect costs.

Over-the-counter medications. Medications that do not require a prescription for purchase by a patient.

Over-utilization of healthcare services. Using more healthcare resources than needed to treat the patient.

Palpate. To examine by pressing with the fingers or palms.

Paramedic. A person trained to provide emergency care.

Pathogen. A microorganism that causes disease. Common pathogens include bacteria, viruses, and fungi.

Pathologist. A medical specialty focusing on the diagnosis of disease through changes in tissues.

Patient day. One day spent by a patient in the hospital.

Patient dumping. The practice of transferring patients that cannot pay their bills to other hospitals.

Pay for Performance. A payment system that attempts to improve quality and decrease cost by paying on the basis of patient outcomes.

Payer. The person or organization that pays the healthcare bill. Private insurance companies such as Blue Cross,and governmental insurance programs such as Medicare and Medicaid are payers.

Pediatrics. A branch of medicine specializing in the treatment of childhood illness.

Peer review. A review of a physician's hospital medical practice by a peer physician. Peer review is often conducted by committees who review medical records. The goal is to improve the quality of care provided by members of the medical staff.

Percodan. A narcotic pain killer.

Performance evaluation. A periodic evaluation by a work supervisor of the quality of work of a subordinate. Performance evaluations are often conducted at the time merit pay increases are awarded.

Personal space. The area surrounding a person that a person regards as his own—the distance from other people that a person needs to feel secure or comfortable.

Pharmaceutical. Relating to the pharmacy.

Pharmacy medication error. A medication error arising in the pharmacy.

Philanthropy. To increase human well being, often through charitable donations.

Physical therapy. The treatment of musculoskeletal disease, injury, and so on through massage, infrared or ultraviolet light, electrotherapy, hydrotherapy, heat, and exercise.

Physician panel. A group of doctors who contract with an insurance company to provide services at a reduced rate.

Pink shop. A gift shop operated by hospital volunteers (in some hospitals called "pink ladies"). Profits from sales in the pink shop are given to the hospital for nursing scholarships or to buy medical equipment.

Plaintiff. The person charged in a civil action.

Pneumonia. An acute (brief) or chronic (long-term) disease characterized by inflammation of the lungs.

Positive Cash Flow. When the amount of cash coming in exceeds the amount going out.

Posterior. "On the back side." A posterior x-ray gives a back view.

Practice protocols. Rules developed to guide doctors in the way they treat specific illnesses.

Pre-certification. A process where an insurance company certifies, before admission, that they will pay for a specific treatment or procedure.

Premium. An amount paid to buy insurance coverage.

President of medical staff. An elected officer of the medical staff who represents the medical staff to the board and administration.

Preventive healthcare services. Services designed to prevent, rather than treat, illness. Examples of preventive medicine include annual physicals, good nutrition, exercise, and the discontinuance of unhealthy habits such as smoking and overeating.

Preventive medicine. Services designed to prevent, rather than treat illness. Examples of preventive medicine include annual physicals, good nutrition, exercise, and the discontinuance of unhealthy habits such as smoking and over eating. Also called preventive healthcare services.

Price competition. Competition between sellers based on price.

Price elasticity. When price influences the volume of sales of a product. When there is price elasticity, as prices go up, the number of goods bought decreases. When prices go down, the number of goods bought increases. There is little price elasticity for life-saving healthcare services.

Private insurance. Some people buy individual or family policies from health insurance carriers. These are usually more costly than the group insurance contracts bought by employers. In addition, coverage is often limited and some people are unable to qualify for coverage.

prn. Acronym for Latin "pro re nata." A medication abbreviation meaning "as needed."

Prospective payment system. A payment system for doctors and hospitals. In a prospective payment system, the bill is calculated before services are given. A prospective payment system is a fixed-price contract. If the cost of the services provided exceeds the prearranged amount, the healthcare provider must absorb the loss. Prospective payment systems shift the risk of cost inefficiency from the patient or doctor to the hospital.

Psychiatrist. A physician who treats mental illness, often through the prescription of drugs.

Pump time. The amount of time a patient undergoing cardiovascular surgery is on a bypass machine.

Purchase order. A document prepared by a buyer authorizing a seller to deliver and bill the buyer for the goods listed.

Quality assurance committee. The committee assigned to monitor quality in the hospital.

Quality assurance. Procedures taken to assure a high degree of excellence.

Race. A category within a classification system based on genetic characteristics, such as color of skin, the structure of hair, and so on.

Radio beam. In the context of aviation, a beam emitted for navigation purposes.

Radiologist. A physician specializing in the field of radiology.

Radiology. A branch of science that uses radiant source energy (especially x-rays) in the diagnosis and treatment of disease.

Rapid response team. A team to respond to immediate emergencies, such as a Code Blue.

Reagent. A substance used in the laboratory to detect or measure another substance.

Reimbursement. Synonym for payment.

Residency. A training program following the internship that provides training in a specialized field of medicine. A medical school graduate who wants to be a radiologist, for example, will enroll in a radiology residency.

Respiratory arrest. A situation where a patient has stopped breathing.

Retractor. An instrument for holding or drawing aside structures beside a wound or operating field.

Retrospective statistical analysis. Statistical analysis that occurs after an event, such as the treatment of patients.

Return on investment (ROI). A measure used to determine the financial attractiveness of an investment opportunity. It is calculated by dividing annual income from the investment by the amount of the average annual investment.

Revenue. Funds that flow into an organization because of the sale of goods or services.

Rigor mortis. The stiffening of the body that occurs after death.

Risk Management. A department or specialty that anticipates and tries to prevent risks to employees, patients, and visitors. Slipping on an icy sidewalk would be a risk this program might address.

Risk manager. One who identifies and develops programs to cut the risk of harm to patients and employees.

Room rate. A daily charge by the hospital, designed to cover nursing and hotel (meals, housekeeping, and so on) services. Total per-diem (per-day) charges are found by adding the room rate to ancillary (x-ray, laboratory, pharmacy, and so on) charges.

Rounds. In this situation, the morning visit by a doctor to his or her patients in the hospital. The term originated at Johns Hopkins Hospital in the late nineteenth century, where patient wings radiated off a central circular hall, causing doctors completing their daily visits to do "rounds."

Safranin. A red dye used as a microbiology stain.

Salary schedule. A schedule listing the entry wage levels of different employee classes.

Salary surveys. Surveys to determine what other firms are paying for specific jobs.

Scalpel. A surgical knife.

Secondary Spending. When a person buys a pair of shoes within a community, the shoe seller can then use that money to buy groceries locally and the grocer can take those funds to pay for an automobile. The impact on the local community of the first dollar spent is, therefore, multiplied. This effect is called secondary spending.

Self-insured health insurance plan. An insurance plan where the employer pays the insurance company for the actual costs of employee care. Compare with fully-insured plan.

Self-pay patient. A patient who pays the cost of his or her own healthcare without the aid of an insurance company.

Self-pay. See self-pay patient.

Severity of illness. A measure of how sick a patient is.

Shareholder. An owner in a corporation.

Skimming. The practice of providing only those healthcare services that generate a profit, leaving to others (usually community hospitals) the responsibility to provide services that generate a loss.

Slander. Spoken defamation.

Social Security Death Index. An internet database listing persons with social security benefits who have died. The database lists the person's name, social security number, date of death, and the place the benefit check was mailed.

Sociologist. One who specializes in the history and function of human society.

Specialty care center. A health center that specializes in one area of care.

Speculative venture. A business proposition with high risk.

Spirochetes. A corkscrew shaped bacteria.

Stakeholder. A person who has an interest in an organization, project or concept.

Standard costs. What a procedure or service should cost as determined by a study.

Standard. A performance goal.

Stat laboratory test. A laboratory test needed immediately.

Stat. Abbreviation for statim—meaning "at once, immediately."

State Fire Code. Rules and regulations, many of which deal with construction standards designed to cut death and injury in the event of a fire. Hospitals are bound by law to abide by the state fire code.

Stock. A share certifying the holder owns part of a corporation.

Strategic planning. Developing a long-term plan listing the strategies the company plans to follow to meet its goals.

Sudafed. An over-the-counter medication commonly used for patients with symptoms of hay fever.

Supply. In economic terms, the amount of a good or service a provider will manufacture at a given price level.

Support services. Services that help nurses perform their duties. Examples include housekeeping, accounting, scheduling, and admitting.

Supra-condylar fracture. A fracture above the rounded articular surface at the extremity of a bone.

Surrogate. Substitute.

System. An orderly and complex arrangement of parts.

Systems thinking or **systems analysis.** An approach to problem solving that focuses on the system as a whole, and the relationship of its interconnected parts.

Tachycardia. Excessively fast heartbeat.

Taxonomy. A classification system.

Telemetry. The science of measuring something, sending the measurement by radio signal to a distant station, and then recording or interpreting the results. In a hospital, telemetry, for example, may be used to transmit heart monitor information from a patient to a central nursing station.

Teleological. A school of thought that focuses on "the greatest good for the greatest number." The teleological school believes that "the end justifies the means."

Tertiary care center. A healthcare center that provides the highest level of specialty care.

Therapeutic. Having the ability to benefit the patient medically.

Third-party payer. The intermediary between a patient with insurance and a doctor or hospital. The job of a third party administrator is to receive premiums from employees and employers and pay claims to doctors, hospitals and other healthcare providers. The term third-party payer is used synonymously with the term intermediary.

Thumb print sign. A radiological sign of thickened tissues that encroach on an airway.

Title. A legal document verifying ownership of property.

TOCA strips. A readout of a baby's heart rate and the mother's rate of contractions during delivery.

Topical antibiotic. An antibiotic designed for application to an external wound.

Torts. Breaches of duty (excluding breaches of contract) for which the court will provide a remedy.

Total Quality Management (TQM). A management philosophy that focuses on the creation of continuous quality improvement to provide products that exceed the expectations of customers.

Traditional insurance program. An insurance program design that provides few incentives for cost control. Traditional policies usually: (1) pay billed charges, (2) allow patients to select their own doctor and hospital, and (3) provide little or no prospective, concurrent, or retrospective review.

Transportation aide. A person responsible for transporting food, supplies, or patients throughout the hospital.

Trauma. A mental or physical injury.

Treatment healthcare services. Procedures designed to restore the patient to a state of health. Medication, surgery, and physical therapy are examples of treatment healthcare services.

Treatment protocol. Procedures that should be followed under specific conditions.

Triage. Medical screening of patients to decide priority for treatment.

Ulnar nerve. A nerve running along the larger of the two bones of the forearm.

Union steward. An in-house union representative.

Utilization review. An audit or review, sometimes by an insurance company, to find out if specific services are being over-used by doctors or patients.

Variance. Also known as cost variance. The difference between what something should cost and what it actually costs. If the cost to remove an appendix is budgeted at $3,000 (the standard cost), and the actual cost is $3200, then the variance is $200.

Vector. A magnetic direction used in aviation.

Vendor. A person or company that sells products or services to a hospital. A medical supply company is a vendor.

Ventilator. A mechanical device for artificial breathing.

Venture capitalist. A person who provides the funds to start or expand a business.

Vertically integrated. A vertically integrated company owns companies at all stages of production and distribution. A vertically integrated hospital chain, for example, might own doctor practices, primary hospitals, specialty hospitals, health insurance companies, and nursing homes.

Vertigo. A sensation of spinning or whirling.

Vestibule. An enclosed space between the outer and inner doors of a building.

Virus. The smallest of the infection agents, which, with few exceptions, can pass through fine filters that retain most bacteria. A virus is not visible through a light microscope, and is incapable of reproduction outside a living cell.

Volume discount. A discount given by a seller to a buyer who purchases a large volume of goods.

Voluntary controls. In this book, caps on costs implemented voluntarily by hospitals.

VOR. Acronym for Very High Frequency Omni Directional Range. An aviation radio navigation system.

Working capital. In accounting, the assets that can easily be converted into cash, divided by debts owed in the current year.

Work-in-process. Goods being manufactured for sale that are not yet finished.

Yoke. The "steering wheel" of an airplane.

Ziac. A medication commonly prescribed for high blood pressure.

Index

Order Information

Additional copies can be ordered through Traemus Books. Volume discounts available.

For additional information or to order, call 1-801-525-9643.

To order through the Internet, visit: http://www.traemus-books.com

We accept Visa and Mastercard

To order with a purchase order, mail your purchase order to:

Traemus Books
Shipping
2481 W 1425 South
Syracuse, Utah 84075

Or fax your purchase order to 801-773-7669.

E-mail the author at richard@traemus.com or remcdermott@weber.edu.